*A Strange Way of Killing*

# A STRANGE WAY OF KILLING

The Poetic Structure of
*Wuthering Heights*

MEG HARRIS WILLIAMS

Clunie Press Literary Criticism Series No. 1

First published 1987

British Library Cataloguing in Publication Data

Williams, Meg Harris
  A strange way of killing : the poetic
  structure of Wuthering Heights.
  1. Bronte, Emily. Wuthering Heights
  I. Title
  823'.8        PR4172.W73

ISBN 0-902965-23-9

Typeset by Action Typesetting Limited, Gloucester.
Printed and bound in Great Britain by
Billing and Sons Ltd., Worcester.
For Clunie Press, Old Ballechin, Strathtay, Perthshire,
Publisher to The Roland Harris Trust.

# Contents

# Acknowledgements

To Mrs Martha Harris and Dr Donald Meltzer, who supervised the process of writing this book; to Dr Adrian Williams who made writing amidst small children possible; to Professor Robert Keefe who gave detailed attention to many sections; to Miss Joie Macaulay and Dr Margot Waddell for reading and correcting the typescript; to the Regents of the University of California for permission to reprint from 'Book Magic: Aesthetic Conflicts in Charlotte Brontë's Juvenilia', to be published and copyrighted by them in *Nineteenth Century Literature*, June 1987.

# Introduction

'A strange way of killing' is the phrase given by Emily Brontë to Heathcliff, through which to express his awareness of the extraordinary metamorphosis which has been wrought upon his mind and body by the influence of Catherine's ghost. It evokes the climactic sequence which is the key to the structural resolution of *Wuthering Heights*; and it emphasizes the paradoxical impact of powerful experience. *Wuthering Heights* itself has this sort of paradoxical impact upon its readers; the pattern for our own response is set by the evolution of experience imaged in the book. In so far as this is a novel, it appears accessible, easy to read and take in; in so far as it is a poem, it presents itself as a mystery, charged with intense and disturbing emotion, leaving the reader 'stunned' like Coleridge's Wedding Guest. E. M. Forster, describing the 'prophetic' quality of the work wrote that

> ... the emotions of Heathcliff and Catherine Earnshaw function differently to other emotions in fiction. Instead of inhabiting the characters, they surround them like thunder clouds, and generate the explosions that fill the novel from the moment when Lockwood dreams of the hand at the window down to the moment when Heathcliff, with the same window open, is discovered dead.[1]

When alive, their passion is 'externalised', 'streaming through the house and over the moors'; when dead, their ghosts 'walk': 'what else could such beings do?' The emotion in the book is not neatly parcelled up within given characters, there to live and die; it is generated by invisible lines of tension, electrical charges, in the landscape. Its unpredictable but inevitable explosions are liable to flash out and inflame the reader also, who is sometimes hardly aware what kind of novel he is reading or what kind of forces are attacking him. The book's aesthetic methods are unique and emotionally disturbing; they threaten to alter the stability of a preconceived outlook. It is an instinctive reaction, faced with this, to formulate a judgement upon the author's artistic or moral inadequacy. One's own confusion becomes rationalised in terms of Emily Brontë's internal split, or inability to realise her 'intentions'. Such rationalisation is often implicit even where it is not explicit. Thus in criticism, many interpretations of *Wuthering Heights* impose reductive overall schemas from without, rather than following the author's own mental process as it evolves through the organic form of her work.

The nature of Emily Brontë's state of mind when on the point of writing *Wuthering Heights*, is suggested in the lines of autumn 1845 describing a 'final bound' from one state to another:

> When the ear begins to hear and the eye begins to see;
> When the pulse begins to throb, the brain to think again,
> The soul to feel the flesh and the flesh to feel the chain!

These lines evoke, not the dullness of actuality after escapist fantasy, but the intensification and then re-formation of sensuous reality under the pressure of a new idea. In precisely this way, the organic form of the novel is moulded under pressure of mystical 'knowledge' received within, not abstracted from, 'flesh'. Aesthetic form is a concrete manifestation of the working of the author's mind, and the vehicle through which its essential, irreducible meaning, has being. With this view of poetic import in mind, the following study of *Wuthering Heights* tries to keep judgement and evaluation at arm's length as far as possible, and to concentrate on describing its poetic structure — the manifestation of emotional meaning. In conventional academic terms, this would probably not be considered a feasible enterprise, because it is not 'objective'. But the aims of this book are in a sense more fundamental. Certainly emotional meaning has to be received through the medium of emotional response, or it simply evades observation. To observe subjectively in a way which discovers structural confines, feeling the existence of the artist's mind against one's own, requires more rigorous adherence to the text and its mystery, than does a Procrustean operation of matching predetermined structures. The aim of this type of 'symbolic' response is not to decode the 'truth' of the text in terms of determinate messages, but to see feelingly how 'heaven and earth are trapped in the cage of form' (to adopt an ancient Chinese definition of poetry, given by A. MacLeish).[2] So what follows in Part I of this book, is a presentational, rather than a discursive or interpretational form of criticism. It concentrates on placing the work, not in a historical or linguistic context, but in the reader's mind. Some of the problems associated with the kind of reading which is a significant life experience, are considered in Part II of this book, with the help of the psychoanalytic concept of 'catastrophic change'.

*Wuthering Heights* is a double-generation story. It repeats what Coleridge would call the 'relations of things', but with a difference, and works through to the thing-in-itself. Its developing structure includes the way the second part of the book relates to the first; and the nature of the relation finally evolved between the two houses. Cutting across the doubleness of time are other contraries in action. In recent criticism these have been defined in a variety of ways: storm and calm; the wild versus the civilised; perversity versus normality; and as aspects of a class or sex war. Emily Brontë's dialectical method tempts one, at points of crisis, to want to choose between ways of life or philosophies, and accept and identify with a partial view: instead of identifying with both sides, experiencing the tension between them and the emotion generated by their friction, and following the struggle through the relations of things to a kind of reality. It is difficult, for example, to feel with both the narrators and the protagonists at the same time; yet the truth or reality of the book lies — not halfway between their viewpoints — but beyond it in a new state imaged through their interaction. This is acknowledged in principle by some of the 'transcendental' interpretations of the novel, but often at the expense of losing contact with its organic reality; they tend to present a skeletal plan rather than the spirit-made-flesh, the emotional substance of its conflicts. To engage fully with these, the reader's identification with the line of tension between Heathcliff and Lockwood is crucial. Heathcliff's structural function, spanning the entire story, underpins every conflict in the emotional landscape, as Charlotte Brontë saw when she complained that 'some of his spirit seems breathed through the whole narrative in which he figures: it haunts every moor and glen, and beckons in every fir-tree of the Heights'.[3] It is inevitable that Heathcliff, who gains heroic stature as the story progresses, should be like Hamlet besieged by the interpreters of his madness: 'You would pluck

out the heart of my mystery . . . yet cannot you make it speak'.
Yet it is through the often-despised Lockwood that Heathcliff
does, indirectly, 'speak', as he himself grapples with the mystery
rather than the cardboard romance of human relationships.
Each figure in the book — whether human, natural or archi-
tectural — demarcates a point in a line of tension, part of a
structural web which traps the knowledge of the book within its
spaces, 'heaven and earth in the cage of form'.

*Wuthering Heights*, published in 1847 under the pseudonym
'Ellis Bell', was received by its contemporaries with a mixture of
admiration, suspicion and moral censure. It was regarded as the
powerful work of a 'primitive' (in the aesthetic and moral sense
— rather as Shakespeare had been before the Romantic critics).
It imaged 'humanity in its wild state', with characters 'that used
to exist everywhere, but especially in retired and remote country
places'.[4] Its truth to life was accepted provided it was distanced
in time and space, and kept at arm's length, because

> it is with difficulty that we can prevail upon ourselves to
> believe in the appearance of such a phenomenon [as
> Heathcliff], so near our own dwellings as the summit of a
> Lancashire or Yorkshire moor.[5]

Many reviewers believed it to be an early work by the author of
*Jane Eyre*, without the refining touches of art and civilisation and
corresponding morality. It was, nevertheless, a work 'baffling
all regular criticism', exhibiting 'a purposeless power, which we
feel a great desire to see turned to better account'.[6] Its
contemporaries looked in vain for the 'moral', for 'We want to
know the object of a fiction';[7] and G.H. Lewes, who admired its
'creative power', concluded the moral was that 'such brutes we
all should be . . . were our lives as insubordinate to law; were our
affections and sympathies as little cultivated, our imaginations
as undirected'.[8] It did not satisfy 'regular' criticism; its want of
'art', in the sense of satisfying pre-existent fashions of taste, was
lamented. Yet despite its 'unpleasing' disagreeable qualities,
several critics admitted a different species of internal aesthetic
logic. The *Atlas* through there was 'keeping in the book — the
groups of figures and the scenery are in harmony with each
other';[9] Sydney Dobell say in it 'the exultation of young wings'
turning 'to exhaust, in a circumscribed space, the energy and

agility which [they] may not yet spend in the heavens'[10] (a metaphor characteristic of Emily's poetry). In similar spirit, the *Britannia* described the mixed feelings aroused:

> The elements of beauty are found in the midst of gloom and danger, and some forms are the more picturesque from their distorted growth amid so many obstacles.[11]

In order to express an appreciation which is not simply a judgement from the standpoint of contemporary expectations, these reviewers adopt the author's symbolic language to frame a parallel metaphor. Through this structural echo, their ambivalent but genuine emotional reaction is conveyed.

The artistic or descriptive approach to criticism, however tentative in the above examples, has potential for a disturbing work such as *Wuthering Heights*, where perceiving the 'elements of beauty' involves a complex emotional response, subsuming not only admiration but perhaps also fear, repugnance, even despair. This type of complex response is the essence of poetry appreciation, and *Wuthering Heights* is, as is often said, a poem of a novel. Meaning is inseparable from form; nothing is irrelevant, superfluous, or accidental. It has inevitability; it has mystery. Through its symbolic language it presents to us the terms on which its 'meaning' has being. Yet owing to its very reality, there is a danger for our contact with it to be one of explosion followed by evaporation; after which, in bewilderment, we might relegate it to the realms of 'adolescent' rather than of 'adult' experience. And like all inspired works, there is a sense in which it has no context — it comes into existence 'out of the air'. Few papers were left by Emily Brontë for scholars to peruse, apart from her manuscript of poems, landmarks of a private world. These, however, provide enough material for a conjectural inner history; and Part III of this book traces the evolution of Emily Brontë's poetic spirit, from playing to creativity. Meanwhile, Charlotte Brontë left voluminous evidence in her juvenile notebooks of the intimate forces shaping family play. The picture drawn from this, and from the antagonistic but dependent relationship between Emily and Charlotte themselves — which appears in their closely related novels *Wuthering Heights* and *Jane Eyre* — illuminates, through complement and contrast, the nature of Emily's 'final bound'.

Finally, in order to give another contextual dimension to Emily Brontë's poetic spirit, I have described in Part IV certain vital links with four of the Romantic poets who preceded her. Although their 'influence' in the common academic sense (which is closer to 'plagiarism') is elusive, as are most 'facts' about Emily Brontë, I hope to make a case for showing that in terms of the implicit, working idea of creativity which is evolved during the process of writing, this is the tradition in which she stands. For Emily Brontë is often regarded, either as academically unapproachable, or as extending the tradition of the Gothic novel in ways which are ultimately banal and trivial. However, stressing her deeper kinship with the Romantic poets, on a level beyond that of wordplay, stylistic devices and philosophical maxims, takes us closer to an awareness of her essentially poetic genius. Emily Brontë's poetic experience, like that of her great predecessors, concerns the heart of the mystery: the aesthetic conflict itself.

# I
# THE POETIC STRUCTURE OF
# *WUTHERING HEIGHTS*

# 1    A Misanthropist's Heaven
(*Chapters 1 – 3*)

In *Wuthering Heights*, the behaviour of a small group of people in a confined locality, realistically evoked through their distinctive speech and the actions of daily life, metamorphoses into a total internal experience of wuthering turbulence and inspired resolution. The scene of the drama is a microcosm of a mental 'universe' at once familiar yet, as in Catherine's terms, 'a mighty stranger'. The lateral dimension of this universe is formed by the two houses across the moor; its depth is measured by the tension-filled gap between the two outsiders Lockwood and Heathcliff; and its vertical dimension, the congruence between the living and the ghostly dead, is established only at the end. Because the artistry of the story is compelling, *Wuthering Heights* does, in a sense, read itself. But the poetic structure of the novel and the mental configuration which this expresses, is bewilderingly complex, and liable to disorient the reader's grasp of space and time once he pauses to analyse the connections being impressed upon him. Introductions to *Wuthering Heights* often try to stabilise the reader by offering chronological charts of plot and lineage. There is a certain primitive appeal in 'proving' that the author was clear-headed about dates, seasons, legalities and terms of pregnancy 'despite' the turmoil left by the book, which is in any case a function of the reader's confusion not the author's. However, ultimately this evades rather than confronts the emotional constellation whose skeleton is the story not the plot, and whose flesh the poetic ambiguities which reverberate within.

The story comprises events in the order in which they are presented to the reader, with unchronological but significant juxtapositions. We recall, then, that *Wuthering Heights* begins in the winter of 1801, when the city-dweller Lockwood arrives in a 'beautiful' but 'desolate' northern country for his first encounter with his new landlord and 'solitary neighbour' Heathcliff, and his first view of Wuthering Heights from within its 'penetralium'. Despite being set on by the dogs, his heart 'warms' towards Heathcliff (a 'capital fellow'), and he returns

3

the next day, to become an unwelcome guest at the tea-table. His acquaintance with the inmates (surly Joseph, the haughty labourer Hareton, the fairy-witch Catherine, and the 'bad nature' of Heathcliff), leaves his habitual interpretation of intimate relationships in a painful whirl of confusion; but despite his desire to escape, his stay is forcibly prolonged by the snow-storm without. He seeks shelter in the recess of a closet-bed, which, however, enshrines the name and intimate diary of an 'unknown Catherine' (Earnshaw-Linton-Heathcliff). His sleep is disturbed by the child-ghost Catherine Linton, wailing to be 'let in' after being lost on the moor for 'twenty years'. Lockwood, after rubbing the ghost's wrist on the broken pane, emits a terrified shriek which brings Heathcliff to the scene; he witnesses his inexplicable 'superstitious' agony as he unsuccessfully attempts to recall the ghost. Next morning Lockwood is guided back to the Grange, shattered and 'feeble as a kitten', to become the bedridden recipient of the 'history' of his landlord, as related by the housekeeper Ellen Dean.

In essence, the novel relates Mr Lockwood's idea of Mr Heathcliff's idea of Cathy's ghost, whose story makes a violent entry with wind at the beginning, and ends in 'quiet breathing' through the grassy mounds. The first three chapters of the novel establish the key relationship between Lockwood and Heathcliff which guides the reader into the depths of the story, demarcating the different levels of reality on which it takes place. The two characters are antithetical in every conceivable way, as Lockwood's string of misconceptions about the landlord and his household makes abundantly clear; yet their relationship is essential to the story and is constructive in a way neither acknowledged nor desired by either of them. Hence the picture of the pair of misanthropes in 'heaven', given in Lockwood's opening paragraph, has more than an ironic function:

> This is certainly, a beautiful country! In all England, I do not believe that I could have fixed on a situation so completely removed from the stir of society. A perfect misanthropist's Heaven — and Mr Heathcliff and I are such a suitable pair to divide the desolation between us. A capital fellow! He little imagined how my heart warmed towards him when I beheld his black eyes withdraw so suspiciously under their brows, as I rode up . . .

Though it soon becomes clear that the 'stir of society' is stagnant by comparison with the 'wuthering' drama in this isolated corner of England, yet in another sense, they indeed make a 'suitable pair' capable of encompassing a 'beautiful' but 'desolate' landscape of the mind. The very tension, or gap in understanding, between them, prises open a mental space suitable for the reception of Catherine's 'ghost', because their different types of incomprehension are complementary. On their first encounter, Heathcliff is firmly set at the pinnacle of his worldly power, with both houses and their heirs mortgaged to his control; yet it is through the unlikely contact with his new 'tenant' that his spiritual imprisonment is made known, and the final phase of the drama initiated. Both men are originally outsiders, alien to the beautiful country and occupying its two houses only temporarily. Lockwood is the ordinary recognisable alien, the city-dweller with slightly more than the average taste for tourism; Heathcliff the extra-ordinary one, of unknown origin and 'nameless' in the historical sense. Yet, in terms of the action of the novel, both exist with a unified purpose: which is to realise and comprehend the nature of the 'ghostly Catherine'. Lockwood's enforced listening, when he is trapped inside Wuthering Heights and then pinioned in his bed at Thrushcross Grange, and Heathcliff's 'infernal torture' as he wrestles in his 'long fight', represent simultaneous aspects of a single creative endeavour to ultimately register the essential meaning, the 'universal idea', of a story spun over two generations.

Both the misanthropes are living their own fictions, in a sense. Heathcliff's fiction, or false romance, is that of his own power or omnipotence — over the native families and their land, heirs and values, and ultimately, over himself. His fiction is maintained by the theme of 'revenge' and the concept of 'avarice' mentioned throughout the novel. Heathcliff endeavours to convince himself that he is the 'owner', and that the more he owns, the more he is 'revenged' — the more he reclaims of his own, his lost name, his lost pride, himself. Heathcliff's fiction becomes exposed only at the end of the story; and its exposure is initiated by Lockwood, who simultaneously, while listening to Mrs Dean's narrative, becomes acquainted with his own (more obvious) fiction: that of the sentimental romanticist. The first meeting of the 'suitable pair' images Lockwood's encroachment

5

onto Heathcliff's mental territory: the 'tenant' impinging on the 'owner'. Lockwood 'warms' toward Heathcliff as Heathcliff 'withdraws'; his first apparently harmless sentence makes Heathcliff 'wince': ' "Thrushcross Grange is my own, sir," he interrupted wincing, "I should not allow anyone to inconvenience me, if I could hinder it — walk in!" ' Lockwood's difficulty in entering the Heights (the locked gate, 'my horse's breast fairly pushing the barrier') prefigures Cathy's ghost wailing 'Let me in'. He disturbs the 'heaven' of Heathcliff's invulnerable ownership of himself, the fixed boundaries of his spiritual objectives. Though Lockwood recognises that Heathcliff's uttered 'Walk in' really means 'Go to the Deuce', it happens that his own romantic fiction is precisely of the nature to make him proceed despite this. Like Isabella later with her 'hero of romance', he woos Heathcliff:

> I felt interested in a man who seemed more exaggeratedly reserved than myself ... I know, by instinct, his reserve springs from an aversion to showy displays of feeling.

Lockwood presses his suit of Heathcliff through his determination not to be a single misanthrope, but one of a 'suitable pair' (like all the other characters except Joseph, he wants company in his subjective 'heaven'). In doing so, inevitably, he gets more than he bargained for, as he is compelled to experience from within rather than romanticise from without. He has to listen to Mr Heathcliff's history, rather than 'bestowing my own attributes over liberally on him'; he has to penetrate the Heights, whose external characteristics he has observed sharply, as capable of withstanding the 'atmospheric tumult' and 'power of the north wind'. He notes also the stone carvings, the date 1500 and the name 'Hareton Earnshaw' displaying the family's history, but again is not enlightened from without:

> I would have made a few comments, and requested a short history of the place, from the surly owner, but his attitude at the door appeared to demand my speedy entrance, or complete departure, and I had no desire to aggravate his impatience, previous to inspecting the penetralium.

The 'history' of Wuthering Heights can be told only from

within; even Nelly, later, explaining her account of intimate events to Lockwood, points out that she feels he is not a 'stranger', and that natives of those parts do not commonly take to strangers 'unless they take to us first'. Lockwood, warming to Heathcliff, expresses his willingness to become part of the 'penetralium'.

For Lockwood is not, as is often thought, shallow and stupid. He is a man of intelligent curiosity, sensitive to others' feelings even when his own have been disturbed (for example, Heathcliff after the ghost; Hareton when ridiculed by Cathy towards the end). Moreover he clearly cannot enact the superficial charade which passes for manifestation of passion in the 'busy world', the 'stir of society', as is shown by the account of his abortive 'seaside' romance of 'looks', which resulted in his shrinking 'icily into myself, like a snail, at every glance retired colder and farther'. His conventional effort to capture a 'real goddess' ended in miserable failure; and Lockwood, fleeing from a bad reputation for 'deliberate heartlessness', comes to the north in part to discover the nature of real feeling — to observe people who live 'more in themselves, and less in surface change'. He is not 'comfortable' in either world: 'my dear mother used to say I should never have a comfortable home' (words which we later remember on his behalf as, after a mauling by the dogs, Zillah splashes 'a pint of icy water' down his neck). His discomfort derives partly from his sensitivity: his misanthropy from being a misfit. With a background of such dubious emotional resilience, he seems ill prepared to withstand a year's tenancy in the neighbourhood of Wuthering Heights, the house whose 'gaunt thorns' testify to the 'power of the north wind' without, and whose internal architecture is equally uncompromising. Ensconced by the fire, he manages to draw forth the stormy spirit of its historical inhabitants, still ensconced in its crevices (dogs 'haunting' recesses, chairs 'lurking' in the shade); he cannot resist 'looking' at the dogs, repeating his seaside mistake in a more dangerous context: 'imagining they would scarcely understand tacit insults, I unfortunately indulged in winking and making faces at the trio, and some turn of my physiognomy so irritated madam, that she suddenly broke into a fury and leapt on my knees'. Lockwood's almost involuntary facial movements again express his discomfort; but this time he

7

creates a genuine storm, turning the hearth into an 'absolute tempest of worry and yelping', which when it subsides, leaves Zillah 'heaving like a sea after a high wind'. The dogs, express- ive of the passionate and violent life lurking in the recesses of the house, leap from their 'hidden dens' to the 'common centre': the common centre being the hearth, with the 'warm' Lockwood expanding in spite of himself — by contrast wih his 'icy shrinking' after the fiction of passion at the seaside. Far from being put off by this reception, Lockwood is encouraged to pursue his relationship with Heathcliff and investigate further the 'sympathetic chord' he imagines between them — despite his awareness of Heathcliff's coolness: 'He evidently wished no repetition of my intrusion. I shall go, notwithstanding. It is astonishing how sociable I feel myself compared with him'. Lockwood's entry has stirred things up at the Heights, in his characteristic, semi-passive way; paradoxically he has initiated a 'stir of society', in 'meddling' with Heathcliff's affairs. As Heathcliff points out, the dogs 'won't meddle with persons who touch nothing': an indication that the metaphor (of protecting his property) is a veneer. Lockwood has not touched his property, but is in the process of touching his heart, revealing his 'soul' (as he describes Catherine). Heathcliff makes an effort to entertain Lockwood, not 'swayed by prudential considerations of the folly of offending a good tenant', as Lockwood interprets, but from the subterranean emotional need for his tenant which, at this early stage, is not stateable because not rationally comprehensible.

Lockwood's second visit to the Heights displays an insistent determination to 'get in' which contrasts strongly with his timorous behaviour at the seaside. Though locked out again, he jumps the gate, runs up the path, knocks 'till my knuckles tingled, and the dogs howled': 'So resolved, I grasped the latch, and shook it vehemently', muttering 'I don't care — I will get in!' This time his acquaintance with Heathcliff is expanded by means of his household and adopted family, the 'mortgaged' children, who during the comic tea-party combine to upturn his previous conceptions of intimate family relationships. Like Mr Heathcliff himself, each has a kind of double, a contrary self: Heathcliff is a 'gypsy' in aspect, a 'gentleman' in dress and manners; Hareton, whose name is carved over the lintel,

8

appears a labourer but his bearing is 'free, almost haughty'; Catherine, shows herself not a 'beneficent fairy' or a pet to be 'possessed' by someone (like the 'heap of dead rabbits') but equally a 'witch', mistress of the 'Black Art' of tormenting Joseph, making a mockery of superstition and sentimentality. The anti-romantic trio of misanthrope, clown and witch are as well or as ill matched as Lockwood's 'suitable pair'. Lockwood approaches the emotional reality of his dream of the first Catherine circuitously, through the romantic misunderstanding of her daughter, in an ironic passage, which, typically, has a sinister undercurrent of truth. Thus his rambling fiction about 'your amiable lady as the presiding genius over your home and heart' evokes a 'diabolical sneer' from Heathcliff who, caught off guard, extends Lockwood's fiction in a manner equally absurd, yet at the same time crystallising the function of the two Catherines and Isabella: 'Where is she — my amiable lady? . . . Oh! you would intimate that her spirit has taken the post of ministering angel and guards the fortunes of Wuthering Heights, even when her body is gone'. Lockwood and Heathcliff between them, concoct an ironic prelude to the appearance of Catherine's ghost, the real 'presiding genius' and 'ministering angel' of Wuthering Heights. Lockwood, on his second visit, is caught in the midst of life in action at the Heights; the whirl of the snowstorm without and general bustle and life of the farm which it brings into focus (the sheep and horses brought under cover, the cows being milked by the light of a lantern), all echo the confused whirl of relations and elements of knowledge within his mind. He exchanges the 'infernal dusk' of his extinguished study fire at the Grange for the scintillating 'radiance of an immense fire' at the Heights, only to find himself symbolically drenched by the inhabitants: first in their 'universal scowl', the 'cloud' within the radiant hearth, then by icy water after an abortive attempt to escape. Like other characters before (or after) him, Lockwood makes himself a prisoner at the Heights in spite of a warning about it (his first visit). He makes a second visit with the aim of extending the 'romance' of his idea of a 'misanthropist's heaven', only to find that this time, the tempest of events outstrips his tourist imagination; as Heathcliff points out, 'I wonder you should select the thick of a snow-storm to wander about in'. Lockwood's ignorance of the landscape and weather, is one with his ignorance of the nature of internal or spiritual signs and portents — of his own nature as much as Heathcliff's. Now his imaginative wanderings trap him in a terrifying encounter with emotional reality in which, as the dispute about guiding him home suggests, his own 'life' is at stake (indeed he returns just in time to prevent the 'search for his remains'). He shortly finds that he has exchanged the dismal dust-cloud at the heart of the Grange only for a storm of another kind: the 'glare of white letters [which] started from the dark as vivid as spectres' at the beginning of his dream of Catherine, image the internal storms he has hitherto avoided experiencing, now reinforced by the whirling snow-flakes which hold him fast at the Heights.

Heathcliff, by refusing to allow Lockwood 'the range of the house' that night (that is, to sleep in the sitting-room), is the indirect but inevitable means of catalysing his own spiritual struggle, as his tenant ends up in the mysterious chamber from which he felt himself 'beaten out' years before. It is the one room which Heathcliff feels he cannot 'own'; whilst also being the one relevant to his spiritual conflict, as it is the means of contact with Catherine. Lockwood has already noted the complex but rigid 'anatomy' of the Heights, with its 'recesses' and tiers of dresser and rafter within the living room, all 'laid bare to an inquiring eye' yet at the same time housing not just shining pewter and legs of ham, but uncompromising spirits 'haunting' the shady spaces and ready to 'bite' on provocation. The closet-bed in which he has his dream, enclosing the only window in the house which it is possible to climb out of, is the ultimate 'recess' in the Heights ('What tenants haunt each mortal cell', in the words of Emily Brontë's poem). Just as the front door displays official Earnshaw history, so the closet-bed and window provide the family's unofficial, subterranean, back-door contact with ostracised or unacknowledged spiritual forces, the otherworld within themselves, the internal wild moors. The enclosed architecture of the chamber of dreams initially makes Lockwood feel 'secure against the vigilance of Heathcliff, and everyone else': providing refuge against them, but not against himself and his experience of them; not against his own dreams. The bed is 'a large oak case, with squares cut out near the top, resembling coach windows', and 'a little closet, and the ledge of a window, which it enclosed, served as a table'. The closet-bed is a sort of travelling 'coach', its window communicating with other realms; it becomes associated with Catherine's coffin (with its side knocked out), Heathcliff's similar coffin (his deathbed, with the window swinging open), and the coach in which Linton (later associated with 'death') arrives, wrapped in furs, fast asleep and incapable of the experience of peering out. Its wooden ledges are carved and marked with Catherine's history in the form of her triple identitiy (Earnshaw, Linton, Heathcliff), paralleling the official stone carving over the front lintel; and it enshrines her intimate diary, written between the printed lines of the musty volumes officially intended for her spiritual guidance.

Ironically Lockwood, endeavouring to lock his mind securely in this wooden refuge, encounters instead the snowstorm within, raised by the writing 'scratched on the paint': 'a glare of white letters started from the dark, as vivid as spectres — the air swarmed with Catherines'. This image later modulates into the storm of feathers, tokens of the life on the moor, which the delirious Catherine raises by plucking her pillow. The spectral, spidery texture of the letters mingles with the mixture of hand-writing, print and sketching over which Lockwood's eyes 'wander' as he begins to disentangle Catherine's emotional route from that of the printed theology. The spidery lines some-times crystallise into images, and it is the 'excellent caricature of my friend Joseph' which awakens Lockwood's interest and acts as guide to Catherine's story (the same Joseph who had refused to guide him back to the safety of the Grange): 'An immediate interest kindled within me for the unknown Catherine, and I began, forthwith, to decypher her faded hieroglyphics'. The educated Lockwood is, in a sense, beginning to learn to read again — not customary script, but the 'faded hieroglyphics' which pertain as if to some ancient mystic rite, the religion of the 'unknown Catherine', a different kind of 'real goddess' or 'angel' from any previously conceived by him. In this, he pre-figures and complements Hareton Earnshaw learning to decipher his own name and identity via the housefront (the obvious, nevertheless a mystery to him until his interest was rekindled by the second Catherine). For Catherine, though remaining 'unknown' to Lockwood in one way, becomes

11

intimately connected with him in another: in terms of the configuration of characters which have imaginative reality for him, within his mind, she becomes 'my ghostly Catherine'.

Lockwood's 'deciphering' is effected through two nightmares, in which he explores the functions of first Joseph then Catherine, the two opposite poles of the Earnshaw household: moralising tyrant, and rebel. Catherine's diary had described how one 'awful Sunday', she and Heathcliff had decided to 'rebel' in the face of the double tyranny of Hindley (with Frances in his 'paradise on the hearth') and Joseph, sermonising in the garret. In the latter's words: 'Miss Cathy's riven th' back off "Th' Helmet uh Salvation", un' Heathcliff's pawsed his fit intuh t' first part uh "T' Broad Way to Destruction"!' Finding no warmth or shelter in the house, either physical or spiritual, and ousted from their makeshift recess under the dresser, they adopt a movable home in the form of the 'dairywoman's cloak' and scamper on the moors. (This escape from restriction we later learn leads to the fateful entry of Thrushcross Grange). For Lockwood, as in another sense for Catherine, her spirit is still on the moors, blown by the elements, seeking anchorage. But before he deciphers her image, he enlarges on her scrawled caricature of Joseph (with which he is already familiar); Joseph is his 'guide' to the printed word of Jabes Branderham's 'Pious Discourse', and Lockwood has to tread his path in the dream, 'floundering' on his journey to the church. Joseph's 'pilgrim's staff' is a 'heavy-headed cudgel', representing the vengeful battering morality to which old Earnshaw entrusted his family. Brought into close contact with this, Lockwood finds he must shed his protective wrapping of inoffensive normality, and speak out in protest. But his accusation of Jabes has the effect of marking him out for persecution: ' "Thou art the man!" cried Jabes'. No longer protected by the laws of decent behaviour, and no longer a conforming member of a civilised society (whose veneer is being stripped off), Lockwood is exposed to the 'tremendous tumult' of 'rappings and counter-rappings' of mob persecution, as he experiences for the first time what it is to be an individual rather than a member of a crowd. The unavoidable inner snow-storm is administered via the fir cones rattling against the window pan, imaging the preacher 'pouring forth his zeal in a shower of loud taps on the boards of the pulpit', as

Lockwood's wooden defences are violently prised open. It is Lockwood's experience of the 'guidance' of Joseph, and his rebellion against it, that befits him to be chosen by Catherine as her messenger, and the presenter of her story; he is singled out from both sides — 'Thou art the man' — isolated from the multitude.

Lockwood's second dream seems 'even more disagreeable' partly because it has a different kind of reality, which makes dream and waking harder to distinguish. The dream becomes an intensified reality, anchored by minute detail to the everyday physical circumstances of Lockwood's actual sleeping position — an effect continued, after Lockwood leaves the chamber, by the manner in which the narrative of the dream is embedded in household routine and indeed the very architecture of the house. The scene of the dream, the oak closet, is exactly that of Lockwood's physical state, and his attempt to unlock the window is recorded more like sleep-walking than a dream of walking. Before, Jabes's 'tumult' had been recognised, on awaking, for the noise of the fir-tree branch; here, the fir-tree (the waking fact) seems transformed, as in fairy tales, into human flesh:

> Instead of [the branch], my fingers closed on the fingers of a little, ice-cold hand! . . . finding it useless to attempt shaking the creature off, I pulled its wrist on to the broken pane, and rubbed it to and fro till the blood ran down and soaked the bedclothes.

It is not the waif, but Lockwood, who finds the violent contact so traumatic that he screams as if he were 'having his throat cut'; the ghost's feelings are thus expressed through him: it is his scream which relays the ghost's presence to Heathcliff, awakening him, piercing the house's security. Lockwood has finally 'deciphered' the vague white-letter image of Catherine, now misty only because seen through the glass: 'I discerned, obscurely, a child's face looking through the window'. Her slightly distorted image supersedes the caricature of Joseph; it is clear enough for Lockwood to recognise later that Catherine Heathcliff is not 'my ghostly Catherine'. The hallucinatory quality of the dream, the vision which is more real than actuality, is caught up later in Heathcliff's struggles to receive

13

the expression of an 'idea' of Catherine, and to differentiate this from other false tormenting 'images' of her. And the return of 'Catherine Linton' in the form of the child who was Catherine Earnshaw, measures the gap which the story has to cover in emotional terms: her life, though ended in one sense, still requires fulfilment or bringing up to date; twenty years a waif, she has 'come home'. (Twenty years takes the story back to the period of Heathcliff's mysterious absence, when the universe turned to a 'mighty stranger' for Catherine). The exile wailing 'Let me in!', can only provide a tormenting function while incomplete, rather than that of guiding or guarding 'ministering angel' of the house. Through the name she announces, she points to her daughter, who was legitimately a child 'Catherine Linton'; and the blood marks the point in adolescence at which both the Catherines emerged from their childhood homes to penetrate the house at the other end of the moor. Catherine points to the confusion and violent break-outs in personal identity which require integration: to the wild disparate elements which require acknowledgement, require to be given a 'home'.

Lockwood's dream of Catherine has a key structural function in the book analogous to Catherine's later description of the quality of dreams in the texture of her mind's life:

> "I've dreamt in my life dreams that have stayed with me ever after, and changed my ideas; they've gone through and through me, like wine through water, and altered the colour of my mind."

Lockwood's dream establishes the central dramatic concern of the book, which is the 'change' of 'ideas' — the blood soaking his bedclothes figuring 'the unknown Catherine' passing through his mind like wine through water. Despite his efforts to attribute the experience to 'bad tea and bad temper' ('what else could it be that made me pass such a terrible night?'), the watery 'tea' of his sensible mind has been coloured outside his control — whether enriched or destroyed, only subsequent events can show. The alteration within Lockwood images past and future changes within the wider 'universal' mental landscape of the novel's action; he is the microcosm to its macrocosm. Through the dream, Lockwood — and we, as readers — become aware of the tension on which the story is based, and the gap in knowledge that needs to be crossed before the ghost can be accepted. This gap is measured by the distance between Lockwood and Heathcliff, with their complementary blindness. Thus Lockwood, in one sense an outsider, appears to intrude on the inner sanctum of Heathcliff's agony of mind (as he does on Joseph's kitchen 'sanctum'), when, beaten out of the dream-chamber, and characteristically 'lost' among the 'narrow lobbies' of the house, he 'involuntarily' overhears Heathcliff's passionate cry: 'Come in! come in! . . . Oh! my heart's darling! hear me *this* time — Catherine, at last!' His words echo the ghost's 'come home . . . let me in', but it is only Lockwood who makes direct contact with the ghost: the wind/ghost/spirit which breaks through the window into Lockwood's consciousness is de-natured, without meaning, for Heathcliff, when he tries to capture it by wrenching open the window: 'The spectre showed an ordinary spectre's caprice; it gave no sign of being; but the snow and wind whirled wildly through, even reaching my station, and blowing out the light.' Heathcliff, despite the force of his will, despite his 'ownership' of this universe and its inhabitants, can encounter only the wind and snow, without the spirit — or spiritual being — it contains. This suggests that Lockwood's function in the story is less extraneous than it appears, and that Heathcliff's unconscious reason for procuring a tenant for the Grange may not necessarily be superficial 'avarice'. Lockwood's experience is not merely a dramatic way of introducing the story to the reader; Lockwood himself brings Heathcliff closer to the 'spirit' for which he searches than he has been for twenty years, although it still eludes him. He finds himself involved in spite of himself: making contact with the story initially from within the penetralium of the Heights (its ultimate recess), and only secondarily learning the 'history' of events. His initial direct experiences, his dream (and our reading of his dream) colours the chronological narrative as wine colours water; despite his ignorance, he is no longer 'a stranger' to these regions of understanding. In spite of his 'locked' romanticising mind, he allows the wind from deeper levels of consciousness to break through the barriers — himself smashing a pane of glass to ease its passage. In this way the story is opened for the reader, in emotional as well as artistic terms;

15

and a way is paved for the final phase of Heathcliff's 'moral teething' (as he terms it later). The outsider or misanthrope who is both 'of the busy world' and not of it, is the chosen one capable of unlocking the tortuous abortive tangle of relationships which exists at the beginning of the book; directing them towards resolution. In this sense Heathcliff and Lockwood genuinely form a 'suitable pair' in the midst of mental 'desolation'. On the metaphorical level on which the structure of the book is identical with its meaning, their relationship is complementary and both sides are necessary. Now that Lockwood has unlocked the situation — like a Pandora's box, ignorant of its contents — his function becomes the passive one of a listener, while Heathcliff's is the active one of resolving the tension of twenty years and more, and of completing his inner drama. Lockwood resolves that 'a sensible man ought to find sufficient company in himself' — irony reflecting on his experience of himself in the dream-closet, which renders him 'feeble as a kitten' and lays him up for the whole winter, a captive listener to 'the story of Mr Heathcliff' through the medium of Ellen Dean. He is ignorant of the fact that the ghost is as much part of his internal 'company' as of Heathcliff's, and is frightened away from direct involvement. Nevertheless his willingness to receive the story at second-hand is simultaneous with, and on a metaphorical level inseparable from, Heathcliff's ability to finish enacting it, and finally to re-enter the dream-chamber from which he felt banished for so many years; making it his death-bed. As if in appreciation of the services of his new tenant, Heathcliff escorts Lockwood back to the gates of the Grange the next morning (the issue of Lockwood's 'guide' finally resolved by his misanthropic partner), through a landscape which has, for Lockwood, changed beyond recognition after the snow-storm — his previous mental 'chart' of landmarks obliterated, and 'the whole hill-back one billowy, white ocean'.

Lockwood is returned in safety if not in comfort to the other end of the misanthropist's heaven, to begin the 'tiresomely active' function of listening, whilst physically incapacitated; 'excited, almost to a pitch of foolishness through my nerves and brain' and 'fearful of serious effects from the incidents of today and yesterday'. On one level the distance between the two misanthropes seems infinite, and (as in Isabella's terms) 'though

16

only four miles distant, there may as well be the Atlantic to part [them]'; yet, for the duration of Lockwood's tenancy, their destiny is linked, for the purpose of making Heathcliff's story known to the outer regions of consciousness, and thereby completing its fateful course, through insight.

# 2     The Eternal Rocks Beneath

(*Chapters 4 – 9*)

*Wuthering Heights*, like Greek tragedy, is ruled by a sense of fatal inevitability, with every development in the pattern of relationships accountable ultimately to an inheritance or 'gift of God' (as Earnshaw labels Heathcliff), left by an ancestor to subsequent generations. This accounts for the amoral quality of the novel, which makes irrelevant both the Victorian search for 'instances of humanity', and the modern social benevolence which weighs up the mitigating circumstances of aberrant behaviour. The reader's sympathy is caught at a much deeper level than that of a rationalising praise or blame; the novel's structure is essentially poetic, in that circumstances are subservient to an underlying emotional problem with which the characters are bound up outside the exercise of their will. The pattern of their actions is determined by the necessity to expose and catharsize the emotional knot. Like Lockwood, the reader approaches the book with conventional expectations, prepared to indulge in a form of romantic literary gossip, and finds that he is sucked into the penetralium of the Heights and the dream-chamber at the heart of its network of 'narrow lobbies'. Here, the observant 'stranger' is confronted with the ghosts that wail in the caverns of his own neglected unconscious — the 'eternal rocks beneath' (as Catherine expresses her idea of Heathcliff's function). Continuing to read the book, he may trace Emily Brontë's own artistic resolution of the tension between the 'Lockwood' and the 'Heathcliff' aspects of the mind confronted and expressed in the opening chapters.

The story, with its simultaneous present and historical action, is — as Nelly says — 'Mr Heathcliff's'. It begins with his arrival at the Heights, and his death, though not quite the last event chronologically, shapes the ending of the tale, and is the last event narrated. The first part of the story concerns his relationship with Catherine, and the second part his relationship with her ghost. This central relationship is played out and made known partly through the other characters, who all enact its primary theme of different kinds of separation and meta-

18

morphosis, serving forces which (though in one sense internal) are felt as external and outside the control of will. The strength of this emotional undercurrent is reinforced by the passive part played by the main narrator, Nelly Dean, who though present at all the crisis points, and a foster-child of the Earnshaws', is unable to have any effect on the action; she is servant to the inevitable unfolding of the story. What is termed by Heathcliff her 'double dealing' is in fact her ability to receive both sides of the story at any given moment of conflict — not in terms of total understanding, but in terms of acute observation which is helped rather than hindered by her individual emotional partisanship (her feeling for Hindley, 'born in the same year', and for her 'children', Hareton and the second Catherine). Nelly states the question of Heathcliff's origins at the end of the novel: 'But, where did he come from, the little dark thing, harboured by a good man to his bane?', at the point in the story when Heathcliff is within sight of his harbour again, having come full circle, seeing himself as a drowning man at last 'within arm's length of the shore' (as in Emily Brontë's poem, 'his home, his harbour found'). In her manner of linking the beginning and end of his 'story', Nelly makes it clear that Heathcliff never comes within her comprehension; despite knowing him from a child, he finds no 'harbour' in her mental landscape, from her vertex of understanding. Certain key moments of mystery evoked by his presence arouse in her the irrational fear that he is a 'goblin', a doppelganger walked out of a Gothic novel ('I had read of such hideous, incarnate demons'). Nevertheless, because she 'serves' his story she accurately reflects his internal needs in practical terms — notably, going to some lengths to bury him according to his instructions.

The second act of the novel's drama, covers the 'feeble', spell-bound phase of Lockwood's mysterious illness. The initiation of this phase corresponds with the introduction of the child Heathcliff into the Earnshaw mind and household, one harvest-time about a quarter of a century back, when Cathy was six and Hindley eleven. It is the image with which Nelly resumes her story. Heathcliff was picked up at Liverpool, the landing-port of starving Irish urchins after the 1845 famine, and gateway to the exotic and mysterious, opening on to the real 'Atlantic'. His transplantation to the land-locked 'out-of-the-way' moor,

19

brings with it a breath of the sea's infinity, and echoes of the unknown. Thus Lockwood, after his personal encounter with Heathcliff's past, needs Heathcliff to guide him back across the moor's 'billowy, white ocean' when his previous 'chart' has been disfigured. Heathcliff is, on one level, simply a main character in a two-phase story; but he also gains another level of existence, closer to the allegorical. He is of no family, no known age (the inscription on his tombstone merely says 'Heathcliff'), and no blood-descendants remain at the end to carry on his earthly line. Yet, like the Green Knight, his strange influence transforms the scene, negating conventional moral values (the decaying church) and forcing new ones to be forged in the vacuum, as it were out of the landscape itself; he finds his 'harbour', eventually, with 'the eternal rocks beneath'. Though Heathcliff is in one sense the ultimate outsider, it is clear that, in another sense, he comes from within old Earnshaw himself. This is suggested by the concrete physical contact between them, when Heathcliff arrives wrapped in Earnshaw's greatcoat: an image symbolising Earnshaw's triumphant realisation of a hitherto unplaced aspect of himself, a legacy to his children in lieu of the toys which he had promised to bring back from Liverpool:

> He threw himself into a chair, laughing and groaning, and bid them all stand off, for he was nearly killed — he would not have another such walk for the three kingdoms. "And at the end of it, to be flighted to death!" he said, opening his great coat, which he held bundled up in his arms. "See here, wife; I was never so beaten with anything in my life; but you must e'en take it as a gift of God; though it's as dark almost as if it came from the devil."

'Heathcliff' is the name of a son who died in infancy. Though not literally an illegitimate son (as is sometimes maintained), he arrives 'at the beginning of harvest', as though representing fruit of a different kind; later, Heathcliff returns after his worldly tranformation, by the light of the harvest moon. His original harbour within old Earnshaw is not a restful relationship for either of them; and Earnshaw, after his three-days' walk and metaphorical giving-birth to this live bundle, the 'gift of God', finds his energies exhausted. He feels internally battered, 'flighted to death', imaging the first violent internal storm later sustained, in different ways, by Lockwood; by Frances, overtaken by death shortly after giving birth; by Catherine in her delirium; by Hareton who narrowly escapes becoming a battered baby; by the second Catherine in her virtual marriage to 'death'; and by Heathcliff himself, 'beaten' by the spirit of Catherine.

Earnshaw himself, though responsible for introducing to the household something more real than the toys requisitioned by the children, cannot cope with the conflicts aroused, either within the family or as reflected within his own mind. After his 'laughing and groaning' excitement has died down, he leaves it to the next generation to determine the ambiguous nature of their inheritance from 'God' or 'the devil'. His wife can make nothing of the gift, and dies shortly afterwards; he himself is inadequate and helpless in the face of the continued 'beating' which would be required to achieve a new stability. He presents to the household the germ of a new idea, which then has to be worked out and assimilated in the pattern of relationships over the next two generations, as they test experientially both its destructive and its creative potential. The nature of Earnshaw's final illness, as his strength crumbles, significantly involves an increasing intolerance and rigidity, representing his final withdrawal from further emotional conflict and the establishment of a split, black-and-white hierarchy between good and bad. Originally he had merely displaced the children's toys (the whip and fiddle lost on the journey), but later, he displaces the children themselves, for an imaginary idea of Heathcliff. Thus, in a state in which 'suspected slights of his authority nearly threw him into fits', Heathcliff becomes a function of his fragile egocentricity and omnipotence: 'This was especially to be remarked if any one attempted to impose upon, or domineer over his favourite ... seeming to have got into his head the notion that, because he liked Heathcliff, all hated, and longed to do him an ill-turn.' Instead of completing the integration of Heathcliff creatively, Earnshaw makes him exclusive 'favourite' and the upholder of his own power and integrity, his fatherliness. His primitive, brittle system of demarcation forces Hindley into the position of 'reprobate': for him, Heathcliff is a 'usurper', initially of his 'parent's affections', then of his own

21

property, son, and life. Meanwhile Cathy, as the only girl, adopts different means of making her power and presence felt, rivalling her father by parodying his weakest spot, acting the 'little mistress': 'and doing just what her father hated most, showing how her pretended insolence, which he thought real, had more power over Heathcliff than his kindness. How the boy would do *her* bidding in anything, and *his* only when it suited his own inclination.' With the 'bonniest eye, the sweetest smile, and the lightest foot in the parish', she develops her charm initially to catch her father's attention by partly mocking his favouritism; but 'Mr Earnshaw did not understand jokes from his children', and later, she inherits his own brittleness, 'maddening at injuries', not 'laughing under them'. Cathy becomes 'inseparable' from Heathcliff, but her father, owing to his rigid demarcations, repudiates her Heathcliff-side: 'I cannot love thee; thou'rt worse than thy brother.'

Unable to comprehend the controversial quality which he himself has brought into the household, he falls back into the rigidly pietistic standards represented by Joseph, 'the wearisomest, self-righteous pharisee that ever ransacked a Bible to rake the promises to himself, and fling the curses on his neighbours'; 'and, the more feeble master became, the more influence he gained.' Joseph, like the gaunt thorns and gnarled currant bushes in the garden, is part of the architecture of the house, remaining there at the end when everyone else has left, and considering himself guardian of the ancient Earnshaw blood-stock. Perpetually old, and abhorring any development or change, he appears to be immune even from the transformation of death. The master's 'feebleness' in his new confusion, consists in his surrendering the living power of judgement to this textbook 'pious discoursing', in the hope that it will supply his deficiencies. This inability to bear internal conflict is captured in the description of his death-scene:

> I remember the master, before he fell into a doze, stroking her bonny hair — it pleased him rarely to see her gentle — and saying —
> "Why canst thou not always be a good lass, Cathy?"
> And she turned her face up to his, and laughed,and answered —

22

"Why cannot you always be a good man, father?"
But as soon as she saw him vexed again, she kissed his hand,
and said she would sing him to sleep. She began singing very
low . . .

Old Earnshaw, unable to face the implications of her serrated
rejoinder to his simplistic question, forces her into a position in
which she can only be on peaceful terms with him by lulling him
into a sleep which is death. Her low singing contrasts with
'spitting and grinning' at the loss of her whip. He seeks oblivion,
through the illusion that she is a 'good lass'. His subsiding into
unconsciousness prefigures Catherine's own death in the face of
the conflict between Edgar and Heathcliff, the irreconcileable
split within. The final picture in the chapter portrays the two
children (Hindley being away at college), glimpsed through the
open door of their room (Lockwood's dream-room) and
manufacturing an image of heaven in that recess of the Heights,
from the restricted materials available to them:

> The little souls were comforting each other with better
> thoughts than I could have hit on; no parson in the world ever
> pictured heaven so beautifully as they did, in their innocent
> talk; and, while I sobbed, and listened, I could not help
> wishing we were all there safe together.

The sentimentality of the picture rests at the door-jamb, with
Nelly; for there are already ominous indications that the
'innocent' heaven is unfit to withstand the test of experience.
Their dream of Earnshaw's new harbour, expressing their idea
of his continuing influence, is not a 'safe' foundation for the
future, capable of weathering the future storms on the horizon.
Thus later at the crisis point of Catherine's decision to marry,
she relates her dream that 'heaven did not seem to be my home';
heaven is the home of a father who cannot tolerate the conception that he may not 'always be a good man'. The door-jamb
divided a fragile, illusory, innocent dream of heaven from the
dangerous world into which the children are soon to be thrust,
feeling homeless and outcast from heaven.

That process begins immediately on Hindley's return, no
longer one of the children, but 'master'. He drives a wedge
between Catherine and Heathcliff, making the sheltered

'children's room' Catherine's only. Though not delivered paternally (but rather from his own position as ousted elder brother), this is in effect a symbolic wedge marking the painful beginning of adolescence — the time when the 'children' can no longer sleep together. In a sense, they never leap this hurdle, and the age of twelve runs through the novel as marking an unravelled emotional knot: hence the child-ghost 'Catherine Linton', and Catherine's delirious dream that 'at twelve years old', she had been 'wrenched from the Heights' and converted into Mrs Linton, a feeling deriving from her 'misery at the separation that Hindley had ordered between me and Heathcliff'. Hindley, in his new position as 'master', returns to fulfil his fantasy of the ideal life of privilege and emotional indulgence from which he felt excluded from the moment of Heathcliff's arrival. He enacts in some ways a pathetic caricature of the ageing Earnshaw's irritable tyranny — as in the episode already reported by Catherine in her diary: 'You forget you have a master here ... I insist on perfect sobriety and silence. Oh, boy! was that you? Frances, darling, pull his hair as you go by.' His ideal of 'perfect sobriety and silence', like any rigid authoritarianism, underlines his internal instability, liable to collapse at the first manifestation of a break in the hierarchy — as, indeed, he collapses when, with Frances' death, his system of idolatry is destroyed. 'He had room in his heart for only two idols — his wife and himself.' The foundation for his 'mastery' is built on the shaky 'paradise on the hearth' which he has erected around Frances and himself, and from which not only the servants (who used to sit 'in the house'), but Catherine and Heathcliff, are excluded: exclusiveness being an essential quality in the heaven of the former outcast: 'there they were, like two babies, kissing and talking nonsense by the hour — foolish palaver that we should be ashamed of. We made ourselves as snug as our means allowed in the arch of the dresser.'

In this context, his choice of Frances is significant. He protects her from the scrutiny of his father, which Nelly accounts for by assuming her lack of fortune or connection, but which seems in fact to lie at a less rational level, associated with a fear of his father's destructiveness. The father who had allowed Heathcliff to 'crush to morsels' the precious fiddle bought at Liverpool, and who had subsequently disowned him (in emotional terms) in favour of that destructive force, could also cast an evil eye on his new, jealously-chosen idol. Hindley (by contrast with the 'spitting' Cathy) had broken down and wept at the fate of his fiddle, his sensitive but fragile spirit collapsing in the face of adversity. Frances then becomes the fiddle ousted by his father. Yet Frances herself, like the crushable fiddle, is 'a rush of a lass', already in the throes of consumption:

> I imagined her as little likely to die as myself. She was rather thin, but young, and fresh complexioned, and her eyes sparkled as bright as diamonds. I did remark, to be sure, that mounting the stairs made her breathe very quick, that the least sudden noise set her all in a quiver, and that she coughed troublesomely sometimes; but, I knew nothing of what these symptoms portended . . .

She is flushed and sparkling, but the animation is partly a cover for ominous symptoms. She already bears Earnshaw's disinheriting curse (in the emotional, not the literal sense). Her terror at the funeral preparations for Earnshaw expresses her intimate connection with the death progressing within her, and particularly with death as embodied by the father-in-law from whom she has, in a sense, been guarded in vain (a fairy-tale curse): 'I thought she was half silly from her behaviour while that went on . . . she began describing with hysterical emotion the effect it produced on her to see black'. Frances is already possessed by the inevitable destructive force; the seeds of the loss of 'paradise' are already sown. From the point of view, or rather the unconscious vertex of Hindley in the general emotional configuration, it appears that Frances has the enemy within her, in terms of both old Earnshaw and his corrupting 'usurper' Heathcliff, the 'imp of Satan'.

Both Frances's gay nature — the 'gay spirit' who loved the Christmas music — and her physical illness, are symbolic of aspects of Hindley himself: the creative, and the potentially self-destructive. In her 'bright eyes', whose brightness derives ambiguously from both life and deathly fever, are mirrored Hindley's own irreconcileable poles of existence: reflecting the hectic, excited, vulnerable nature of his emotional life: potentially gay and musical, but inheriting Earnshaw's instability and inability to face emotional conflict. Hindley chose

25

Frances as the image of his own lost 'fiddle', his musical soul, determined that his new status as 'master' should ensure its protection and preservation. She provided an idol or toy for him to baby and protect, and through whom to assert his new power and try to construct a secure paradise free from outside intervention. But in choosing the consumptive 'rush of a lass' for a soul-mate, he is instrumental in exploding his own myth. Already he is gambling against forces he is powerless to resist: a game played-out literally to the end, against Heathcliff; the earlier incident in which he allowed Heathcliff to take his horse, is enacted repeatedly, not as a function of circumstance, but as a function of his own nature. Hindley's tyrannical system of privilege cannot protect his soul from the intolerable aspects of his own nature which Heathcliff comes to symbolise for him — the rebellion, wildness, destructiveness imaged in the incipient death within Frances. For the 'paradise on the hearth' is founded on his and Frances's mutual self-deception, in which death is denied until the last minute: 'he persisted doggedly, nay furiously, in affirming her health improved every day'; finally Frances dies 'while leaning on his shoulder, in the act of saying she thought she should be able to get up to-morrow.' Hence her death, by undermining his whole system of 'mastery', the only way in which he felt he could protect the lively spirit within himself, results in his total mental collapse. The 'tyranny' of his illusory system forces him to take Frances's death in the light of a personal defeat, in which the alien, the 'imp of Satan', has won, and the dark forces brought into the family with Heathcliff have asserted their pre-eminence: 'he grew desperate; his sorrow was of that kind that will not lament; he neither wept nor prayed — he cursed and defied — execrated God and man, and gave himself up to reckless dissipation.' Hindley's collapse is inevitable, given the failure of integration within himself; the seeds of his final degradation are sown simultaneously with those of creativity — taking on independent life in the form of Hareton. Nelly later wonders why Hindley failed as a father, in contrast to Edgar, apparently the weaker man and presented with a weak, premature child. The fact is that Hindley's doom is sealed by the death of Frances, reinforcing his sense of exiled failure and crushed integrity; his omnipotent gamble with death leaves him a ruined shell. He cannot redeem death through a creative relationship with Hareton, the healthy baby, because in a sense he already regards his son as the property of the enemy. Hindley's identity crumbles finally with the expulsion from a 'paradise' in which he needed to feel himself invincible. Consequently his subsequent pathetic attempts to ensure 'justice' for Hareton are foiled, not by Heathcliff who is merely the agent, but by himself. Hareton ultimately receives, or earns, 'justice' of a complex not a straightforward nature, derived from his two complementary 'devil-daddies'. Hindley's character is, at Frances's death, already set in relation to his father's ambiguous 'gift'; he makes the Heathcliff-within-him a 'devil'; ensuing events merely confirm the underlying structure of the 'eternal rocks beneath'.

The fact that Hindley's love for Frances is part of a distorted creative system, is shown before the failure of his relationship with Hareton, in the effect of their exclusive 'paradise' on the other 'children'. Ejected from the warmth of the central hearth, Cathy and Heathcliff become dependent on the heath for space in which to develop their relationship. In an endeavour to recover the 'innocent' heaven of their old closet-bed, they construct other makeshift play-houses from whose shelter to explore and pour scorn on the other 'heavens' from which they seem outcast. On the 'awful Sunday' made known to Lockwood through Catherine's diary, they huddle under the 'arch of the dresser', then in the confined back-kitchen, and finally, finding no room at the Heights, adopt a mobile shelter in the form of the dairywoman's cloak, and escape to the moor. They are finally squeezed out of the Heights when the dual tyranny of Hindley and Joseph is at its height; hurling the starving fare of 'Th' Helmet uh Salvation' and 'T' Broad Way to Destruction' into the dog-kennel, they notice a beacon-light from the Grange, and go 'to see whether the Lintons passed their Sunday evenings standing shivering in corners, while their father and mother sat eating and drinking, and singing and laughing, and burning their eyes out before the fire.' Their vision of this particular heaven is relayed by Heathcliff alone, now the sole outcast, whose return from its brightness is seen by Nelly via 'the light of a lantern glimmering through the gate' later that night:

27

Ah! it was beautiful — a splendid place carpeted with crimson, and crimson-covered chairs and tables, and a pure white ceiling bordered by gold, a shower of glass-drops hanging in silver chains from the centre, and shimmering with little soft tapers . . . We should have thought ourselves in heaven!

The dazzling imagery of the crimson colouring shot through with flashes of light (glass-drops, silver chains, white and gold, shimmering) echoes the 'paradise on earth' from which they are excluded at the Heights (the fire, the white floor, the shining pewter), yet (like Frances's flushed face and 'diamond' eyes') it has its sinister side, its microcosmic hell:

"Isabella . . . lay screaming at the farther end of the room, shrieking as if witches were running red-hot needles into her. Edgar stood on the hearth weeping silently, and in the middle of the table sat a little dog shaking its paw and yelping . . . We laughed outright at the petted things, we did despise them!"

It gradually appears that the Grange is not really antithetical to the Heights, but rather plays the same theme tune transposed into another key. Despite Heathcliff's scorn (and his belief that he speaks equally for Cathy), our sense of déjà vue here derives from the remembrance of Earnshaw's return with his unwanted 'gift', Heathcliff himself; with Hindley weeping like Edgar and Cathy 'spitting' not unlike Isabella 'screaming' and 'shrieking'. Unlike the Earnshaw children, the Lintons possess their desired 'pet' or toy; but that pet is shortly to be replaced by Catherine herself with her wild Heathcliffian nature, altering the course of their future lives irrevocably. Her irresistible longing to be a 'pet' and a 'petted thing', like the Lintons or Frances, never fulfilled in childhood and never understood by Heathcliff, results inevitably in her new position as queen of the Linton hearth and centre of illumination, superseding the glass chandelier with her own radiance:

"They . . . wheeled her to the fire, and I left her, as merry as she could be, dividing her food between the little dog and Skulker, whose nose she pinched as she ate; and kindling a spark of spirit in the vacant blue eyes of the Lintons — a dim reflection from her own enchanting face — I saw they were full of stupid admiration . . ."

Her new glow equals and contrasts with Frances's hectic flush. Though in one sense a victim, she appears in another sense queen and benefactress; not just the Linton children, but symbolically the two dogs, become recipients of her bounty: the pet 'heap of warm hair' (echoing Lockwood's 'heap of dead rabbits') and the savage guard-dog, being twin sides of a motif running throughout the book at points of passionate transition. Cathy's guide into the Grange is the pet dog, who issues forth from the crimson room in another form, that of Skulker the bulldog, with his 'huge, purple tongue hanging half a foot out of his mouth, and pendant lips streaming with bloody slaver'. The 'devil' of a dog represents a metamorphosis of the image of the chandelier pendants dripping light in the crimson room, the hell emerging from within its heavenly brightness. The dogs and the blood link this key episode with Lockwood's entry into the Heights; with Isabella's elopement (leaving her pet springer gasping at the end of a rope) and knife-marked return; and with the second Cathy's first confrontation with Hareton at the Heights, through a fight between their dogs. The central constellation of imagery of blood, glass and hieroglyphics, relates back to Lockwood's original dream, rubbing the exiled Catherine Linton's bleeding wrist on the shattered glass; and prefigures Hindley's slashed wrist when Heathcliff bursts through the solid Earnshaw housefront: an entry prophesied here in his vision of 'painting the housefront with Hindley's blood' (a new kind of Earnshaw inscription). Heathcliff's related threat of 'shattering [the Lintons'] great glass panes to a million of fragments, unless they let her out' also prefigures the translucent but fragile 'heaven' in which he returns to find Catherine Linton years later, sitting in a window whose panes 'reflected a score of glittering moons': a situation apparently 'wondrously peaceful', but underneath, dangerously explosive.

For Catherine has to pay heavily for her new position as Linton queen. Though possessing 'the lightest foot in the parish', she is significantly barefoot and unable to run fast, hence is vulnerable to the grasp of the crimson 'devil', the metamorphosed 'pet', who exists within her as much as without her. Like the mermaid in the fairy-story, she pays for her prince by cutting off an essential part of herself (her fish's tail, as it were, associated with her life with Heathcliff on the wild sea-like

moor); walking on 'red-hot needles' (like Isabella) she accepts
the infernal aspect of the crimson room without complaint: 'She
did not yell out — no! She would have scorned to do it, if she had
been spitted on the horns of a mad cow'. Much later, she tells the
uncomprehending Ellen that all those years, she has been 'tormented, haunted', 'in agony'. That particular agony begins,
years before the marriage itself, with the pain of an internal split
that she cannot harmonise, but that she precariously covers over
through the illusion that she is 'loved' by everyone and consequently reigns in both kingdoms: 'I always thought, though
everyone hated and despised each other, they could not avoid
loving me'. Her agony begins when she becomes the twelve-
year-old 'Catherine Linton', whose ghost is still attempting to
re-enter her 'home' some twenty years later: that is, to unite the
split, and achieve integration between Linton, Earnshaw and
Heathcliff. Her separation from Heathcliff at the beginning of
adolescence is only superficially caused by the external factor of
Hindley's tyrannical order, and by the chance seizure of a
Grange bulldog. On a deeper level it is instigated by Catherine
herself, as Heathcliff knows: 'Because misery, and degradation,
and death, and nothing that God or satan could inflict would
have parted us, *you*, of your own will, did it.' Heathcliff is wrong
only in attributing it to her 'will' — the impotence of willpower
in the face of emotion being the last lesson he himself has to
learn. The internal rift within Catherine marks a subterranean
shift in the 'rocks beneath' of her character and in the whole
pattern of revised relationships initiated by old Earnshaw's 'gift
of God'.

This subterranean shift culminates three years later in the
storm which comes 'rattling over the Heights', described in
terms of an earthquake striking at the heart of the house, the
chimney-stack, and marking the complete separation of
Catherine and Heathcliff. The events which lead up to this
storm consist in the gradual ostracism and degradation of
Heathcliff, simultaneous with an undercurrent which
establishes his central irreplaceable position in the life of the
house and family. These twin, though contradictory, movements, coalesce in the emergence of the 'double nature' of
Catherine, which first becomes apparent at Christmas on her
return from five weeks of superficial civilising at Thrushcross

Grange. The 'bright graceful damsel' who descends from her horse like Cinderella, appears to have united the two neighbours, bringing glamour and colour with her, and reinvigorating the spirit of Wuthering Heights. The Christmas episode stands out in the book as its most concentrated piece of social description; it represents the social union of the Lintons and Earnshaws — neighbourhood life at its most traditional, with the slightly nostalgic sense that this is the way it used to be in the past (suggested by Ellen's memory of how 'old Earnshaw used to come in and give her a Christmas box'). The 'shining kitchen utensils, the polished clock, the silver mugs, the speckless purity of the floor', together with the reception of the Christmas singers, excel in liveliness the glamour of the Grange's crimson parlour. But the insistence of the Linton parents and the 'master and mistress' of the Heights that the 'naughty swearing boy' Heathcliff should be excluded from the festivities and from all contact with the 'darling' children, reveals the hollowness of the Christmas socialisation, and simultaneously, the alien presence which smoulders disregarded at its centre. In a new cluster of references to his 'darkness' — his face 'dismally beclouded', his 'dusky fingers', 'skulking behind the settle', Heathcliff seems isolated from the house, and in particular from the new Catherine: 'Why, how very black and cross you look! and how — how funny and grim! But that's because I'm used to Edgar, and Isabella Linton. Well, Heathcliff, have you forgotten me?' Inevitably, because of the elders' attempt to block Heathcliff from contact, there is a clash between the two 'rivals': because he is accused of 'touching' the pies he throws apple sauce at Edgar. The refusal to allow him 'his share of the dainties' and to banish him from sight and hearing merely roots his position more deeply: 'I'm trying to settle how I shall pay Hindley back. I don't care how long I wait, if I can only do it . . . while I'm thinking of that, I don't feel pain.' Heathcliff, not allowed to join the dance, expresses his presence by drawing Cathy out, first under the table (as she pretends to lose her fork: 'She hastily dived under the cloth to conceal her emotion'), then up to the garret where he is locked up. She affirms that 'the music sounded sweetest at the top of the steps', implying that their conversation together is the sweeter music, and seeking out the alternative disguised festivity or old

31

'heaven'. The Christmas party illuminates the nature of a society in which emotion cannot be played out or recognised in public, as part of the general 'dance', but is thrust into dark corners, behind locked doors, under covers. Cathy is acting not only as herself, but also as representative of the Earnshaws, when she takes on herself the function of joining Heathcliff in the garret; though unable to integrate both sides of her nature, she recognises the pull of the alien, apparently powerless element, and responds to it. And Heathcliff is an indispensable part of their existence, though locked away like Rochester's mad wife.

Other than Cathy herself, Nelly is the only one of the household capable of facing and stating Heathcliff's existence, in her position as 'double-dealing' observer of all aspects of the story. It is her historical persistence, her memory of old Earnshaw and his 'fondness for Heathcliff', that makes her recognise the appropriateness of 'arranging' Heathcliff and drawing out his disguised 'princeliness', just as she has cleaned and decorated the house in the traditional manner, making it 'cheerful with great fires befitting Christmas eve'. She 'steals time' from her official duties to act as mirror to Heathcliff, reflecting and exposing his nature as a strange kind of Christmas spirit:

> "I'll steal time to arrange you so that Edgar Linton shall look quite a doll beside you: and that he does — You are younger, and yet, I'll be bound, you are taller and twice as broad across the shoulders — you could knock him down in a twinkling; don't you feel that you could? . . . Come to the glass, and I'll let you see what you should wish. Do you mark those two lines between your eyes, and those thick brows, that instead of rising arched, sink in the middle, and that couple of black fiends, so deeply buried, who never open their windows boldly, but lurk glinting under them, like devil's spies? Wish and learn to smooth away the surly wrinkles, to raise your lids frankly, and change the fiends to confident, innocent angels . . . And now . . . tell me whether you don't think yourself rather handsome? I'll tell you, I do. You're fit for a prince in disguise. Who knows, but your father was Emperor of China, and your mother an Indian queen, each of them able to buy up, with one week's income, Wuthering Heights and Thrushcross Grange together?"

This description of Heathcliff is the only setpiece in the book; other physical descriptions are generally brief and incidental, evoked to make some point relevant to the context of the action. Yet this, also, gains its effectiveness from the context: it sets the presence and power of Heathcliff in balanced opposition to the social festivities. The darkness of the 'prince in disguise' has its own glamour: banished from the general dance, he nevertheless draws the new princess (acknowledged now as 'quite a beauty') away from their company to his, exiled and locked in a far garret — another version of their closet-bed, the dark playhouse. Earnshaw's alien, untraditional 'gift' smoulders at the centre of the Heights and already involves the Linton children who, unlike their parents, cannot resist measuring themselves against its compelling negative fascination (as with Edgar 'peeping from the doorway' in curiosity, or Isabella's earlier 'Frightful thing!'). It is only a matter of time before Nelly's fantasy about him buying up both houses, is fulfilled. Nevertheless, the concept of power which she mirrors and registers here, on behalf of the reader and the stage which the story has reached, is later to be overturned, in a manner incomprehensible and unstateable as yet. She still conceives of power in terms of 'knocking him [Edgar] down', as does Hindley: 'Next time, Master Edgar, take the law into your own fists'. And the primitive concept of knocking people down, and buying up property, is complemented only by the equally innocent one of changing 'devil's spies' to 'angel's eyes'. Neither concept can comprehend the implications of Heathcliff's situation; hence it is that he can envisage no way out other than the impossible one of becoming 'angelic' in nature and feature ('if I knocked him down twenty times, that wouldn't make him less handsome, or me more so'), or that of revenge against the other tyrant, 'paying Hindley back'. Nelly, setting the looking-glass to Heathcliff and showing him 'what you should wish', is able to receive the emotional and intellectual reverberations of the current state of the story — but no further.

This applies to Lockwood, who is given a break at the end of the Christmas section, to interpose with his chorus-like comments, measuring the reader's digestion. The Christmas union of the Lintons and Earnshaws by the music of the Gimmerton band, represents the nearest equivalent to the 'stir of society' Lockwood has left behind. Yet Nelly's balanced presentation of the the life of Heathcliff and the life of society, or rather of the Heathcliffian life within society (though banished), percolates through to Lockwood in the form of a distinction between social appearances or forms and underground currents of passion:

> I perceive that people in these regions . . . *do* live more in earnest, more in themselves, and less in surface change, and frivolous external things. I could fancy a love for life here almost possible; and I was a fixed unbeliever in any love of a year's standing.

The confines of space in 'these regions', and of time in 'a year', bound a mental universe which is in fact Lockwood's own just as much as that of the main protagonists. Nelly points out that 'here we are the same as anywhere else, when you get to know us' and that her understanding stems as much from 'sharp discipline' and studying, as from the literal confines of her situation. Nevertheless for Lockwood, those literal confines of space and time have a metaphorical significance: they represent an artistic, structural boundary round an extended image of mental action. Nelly's account of Mr Heathcliff's story is at the same time a mirror of his own mind, for the first time held up for his inspection; it is Lockwood, more than Nelly, whose physical restrictions (especially since imprisoned in bed) compel him to 'cultivate [his] reflective faculties for want of occasions for frittering [his] life away in trifles.' The concept of a 'love for life' has meaning for him for the first time. And though he eventually shies away from direct participation in the 'love' which evolves during his year's tenancy, yet his secondary critical experience of listening and reflecting is in effect an imaginative effort of love; and it has, moreover, a subterranean stimulatory effect on the ultimate real romance of the second generation. Uneasily weighing the balance between 'living in oneself' and 'surface change', and observing the development of Heathcliff, he becomes aware for the first time of the 'rocks beneath' the surface of his own mental landscape. With his superficial values, or preconceptions, obliterated by a fall of snow, he turns to introspection (with some guidance from Heathcliff himself), in an attempt to decipher the internal hieroglyphics, and find his way 'home'. Lockwood is, in effect, Emily Brontë's critical reader; his difficulties exist not merely as comic background, but in order to direct the reader to the difficulty of his own experience in differentiating a seaside fiasco, one of society's romances, from a love for life. Despite his discomfort, and the necessity for six months' refuge in the 'busy world', Lockwood stands the test in that he returns to hear the story to the end, and to observe the ultimate harbour found by Earnshaw's gift of God.

Heathcliff's position at the heart of the Earnshaw household is established, by action this time rather than words, on the day of crisis on which he is banished from the Heights by Cathy — a form of self-banishment. This occurs three years after the Christmas which established the rivalry between himself and Edgar, during which period has occurred the birth of Hareton and death of Frances, and the Heights has become an 'infernal house' shunned by respectable society, owing to Hindley's dissipation. The hellish or destructive aspect of his relationship with Frances is now imaged in terms of his failure to 'recognise' his own son — the creativity which he rejected when he found himself not its 'master':

> "Oh! . . . I see that hideous little villain is not Hareton . . . if it be, he deserves flaying alive for not running to welcome me, and for screaming as if I were a goblin. Unnatural cub, come hither! I'll teach thee to impose on a good-hearted, deluded father".

Hindley is identified with the 'goblin', his personal delusional idea of Heathcliff, which he therefore sees reflected in his son's idea of him, as a 'devil daddy'. It is while this delusional, self-destructive state is at its height (in his 'madman's rage'), that Hindley hands over the reins to Heathcliff (as in the horse episode of their childhood); and the prince in disguise becomes the disguised guardian of the Earnshaw stock, in Hindley's default. This is symbolised by the episode in which Heathcliff rescues Hareton from his father, who unintentionally drops him from the banisters. Although Nelly recounts this episode in the rational terms of a double accident (neither Hindley's dropping the child, nor Heathcliff's catching him, being a function of deliberate will), it is told with an air of inevitability; her acute observation pinpoints its symbolic features in the total context of events. Heathcliff emerges from the lower depths of the house, as he does from background or shadow at other critical points in the book, as if he were part of its internal structure of narrow lobbies. It is this 'noise' which distracts Hindley's (and Ellen's) attention, causing his 'careless grasp', 'almost forgetting what he had in his hands':

> "Who is that?" he asked, hearing some one approaching the stair's foot. I leant forward also, for the purpose of signing to Heathcliff, whose step I recognised, not to come further; and, at the instant when my eye quitted Hareton, he gave a sudden spring, delivered himself from the careless grasp that held him, and fell. . . . Heathcliff arrived underneath just at the critical moment; by a natural impulse he arrested his descent . . .

It is not Nelly alone who recognises Heathcliff's step; it is also Hindley who is disturbed by the sensed presence of Heathcliff, whom he associates with all his trouble, and whom he degrades in order to project or externalise his own self-degradation. The episode of exchanging the 'grasp' of the child, is not told as an accident, but as an unconscious function of the relationship of the two men, and indeed of the child, who actively 'delivers himself'. As always, Nelly is powerless at the crucial moment — for an instant her eye quits Hareton, her charge, symbolising the way that she is forced to give up her own method of upbringing and surrender him to Heathcliff's. Hareton is not brought up under her eye, after the age of five, but from the time she 'begins to teach him his letters' he is removed to Heathcliff's guardianship: again not merely a circumstantial event, but an inevitable function of the total constellation of characters. Later, on the day when she is drawn to see Hareton at the Heights by her hallucination of seeing the child Hindley at the same age, at the crossroads, she discovers, not a version of Hindley, but a version of Heathcliff; 'The apparition had outstripped me; it stood looking through the gate', but it denounces 'Devil Daddy' and expresses loyalty to 'Mr Heathcliff'. During the ten months of their separation, the child appears to have forgotten her: 'Nelly, if she lived in his memory at all, was not recognized as one with me.' Her bribe of oranges conjures up not Hindley, but the real spirit behind him, the 'goblin' Heathcliff who appears 'on the door stones' and terrifies her into flight. In this loss of contact with Hareton, Nelly is in a way echoing and paralleling the experience of her 'early playmate' Hindley who lives so vividly in her memory, 'as fresh as reality' — the evidence of their childhood games still present in the store of stones and shells collected within the signpost. Unlike Hindley, she lives to weather subsequent emotional dynastics, and thus in a way perpetuates his influence, alongside that of Heathcliff, when Hareton comes under her eye again.

Meanwhile, the 'goblin' Heathcliff, in spite of his deliberate degradation of Hareton to 'revenge himself' on Hindley's treatment of him, continues to be the 'instrument of thwarting his own revenge' that he had become (in Nelly's words), when he rescued Hareton as a baby. After Hindley's funeral his 'ownership' of the child is clinched:

> He lifted the unfortunate child on to the table, and muttered, with peculiar gusto,
> "Now, my bonny lad, you are mine!' And we'll see if one tree won't grow as crooked as another, with the same wind to twist it!"
> The unsuspecting thing was pleased at this speech . . .

But Heathcliff omits the concept of love from his calculations. Though far from a model of 'normal' paternal behaviour, the relationship which he establishes with the boy is real, by contrast with Hindley's which is delusional; and it consequently outgrows his neatly diabolical intentions. Hareton takes root in his imagination as 'a personification of my youth', catharsizing his past experience; blown by a different wind, the tree of Hareton's growth grows differently, and redirects that of Heathcliff at the same time — Nelly notes 'evidence of a wealthy soil that might yield luxuriant crops'. Later, the 'thousand forms . . . and ideas he awakens, or embodies', express for Heathcliff a new realm of spiritual reality, deriving from the 'love' he 'would have felt' for him, never explicitly acknowledged. Hareton reciprocates by regarding him as a father more real than his own: 'How would you like me to speak ill of *your* father?' he corrects Cathy. The bond between Hareton and Heathcliff becomes instrumental in repeating history with a difference, and in gradually evolving a concept of power other than that of revenge, ownership, or omnipotent willpower.

Heathcliff's progressive ostracism and degradation at Wuthering Heights coincides with a parallel, underground movement in which, paradoxicaly, his indispensability becomes affirmed. These twin developments culminate in his ultimate departure from the house on the day of crisis in which a series of 'accidents' suggest his new function as guardian of the 'last of the Earnshaw stock', and as the 'eternal rocks beneath' the character structure of Catherine and of the moorland society as a whole. His central position in the Earnshaw heritage, suggested by saving Hareton from his father, is confirmed only when he feels himself banished — not by the enemy, Hindley, but by Catherine, the Earnshaw who is inseparable from himself. The grounds for their separation were laid during the venture to Thrushcross Grange three years earlier, and are now displayed openly as Edgar walks in and Heathcliff walks out: 'The contrast resembled what you see in exchanging a bleak, hilly, coal country for a beautiful fertile valley'. The open exchange is inevitable, since the adhesive relationship of Cathy and Heathcliff has reached a point of stagnant frustration, incapable of continuing beyond the twelve-year-old stage where is stuck, into adult sexuality. Heathcliff 'had ceased to express his fondness for her in words, and recoiled with angry suspicion from her girlish caresses, as if conscious there could be no gratification in lavishing such marks of affection on him.' Correspondingly Catherine, though blindly continuing her 'girlish caresses', finds Heathcliff 'no company at all': 'You might be dumb or a baby for anything you say to amuse me, or for anything you do, either!' By contrast, her relationship with Edgar is at least susceptible of further movement, in a quarrel which breaks 'the outworks of youthful timidity' so that they 'forsake the disguise of friendship, and confess themselves lovers'. For at fifteen, Catherine is the 'queen of the country-side'; she emerges from her two homes, the crimson parlour of the Grange and the 'infernal house' at the Heights, like Proserpine, queen of the underworld. And it is significant that the key quarrel between herself and Edgar, is sparked off by the quarrel between herself and Heathcliff, who receives her first complaint about his 'company' 'in much agitation'. The corresponding agitation within herself, derives from her foreboding of the clash between them, representing the internal rift which she is unable to accommodate; hence Heathcliff, though he departs from their presence, is in a sense the cause of their quarrel and the stimulatory factor in their change of state from 'friends' to 'lovers'. During the quarrel Cathy exhibits to Edgar, for the first time, what Nelly terms 'a glimpse of her genuine disposition' — the wildness associated with her Heathcliffian nature. In the process, her equanimity is destroyed, and her uncontainable inner disturbance and bruising explodes in the crimson colouring which she stirs up all round her, like wine through water: 'her whole complexion in a blaze', 'her ears red with rage', 'a decided purple witness' in Nelly's arm, and the shaken Hareton who 'waxed livid'. Underneath the princess's skin, the 'silly dress' which antagonised Heathcliff, is an eruption of blood, as on her first entry into the crimson room. The establishment of 'lovers' involves imagery of prey erupting through the civilised game; Edgar 'possessed the power to depart, as much as a cat· possesses the power to leave a mouse half killed, or a bird half eaten'. And their relationship is sealed, not stopped, by the recognition of underlying primitive, violent, forces which at the same time include their first attempt at sincerity. In this way Heathcliff, via Catherine, enters the Linton household, becoming part of their emotional network as much as of the Earnshaws'. Already, the lovers exist as an interdependent threesome, later imaged in the three headstones on the moor; as later, the progress of Catherine's pregnancy is marked by further eruptions of violence in the Linton 'heaven', and begins at the point of Heathcliff's return, under the harvest moon.

The culminating scene of this day of action, which finally brings the 'storm rattling over Wuthering Heights', disturbing its weatherproof fabric, is Catherine's 'confession' to Nelly, in which she attempts to analyse her 'double nature' regarding Edgar and Heathcliff. The first 'accident' of the day was the meeting between these two; the second the dropping of Hareton; the third is Heathcliff's overhearing enough of Catherine's confession to stimulate his departure from the Heights. Nelly, smarting from Catherine's 'recent behaviour', is loathe to receive her confidences; but, as always, she serves the emotional needs of the main protagonists. Catherine's initial need, in this

39

case, is to shed the 'silly dress' aspect of her romance with
Linton, the superficial appearance in which 'all seems smooth
and easy — where is the obstacle?', so that she can formulate the
hidden demands of 'soul' and 'heart': ' "Here!" and "here!"
replied Catherine, striking one hand on her forehead, and the
other on her breast. "In whichever place the soul lives — in my
soul, and in my heart, I'm convinced I'm wrong!" ' Nelly
expertly disposes of the 'silly dress' by means of a 'judicious
catechism', to which Catherine responds with complete conven-
tionality and insincerity: 'I love the ground under his feet, and
the air over his head, and everything he touches, and every word
he says — I love all his looks, and all his actions, and him
entirely, and altogether. There now!' She repeats her catechism
as she would have repeated the many chapters the curate made
her 'get by heart' as a punishment; the repetition exorcises the
silly dress, exposing its hollowness, enabling Catherine to turn
to the central problem, which is how to recognise, express and
cultivate *real* feeling. It becomes clear that the problem of living
more 'in oneself' and less in 'surface change' (in Lockwood's
terms), is inseparable from that of expression. Catherine wants
to give Nelly 'a feeling of how I feel'; but in order to do so, she
has to abandon Nelly's 'judicious' format altogether (now that
it has served its negative purpose), and branch out into other
means of expression, using the imagery of dreams: the 'queer'
dreams which mark traumatic points of change in life: 'dreams
that have stayed with me ever after, and changed my ideas;
they've gone through and though me, like wine through water,
and altered the colour of my mind.' Nelly is disturbed by
Catherine's switch in rhetoric, dreading 'something from which
I might shape a prophecy, and foresee a fearful catastrophe'; she
prevents Catherine from telling the dream, and consequently
from making available for analysis the image of a 'catastrophe'
before it might take place in action. She cannot bear the fore-
sight of catastrophe. Nelly has the sensitivity to receive its
reverberations (admitting that 'now and then' she also has
dreamt 'queer dreams'), but not the power to structure its image
and analyse its meaning; this function belongs ultimately to
Heathcliff at the culmination of several more transpositions of
mental action. For Catherine's confession is, in a sense, before
its time, in terms of the state of understanding expressed by the

novel so far; it reaches out to the future, as a guide to its direction; it attempts to formulate that which is not yet expressible. And Nelly, to the end of the novel, retains her outlaw mental pocket of 'superstition', to which she relegates matters she finds it impossible to integrate.

Catherine tells another dream, as second-best, in which she foresees her exile within the Linton 'heaven' she has chosen with Edgar's 'fertile valley': 'I broke my heart with weeping to come back to earth; and the angels were so angry that they flung me out, into the middle of the heath on the top of Wuthering Heights, where I woke sobbing for joy.' Edgar and Isabella are frequently described as having 'angel's eyes'; and Catherine, in one sense their goddess and mistress, is also their prey (the 'bird half eaten'), their pet dog pulled in two; she pays for her privilege by 'breaking her heart' (later saying Edgar and Heathcliff have 'broken my heart'), and by the alteration in her constitution which leaves her unable to be 'crossed'. Only if never disturbed can she maintain the illusion of an 'angelic' marriage; which means at the same time that the marriage can never develop through confrontation, never become real. But the 'shape' of her 'prophecy' of exile and heart-splitting is not fully formed, remaining partly in 'the other' dream. Yet the content of this dream, though untold, is in a strange way evoked by the context of the confession, which suggests that it has something to do with her future child (seen beyond the idea of marriage), and with the future ghost of her own child-self, when she ultimately finds her home in the middle of the moor under the peat-moulds, after expulsion from the Linton paradise. For during the whole conversation, Nelly is nursing Hareton to sleep with a ghoulish lullaby ('The Ghaist's Warning') about crying children and mothers beneath the mould:

> It was far in the night, and the bairnies grat,
> The mither beneath the mools heard that.

Hareton's mother is beneath the mould, as Catherine will be when Nelly is nursing her own 'moaning doll' of a child; and Hareton has recently denounced 'wicked aunt Cathy' and 'shrieked himself almost into convulsions' at the touch of his father, who was accused by Nelly of being 'worse than a heathen': 'I wonder his mother does not rise from her grave to

41

see how you use him'. Yet Nelly is unaware of the irony of insisting that 'We're dismal enough without conjuring up ghosts, and visions to perplex us. Come, come, be merry, and like yourself! Look at little Hareton — *he's* dreaming nothing dreary. How sweetly he smiles in his sleep!' To this, Catherine replies sharply, 'Yes; and how sweetly his father curses in his solitude! You remember him, I dare say, when he was just such another as that chubby thing — nearly as young and innocent'. (As Nelly's hallucination at the cross-roads is soon to show, she does indeed 'remember' Hindley; but the superimposition of past and present crises is ejected from her mind in the form of superstition, from which she flees, 'as if I had raised a goblin'.) Nelly's romanticisation of Hareton's mental state is as far from the truth as in Catherine's catechism. Catherine's 'queer dream' may remain untold, in the literal telling of words, but its 'shape' cannot be hidden from the story, any more than Hareton can really be immune from 'ghosts and visions' when he is lying embedded in the midst of them, in an 'infernal house'. The presence of the apparently sweetly-dreaming child during the confession, underlines the unsolved existence of the past within the present (Hindley within Hareton), and also prophesies the shape of these problems continued into the future. In a sense Cathy is part of Hareton's dream, the ghostly mother, just as simultaneously, he is part of her untold dream: both expressing the chaos of their inherited 'gift of God' and foreboding about the shape of their future identity.

The conversation between Catherine and Nelly tells a dream, not only for Hareton, but also for Heathcliff, who is also lying in a posture of sleep, behind the settle: his presence consciously unknown to both of them, though the shape of the confession as it progresses seems to indicate their acceptance of emanations from him. Lying, typically in a hidden dark corner, in the 'shadows' of the house, Heathcliff seems to represent Cathy's unconscious 'rocks beneath', which — however — she can only formulate when his physical presence becomes absent. His departure at the key turn in her confession is essential not merely in terms of the plot's apparently fateful coincidence, but in the symbolic terms of Cathy's registering her 'feeling of how I feel'. Only when his absence is felt, can she attempt to put her attachment to him on the plane of verbal expression, and try to analyse the meaning of his presence. Her rhetorical question 'Who is to separate us, pray?' is answered much later by Heathcliff: 'you, of your own will, did it'. One suspects that, as in the case of Hindley sensing Heathcliff, it is not just Nelly who 'became sensible of Heathcliff's presence' as he steals out, but also Catherine, evoking a transition in her argument:

> "So he shall never know how I love him; and that, not because he's handsome, Nelly, but because he's more myself than I am. Whatever our souls are made of, his and mine are the same, and Linton's is as different as a moonbeam from lightning, or frost from fire."

Her relationship with Heathcliff can only develop beyond its stultified lack of communication when their 'sameness' is wedged apart for inspection from another vertex, in the light of the Linton 'moonbeam'. In her final lyrical speech Catherine atempts to express the reality of Heathcliff's significance, trying to find terms for describing the 'self' beneath the 'surface change'. It is as if his absence evokes a new poetic intensity, a new verbal blossoming. She discards the criterion of personal 'pleasure' along with the superficial answers to her catechism, as merely the 'satisfaction of my whims': instead,

> "This is for the sake of one who comprehends in his person my feelings to Edgar and myself. I cannot express it; but surely you and everybody have a notion that there is, or should be, an existence of yours beyond you. What were the use of my creation if I were entirely contained here? My great miseries in this world have been Heathcliff's miseries, and I watched and felt each from the beginning; my great thought in living is himself. If all else perished, and *he* remained, I should still continue to be; and if all remained, and he were annihilated, the universe would turn to a mighty stranger. I should not seem a part of it. My love for Linton is like the foliage in the woods. Time will change it, I'm well aware, as winter changes the trees. My love for Heathcliff resembles the eternal rocks beneath — a source of little visible delight, but necessary. Nelly, I *am* Heathcliff — he's always, always in my mind — not as a pleasure, any more than I am always a pleasure to myself — but as my own being — ''

Her concept of Heathcliff as symbolically encompassing her feelings to Edgar and herself, suggests her awareness of their interdependence, beyond the superficial status as rivals, mutually exclusive alternatives: as does her image of the 'rocks' and the 'foliage' as part of one landscape. Certainly, she begins by allying Edgar and Heathcliff in the standard terms of property and power: 'did it never strike you that, if Heathcliff and I married, we should be beggars! whereas, if I marry Linton, I can aid Heathcliff to rise, and place him out of my brother's power?' But her subsequent speech, reacting to Nelly's indignation, reaches far beyond these criteria to foreshadow or prophesy concepts of integration which cannot yet be embodied, at this stage of the action. She sees Heathcliff as in a sense 'necessary' to the creative potential of her marriage: to continue its existence beyond the lifespan of summer foliage, the egocentric status of earthly time, and into 'eternity', an 'existence beyond' her. By complete contrast with the princess-fantasy of marrying Edgar to become the 'greatest woman of the neighbourhood', she attempts to express her identity, through Heathcliff, in terms outside herself: as a function of the universe, rather than its centre. Consequently the moorland landscape stretches to infinity, and eternity, rather than seeming limited and circumscribed by society's small stir, into a petty insular 'neighbourhood'. She had described Heathcliff as 'dumb or a baby' when it came to 'amusing' her (by contrast with the 'sweeter music' at the time of the Christmas conversation in the garret); now, as Heathcliff leaves, her words seem to follow as she verbalises an 'existence beyond oneself', and her own expression gains a new prophetic eloquence. As the universe turns to a 'mighty stranger' and Heathcliff himself becomes a kind of ghost, so Catherine learns to speak for the dumb, dreaming Earnshaw 'baby' — not Hareton alone, but the 'baby' within them all, hitherto voiceless. She speaks not only for herself, but for the Earnshaw household and now the Lintons too, when she tries to translate Earnshaw's 'gift of God' in terms of the concepts of 'necessity' and 'usefulness' rather than as a toy serving personal prestige or egocentric despotism with its hollow illusory power. She tries to envisage a function for Heathcliff in terms of a wider creative system, universal rather than social, riding the changes brought by time rather than circumscribed and destroyed by them. Her description of Heathcliff balances that of Nelly earlier, but in the realm of ideas rather than of visible characteristics: the spirit of the alien gift, housed at the Heights but relegated to corners and shadows, becomes internalised as the body exits; it becomes a 'thought': 'my great thought in living is himself'. In the same way, Heathcliff later internalises his knowledge of Hareton through 'forms and ideas', and of Catherine herself, first as 'my soul' then as 'one universal idea', echoing her words here; and his subsequent powers for verbal expression (which by the end come to match Catherine's), indicate the process of painful self-education which brings him to this internalised knowledge.

Catherine, then, is presented with a choice of 'marrying' Edgar or Heathcliff, neither of which is the correct solution, since the choice itself has been wrongly defined. Yet in her speech, she manages to go beyond those standard definitions which she feels imprison her own nature. Expressing the concept of an 'existence' which is no longer 'entirely contained here', she senses that her own story, which began with an historical inheritance, cannot be 'contained' or fulfilled within her own lifetime, within the restrictive conditions imposed on her by fate or society. Nelly, of course, recoils in horror at Catherine's 'nonsense' and the nature of her 'secret'. Her condemnation is expressed in terms of morality — 'a wicked, unprincipled girl' — but is really her fear of the alien ideas themselves, that emanate from the human Heathcliff in his other dimension as a 'gift of God or the devil'. To the end, she maintains a split between 'superstition' and 'normality' — mirrored in her view of his 'goblin' nature as opposed to his ordinary existence and 'familiar voice': 'Is he a ghoul, or a vampire? ... what absurd nonsense it was to yield to that sense of horror'. She relegates his mystery, along with ghosts and dreams and the Gothic romances, to a realm kept banished beneath the surface, though it occasionally erupts as 'nonsense' which she finds incomprehensibly terrifying. Meanwhile, Catherine herself is forced to retract the alien feelers of her imagination, and to fulfil her ordinary, fated part in the unfolding of the action. The ideas in her speech had an existence 'beyond herself'; she cannot contain their implications within herself, or complete the integration which they shadow, within her own personality or within her own lifetime. Instead, she succumbs to the structural rift within herself symbolised by the choice between Edgar and Heathcliff. In entering the Linton heaven from which she knows she must be thrown out, and losing Heathcliff, she becomes 'estranged' from the 'universe', no longer 'herself', on one level ceasing to exist. The storm that comes 'rattling over the Heights in full fury' that night, marks Heathcliff's removal and the rift in Catherine's heart. What she later calls her 'shattered prison', is here imaged in the 'violent wind' and thunder which result in part of the east chimney-stack being knocked down, 'sending a clatter of stones and soot into the kitchen fire. We thought a bolt had fallen in the middle of us'. The house's hearth is split, and Nelly feels 'some sentiment that it must be a judgement on us also'. The judgement is borne on behalf of the house, not by the obvious 'Jonah' (Hindley), but by Catherine; the storm passes, 'leaving us all unharmed, excepting Cathy'. The storm is called up by the dark, Heathcliffian corner within Catherine, the rocky base or black 'coal country' which erupts like a volcano and shifts the stratification of the 'eternal rocks beneath'. The 'bolt' which seems to fall in their midst has the poetic effect in the narrative of marking the shattering knowledge, belonging in fact to the house and all its inhabitants, but embodied at this point by Catherine, whose 'constitution' henceforth alters irrevocably after the fever caught during her exposure to the storm (and which, incidentally, demolishes old Mr and Mrs Linton 'within a few days of each other'). At this point in Mrs Dean's narrative, Lockwood himself succumbs sympathetically to a fever; 'four weeks' torture, tossing and sickness' which incapacitate him even as listener. It is poetically appropriate that at this point the direct link between the 'misanthropes' is re-affirmed, to sustain Lockwood's listening powers. Thus it takes a visit from Heathcliff himself ('scoundrel! — not altogether guiltless in this illness of mine'), in addition to a gift of grouse, to encourage him to request the continuation of 'the history of Mr Heathcliff, from where [it was] left off, to the present day'.

# 3    A Moral Teething

(*Chapters 10 – 17*)

In the complicated central section of the book, the 'prophecy' of
'fearful catastrophe' foreshadowed in Catherine's told and
untold dreams, is fulfilled. It is a multiple catastrophe, involving
a change of state in all the protagonists, brought about through
the double action of Isabella's 'romance' with Heathcliff, and
Catherine's pregnancy and progress towards death. The stories
of the two 'rivals' for Heathcliff, parallel one another in significance like masque and antimasque. Simultaneous in time, their
narration is interleaved, with Grange and Heights viewpoints
penetrating one another through Isabella Linton's narratives
from her new home at the Heights, and Heathcliff's secret
haunting of the Grange. Together the twin stories weave a
tapestry of meaning around the central figure of Heathcliff and
the process he terms his 'moral teething'. The image of his
'teething' on Isabella and on Hindley, is echoed by the implicit
imagery of birth and labour resulting in the 'unwelcomed
infant' the second Catherine; it indicates a major adjustment
being made in the underlying fabric of the Linton-Earnshaw
emotional network. Heathcliff's 'labour of Hercules' on the
persons 'belonging' to Catherine, is a kind of anti-romance
about a knight winning his spurs, a degraded hero performing
the impossible. Instead of spurs, a 'tooth' is evolved, with the
emergence of the first headstone outside the traditional burial
places of the Lintons and Earnshaws. The ancient rocky bone-
structure shows through the mould, and a new dimension of
action is created, a tension between bone and spirit, establishing
new lines of power between different levels of existence.
Simultaneously, Isabella's hostaged 'soul' escapes from its
'purgatorial' prison at the Heights; Catherine's soul escapes
from its 'shattered prison'; and the second Catherine is born
from the same confines of her mother's body. Nelly looks back
on this painful process, shot with imagery of blood, bone and
weapons, as a 'dismal period'; but it lays the essential
foundation for the development of the second generation.
Catherine and Hindley die; Isabella leaves the country; Edgar

retires, leaving the stage clear for the new actors.

The process begins with the return of Heathcliff, to disrupt the translucent, ephemeral 'deep and growing happiness' of the Linton household, which is based on tenuous coalition rather than on internal harmony. His reappearance in the neighbourhood, and renewed anchorage at Wuthering Heights with Hindley, is described in terms of the emergence of an inevitable and ancient growth with the landscape, finally taking shape from amongst its shadows and becoming recognisable once again:

> On a mellow evening in September, I was coming from the garden with a heavy basket of apples which I had been gathering. It had got dusk, and the moon looked over the high wall of the court, causing undefined shadows to lurk in the corners of the numerous projecting portions of the building. I set my burden to rest on the house steps by the kitchen door, and lingered to rest, and drew in a few more breaths of the soft, sweet air; my eyes were on the moon, and my back to the entrance, when I heard a voice behind me say —
> "Nelly, is that you?"
> It was a deep voice, and foreign in tone; yet, there was something in the manner of pronouncing my name which made it sound familiar. I turned about to discover who spoke, fearfully, for the doors were shut, and I had seen nobody on approaching the steps.
> Something stirred in the porch; and moving nearer, I distinguished a tall man dressed in dark clothes, with dark face and hair.

Heathcliff is touched into recognisable existence by the harvest moon, his dark shape emerging from the character of dark shadows caused by the moon's light; he is one of the 'undefined shadows' behind Edgar's moonlit calm. He stirs in the porch, as in the lobbies of the Heights, like a structural feature of the house newly-discovered in the distinctive light. Nelly's position figures her function as receptor for both the light (her eyes on the moon), and the voice from the darkness behind her: 'double-dealing' as always, she is to tell both sides of the tale, as eventually she twists Edgar's fair lock of hair with Heathcliff's dark one in the locket of the dead Catherine. Catherine had described the composition of her soul and Heathcliff's as 'the same, and Linton's is as different as a moonbeam from lightning, or frost from fire'. Here, Heathcliff is an inherent part of the beauty of the 'mellow evening' in which Catherine and Edgar are also embedded, sitting in darkness, amidst a 'score of moons'. The menacing, sinister connotations of his 'lurking' coexist with a premonition of the potential harmony of the different qualities richly textured in the scene. The fruitfulness suggested by the basket of apples recalls Heathcliff's original arrival at harvest time inside the coat of old Earnshaw, usurping not only the toys intended for Cathy and Hindley, but the 'pocketful of apples and pears' promised to the child Nelly. The prince returns in a new guise — his features changed, yet 'I remembered the eyes'. He is both alien and at home: his voice 'foreign in tone', yet with something 'which made it sound familiar'. His return is coincident with the beginning of Catherine's pregnancy, marking it both with the harvest moon and with sinister shadows, and initiating the delayed action of the latent mental and physical illness which began with her unintegrated 'double life'.

The description of Catherine and Edgar seated in the open window, against a background of house on one side and landscape on the other, suggests the charmed, unearthly stillness of their emotional state, and its openness to outside influence, as if prepared to receive Heathcliff once again:

> They sat together in a window whose lattice lay back against the wall, and displayed, beyond the garden trees and the wild green park, the valley of Gimmerton, with a long line of mist winding nearly to its top (for very soon after you pass the chapel, as you may have noticed, the sough that runs from the marshes joins a beck which follows the bend of the glen). Wuthering Heights rose above this silvery vapour — but our old house was invisible — it rather dips down on the other side.
>
> Both the room, and its occupants, and the scene they gazed on, looked wondrously peaceful.

There are 'no lights from within'; their silhouettes, rising from the darkness of the interior, and framed by the open lattice, are defined against the moonlit landscape without, like Nelly —

Heathcliff's messenger — between the moon and shadow. By contrast with Wuthering Heights, the boundaries of the Grange are fluid, particularly since the rule of Edgar Linton. The locks, gates, bulldogs, servants carrying bludgeons, backed by faith in 'the magisterial heart' (as Heathcliff satirically terms it), all still exist; but rather as tokens than as the means of enforcing power. Edgar Linton, since his marriage to Catherine, has his eyes opened to other meaning in life, so does not carry on his father's tradition wholeheartedly, and after her death withdraws from public life altogether. The fluid boundaries are here suggested by the perspective in which the figures of Catherine and Edgar seem to melt outward into the evening's moist atmosphere, linked by a 'long line of mist', a 'silvery vapour', with the invisible but localised image of the old house — the house which has just become the home of Heathcliff once again. And the Grange itself 'reflects a score of glittering moons' from its windows: imaging the silvery Linton heaven which, unlike the crimson room earlier, seems part of the natural moorland landscape, linked by the stream's silver thread with the Heights. The picture is reminiscent of the melting sensuous interchange in Emily Bronte's poem 'The Prisoner': when 'Winds take a pensive tone, and stars a tender fire . . . But first a hush of peace, a soundless calm descends', before the dawning of 'the Invisible', as sense measures 'the gulf' (here the distance between the two houses) 'and dares the final bound'. Elements from this image in both poem and novel, recur at the end of the book, reorganised and seen from the standpoint of Wuthering Heights. The image of the two lovers at the window, seen by Lockwood from the 'amber light' within, and the image of Heathcliff in the window, seen by Nelly from within, against the stream going down towards the Grange, compound this earlier point of change at the moment of Heathcliff's return.

But the 'wondrous peace' in the Linton household is a tenuous one, dependent upon the preservation of a state of inaction: 'for the space of half a year, the gunpowder lay as harmless as sand, because no fire came near to explode it'. Now Heathcliff, 'his eyes full of black fire', makes the moonlit heaven explosive, as it is not equipped to sustain vexations: Edgar 'averred that the stab of a knife could not inflict a worse pang than he suffered at seeing his lady vexed'. The sparks in heaven are not just Catherine's but the Lintons' — developing Heathcliff's observation of long ago that she 'kindled a spark of spirit in the vacant blue eyes of the Linton children'. Now, the Linton sparks fly out of Catherine's control. Edgar is brought to a point where he gives Heathcliff a 'burning' blow in the gullet; Isabella is seen as 'kindling' and 'sparkling irefully': with her 'dove's eyes — angel's' she becomes a 'tigress' marking Catherine's skin with 'crescents of red', for which Catherine invokes retaliation from Heathcliff: 'You'd hear of odd things, if I lived alone with that mawkish, waxen face; the most ordinary would be painting on its white the colours of the rainbow, and turning the blue eyes black'. These impressions of violence are received again by Catherine via Heathcliff when she herself is shrouded in white: 'on his letting go, I saw four distinct impressions left blue in the colourless skin'. In the process of the conflagration, the weakness of apparently strong and long-established ties becomes exposed: not just between Edgar and Catherine, but between Edgar and Isabella, and Catherine and Heathcliff. Catherine experiences Heathcliff's return both as a 'jubilee' of joy, and as a catastrophe: 'too excited to show gladness; indeed, by her face, you would rather have surmised an awful calamity'. Her response to Nelly's warning of approaching conflict is the grim joke: 'And then we shall fight to the death, shan't we, Nelly? . . . No, I tell you, I have such faith in Linton's love that I believe I might kill him, and he wouldn't wish to retaliate.' The ensuing action becomes in fact a 'fight to the death' — her own death, consequent on the destruction of her illusion of power over the other three (her own interpretation of being 'loved' by everyone): all of whom insist on independently pursuing their own method of 'loving' her.

After the shock of Heathcliff's initial appearance, the situation appears to quieten down for a while, as he establishes his 'right to be expected'; Catherine maintains her equilibrium owing to her unchallenged self-idealisation — 'Goodnight — I'm an angel!' — although, as her sense of 'an awful calamity' shows, she awaits her inevitable expulsion from the Linton heaven, foreshadowed in her dream. It is the 'not anticipated misfortune' of Isabella's 'fantastic preference' for a 'nameless man', that extends and dramatises the original rift within Catherine, which otherwise might have been glossed over by the civilised veneer maintained by the children as adults. Isabella's attraction toward Heathcliff is based not on her assessment of his character but on her identification with Catherine: 'He has an honourable soul, and a true one, or how could he remember her?' Her romanticisation of Catherine's relationship with Heathcliff enacts, in a way, a part of Catherine's own story which had never previously found expression. For Catherine's own idea of her queenliness is founded on her original reception in the crimson room when she became the centre of attraction instead of the pet dog, and reciprocally gave of her bounty to the 'petted things' the Linton children (and their pets), re-directing their existing hierarchy around herself. Now, she conceives of herself as 'a foolish mother' to Isabella, she and Edgar being 'spoiled children': 'I call her a darling and flatter her into a good temper'. She makes Isabella the 'naughty fondling' or pet that Frances had tried to make of her; and her acceptance of maternity is based on the illusion of her indulgence toward the Linton 'children' and Heathcliff: 'my constant indulgence of one's weak nature, and the other's bad one'. Consequently she is unable to cope when Isabella's fiery temper and self-will (her latent Catherine-like aspects) rebel against her fond guardianship, daring to 'rival' her supremacy, and calling her a 'dog in the manger' who 'desires no one to be loved but yourself'. Isabella, in her own identification with Catherine, and attachment to Heathcliff, begins to re-live aspects of the old, lost, sublimated Catherine which are now insupportable to the 'foolish mother' cum 'angel'. It is not the idea of Isabella's stealing Heathcliff that terrifies Catherine as a real danger; but the uncontrollability of her new stab at independence, suggesting the possibility of 'sending my image into eternal oblivion', the loss of her artificial self-image. When Catherine loses her control over Isabella, she succumbs to a 'fit' which recalls the child Isabella screaming as if witches were 'driving red-hot needles into her', in the context of quarrelling over the ownership of a pet: 'There she lay dashing her head against the arm of the sofa, and grinding her teeth, so that you might fancy she would crush them to splinters!' Their identity, to some extent, is exchanged; Catherine's 'image' becomes shattered into separate components ('oblivion', she fears) — into Isabella as into Hindley and Hareton, all seized by Heathcliff as teething prey. The central chandelier splinters into broken glass, as the image of the 'score of moons' loses its precarious tranquil beauty.

It is only the 'fantastic' concept of an alliance between himself and Isabella Linton, that awakens Heathcliff's fury against Catherine, hitherto quiescent. He perceives not just the opportunity, but the neglected emotional necessity for 'revenge' on the Linton aspect of Catherine which has up to now been out of his grasp and comprehension. The concept of 'revenge' becomes real, not just because Isabella 'belongs' to Catherine in social terms, but because he senses the emotional identification between them. His revenge is not a function either of 'avarice' or of motiveless sadism (though he uses these concepts to explain his actions, to himself and to Nelly). Rather, it is an attack on Catherine Linton which he cannot make directly, nor even, for long, allow himself to feel directly:

> "And as to you, Catherine . . . I want you to be aware that I *know* you have treated me infernally — infernally! Do you hear? And if you flatter yourself that I don't perceive it, you are a fool — and if you think I can be consoled by sweet words you are an idiot — and if you fancy I'll suffer unrevenged, I'll convince you of the contrary, in a very little while. Meantime, thank you for telling me your sister-in-law's secret — I swear I'll make the most of it, and stand you aside!"
>
> "What new phase of his character is this?" exclaimed Mrs Linton, in amazement. . . .
>
> "I seek no revenge on you . . . That's not the plan. The tyrant grinds down his slaves — and they don't turn against him, they crush those beneath them."

Later, he elaborates this method of indirect revenge with: 'The more the worms writhe, the more I yearn to crush out their entrails! It is a moral teething'. The 'new phase' of his character 'amazes' Catherine herself, and the separation it entails marks a new phase in the development of their mutual knowledge, beyond the present plateau of immobility reached by their relationship. The sado-masochism of Isabella's 'romance' is prompted initially by Catherine, who, finding she cannot control Isabella, furiously offers her instead as a sacrifice to one whom she presents as a 'fierce, pitiless, wolfish man':

53

"I never say to him let this or that enemy alone, because it would be ungenerous or cruel to harm them, I say — 'Let them alone, because *I* should hate them to be wronged!': and he'd crush you, like a sparrow's egg, Isabella, if he found you a troublesome charge."

And again, to Heathcliff: 'I won't repeat my offer of a wife — it's as bad as offering Satan a lost soul'. And both Isabella and Heathcliff, in their efforts to grapple with an 'image' of Catherine, live up to her expectations and fulfil her image of themselves — initially at least. Catherine has always been Heathcliff's interpreter to the world, first to the Earnshaws, then to the Lintons (Nelly advises Isabella that her judgement of his character must be a true one). Heathcliff is therefore in a sense forced to act out her own idea of him, via Isabella's 'hero of romance'. The sado-masochism is primarily Catherine's and secondarily Isabella's, but it has to be worked out and exorcised through Isabella's independent education in hatred.

Isabella's elopement with Heathcliff marks the beginning of Catherine's 'brain fever', and is as instrumental as the rift between Edgar and Heathcliff brought into the open during the quarrel when she throws the 'key' into the fire (the key to her burning brain, denied them both). Catherine experiences the rupture with Isabella as a similar process of sacrificing some aspect of her soul or internal child which has proven her to be, not just a 'foolish', but a bad and a weak mother (instead of indulging the 'bad' or 'weak' nature of others). Not only Isabella but also Heathcliff has shaken her omnipotence and broken free; Heathcliff takes his 'wife' in one sense on Catherine's 'offer' but in another sense rejecting her terms, implying that he can 'do without the approbation' not only of Edgar but also of herself. When Heathcliff hangs up Isabella's pet springer in the garden, he is tormenting not only the pet Isabella but also the pet Cathy became on her entry into the crimson room — the Linton girl which he regards as a repulsive 'centipede' or reptile (as he does the second Cathy, the 'snake'). The dog twitching in the darkness ('something white moved iregularly'), like a shed skin, or a 'creature from the other world', is the 'sparrow's egg' or 'canary' become a 'lost soul' sacrificed to Satan. Only when Isabella recovers from her 'first desire to be killed by Heathcliff (the masochistic romance), can the hostage of her soul be released: symbolised by her recovering the pet dog, which 'yelped wild with joy at recovering its mistress': 'I knocked over Hareton, who was hanging a litter of puppies from a chairback in the doorway; and blest as a soul escaped from purgatory, I bounded, leaped, and flew down the steep road'. And Isabella's ultimate release is, like that of all the 'prisoners' at the Heights, self-effected; nothing has changed except her attitude to her jailer Heathcliff, and herself. It is not the first time she has 'made the attempt' (she admits to Nelly); but the attempt only becomes successful when her self-education is completed. This is the same moment, that Heathcliff, correspondingly, ceases to have any further use for her as an aspect of his relationship with Catherine — who becomes herself a ghost in purgatory.

Isabella's romance with Heathcliff is, as she suggests implicitly, a venture into the 'madness' — that is, the wild, inexplicable — deep within herself; and expressed partly in terms of the fascination of Catherine. Just as Heathcliff thinks of the beings 'belonging to her' on the night of their elopement (wishing he could hang them all, 'excepting one'), so does Isabella marry into Heathcliff's entire adopted family at the Heights: 'The concentrated essence of all the madness in the world took up its abode in my brain the day I linked my fate with theirs'. Her venture into the 'madness' awakened in the Linton household by Catherine and ultimately by Heathcliff, is made also on behalf of Edgar, who cannot bear to face Heathcliff directly, or the Heathcliff within Catherine: 'he dreaded that mind, it revolted him'; its exhibition cuts him 'like the stab of a knife' — a stab ultimately sustained by Isabella at the moment of her escape. And Edgar, though he cuts off his relationship with Isabella, cannot escape the consequences of a 'Linton Heathcliff'. Isabella, in her exploration of the Heights from within the penetralium, encounters ghosts and other transformations of beings familiar to her. Hareton's dog Throttler, initially roused to attack her, later becomes an 'unexpected aid' when she recognises it as 'a son of our old Skulker' who had first dragged Catherine into the Grange. She explores the other side of Catherine, the non-beautiful images excluded from the Grange, the shadows behind the moonlight: in the 'ruffianly'

Hareton himself, 'with a look of Catherine in his eyes, and about his mouth', and in Hindley, whose eyes are 'like a ghostly Catherine's, with all their beauty annihilated'. Catherine's eyes are her overwhelming and enduring feature, bequeathed to her daughter, and regarded by Heathcliff as the window on her soul (he cannot bear to see her eyes, when she is dying). Meanwhile Isabella is regarded by Joseph as embodying some of Catherine's characteristics: 'Weel done, Miss Cathy!' he applauds when she throws her porridge bowl to the ground. And with the symbolic cut from Heathcliff on her departure (a meta-phorical tooth-mark), she seems to take on some of Catherine's lost childhood resilience, 'half savage, and hardy, and free' (as Catherine remembers herself), 'laughing at injuries, not maddening under them' — as she bursts 'out of breath, and laughing' back into the Grange parlour.

Isabella's education in hating Heathcliff begins when she writes to Nelly: 'I sometimes wonder at him with an intensity that deadens my fear'; and her fear, though not dispelled or lessened, gradually becomes subordinate to her understanding. The achievement of hatred represents the mid-point of her education:

> "This morning she announced, as a piece of appalling intelligence, that I had actually succeeded in making her hate me! A positive labour of Hercules, I assure you! If it be achieved, I have cause to return thanks — Can I trust your assertion, Isabella?"

But Heathcliff's 'labour of Hercules' has further, unforeseen consequences, as Isabella eventually comes to an intuitive understanding of the nature of the image of Catherine behind Heathcliff. She displays this, implicitly, on the night of Catherine's funeral, when she and Hindley lock Heathcliff out of the house — for the first time, as if unconsciously aware that this is a crisis point in terms of Heathcliff's union with the spirit of Catherine. Then the accuracy of Isabella's understanding is measured by the depth of torment she can arouse in Heathcliff in relation to his 'deity' now become 'senseless dust and ashes'. In perceiving that 'pulling out the nerves with red-hot pincers, requires more coolness than knocking on the head', she contrasts with Hindley and his 'double-edged spring knife' — a weapon she once 'coveted', but comes to recognise as a 'spear pointed at both ends', recoiling on its user. Hindley with his primitive methods, is unable to free himself from his masochistic, self-degrading use of Heathcliff (who becomes, in Isabella's terms, his 'evil genius'); whilst Isabella sharpens the weapon of her perception against his example. Her ultimate release is earned by her interpretation of Heathcliff's and Hindley's destructive inter-dependence and its relation to the governing spirit of Catherine, behind them. The next morning she explains to Hindley how Heathcliff 'teethed' on him: he 'trampled on, and kicked you, and dashed you on the ground ... And his mouth watered to tear you with his teeth'. She develops the image of his 'cannibal teeth' as they had appeared through the window the night before, when he was locked out:

> His black countenance looked blightingly through. The stanchions stood too close to suffer his shoulders to follow ... His hair and clothes were whitened with snow, and his sharp cannibal teeth, revealed by cold and wrath, gleamed through the dark.

Now, Isabella notes that the flashing sharpness is absent from Heathcliff's dark, dusky imagery: 'his eyes rained down tears among the ashes, and he drew his breath in suffocating sighs ... The clouded windows of hell flashed a moment towards me; the fiend which usually looked out, however, was ... dimmed and drowned'. Heathcliff's bite is taken out; snow and watering mouth have become tears, fire become ashes; the 'fiend' is 'drowned'; Heathcliff's countenance itself seems 'turned to stone' (the 'rocks beneath', without their soul); for as he explains later, 'I could *almost* see her ... yet I *could* not! ... She showed herself, as she often was in life, a devil to me!' Isabella recognises the loss of his live 'devil', Catherine; and proceeds to point out the dead Catherine within Hindley also:

> "Now that she's dead, I see her in Hindley; Hindley has exactly her eyes, if you had not tried to gouge them out, and made them black and red ... But then ... if poor Catherine had trusted you, and assumed the ridiculous, contemptible, degrading title of Mrs Heathcliff, she would soon have presented a similar picture!"

Isabella taunts Heathcliff with a 'similar picture' of unnerving accuracy: a picture of the Catherine who is his 'soul' and whom he feels he has killed — Hindley's eyes being Catherine's with their 'beauty annihilated', the picture of death which Heathcliff found unbearable in Catherine herself. Isabella reminds Hindley that 'Catherine used to boast that she stood between you and bodily harm'. The bodily harm suffered by Hindley is another way of clinching the fact of her loss: a loss only partly due to physical death, but more particularly due to the destruction of her spirit. In knocking down the 'stanchions' of the window which stand between Hindley and bodily harm, to make a forced entry, Heathcliff in a sense inflicts violence on Catherine also (always associated with the body of the house). Now, the degraded, fragmented images of a dead Catherine — seen within Hindley and secondarily within Isabella — block him from the image of her live spirit, which he had been convinced he would 'find' at the Heights. Catherine's fear of her image being 'sent into eternal oblivion' seems to have been justified: she herself seems dissipated and destroyed, now that the first generation is being 'driven asunder'.

Nevertheless Isabella's interpretation of the death of Catherine fulfils a necessary positive function. In guessing at the 'morality' or meaning behind the 'teething', she helps to define the search for knowledge (of Catherine) of which it forms a part — albeit, at this point, a negative knowledge, described by her as 'perverted taste'. In taunting Heathcliff out of his 'diabolical prudence', and indirectly stimulating Hindley also to active violence, she becomes in a sense the 'happy chance' desired by Heathcliff long ago when he muttered that Hindley's 'constitution' would defy an early natural death, 'unless some happy chance out of the common course befall him'. Though she leaves behind with Hindley his 'evil genius' of masochism, she has also catalysed his approaching deliverance by death, into which he fades quietly six months later, after the inevitable failure of his last attempt to secure 'justice'. Her last picture is of Hindley and Heathcliff 'locked together on the hearth' (like Lockwood with the dogs), covering her own release from 'purgatory'. She is purged of her 'romance', as Lockwood, by this stage, is purged of his: 'Let me beware of the fascination that lurks in Catherine Heathcliff's brilliant eyes'. Unlike Hindley, she escapes with a token mark of teething, the bleeding cut beneath the ear: not literally beaten to 'the colours of the rainbow'; recovering from looking 'a thorough little slattern', she leaves having 'no objection to dressing myself decently'. Nevertheless the story of Heathcliff's symbolic mark on her is to be perpetuated in the existence of Linton Heathcliff.

The mutual knowledge gained by the conclusion of Isabella's romance and Heathcliff's teething, is counterpointed by the conclusion of Catherine's romance as queen of both worlds and her 'brain fever' as she tries to face the reality of 'mother' to the child within her (by contrast to the delusory 'spoiled children'), whose growth and birth are in a sense activated by both Edgar and Heathcliff. Moreover Heathcliff's part in her complicated change of state, represents another aspect of his teething — which is itself crucial to the establishment and recognition of his own identity. It is his part in the creative romance resulting in the second Catherine, as opposed to the destructive one resulting in Linton Heathcliff. Catherine's illness is neither play-acting as Nelly assumes at first, nor an act of will, but the inevitable result of her inner rifted condition: 'I couldn't explain to Edgar how certain I felt of having a fit'. During the delirium preceding the 'brain fever' proper, she re-lives the original 'separation' between herself and Heathcliff: the first catastrophic change in her life with which she never came to terms, resulting in successive 'separations' or moments of change progressively weakening her body and mind:

> 'I thought as I lay there, with my head against that table leg, and my eyes dimly discerning the grey square of the window, that I was enclosed in the oak-panelled bed at home . . . the whole last seven years of my life grew a blank! I did not recall that they had been at all. I was a child; my father was just buried, and my misery arose from the separation that Hindley had ordered between me, and Heathcliff — I was laid alone, for the first time . . .''

In imagination, she is back in the original closet-bed, Lockwood's dream chamber, her delirious visions explained by Nelly as deriving from 'cold water and ill temper' — recalling Lockwood's 'effects of bad tea and bad temper'. The images of her delirium present clearly the images for Lockwood's key dream: the 'fiery Catherine' 'no better than a wailing child'; the snow-like storm of white feathers which she shortly creates; the 'wind sounding in the firs by the lattice' which comes 'straight down the moor'. The open window and the icy wind ('keen as a knife') which provide a direct link with the old house, felt as a 'chance of life' not 'death', suggest the drawing-out of her soul into the wind-spirit or ghost it becomes when she knocks on Lockwood's window. She is metamorphosing into a 'creature of the other world' like Isabella's springer, her 'abstracted gaze' contemplating the 'outer darkness' and imagining her life within the grave. The enclosing bed becomes associated with her premonition of the coffin, 'my narrow home out yonder', for the child-ghost 'come home' (Joseph is 'waiting till I come home that he may lock the gate'): 'It's a rough journey, and a sad heart to travel it: and we must go by Gimmerton Kirk, to go that journey!' In one sense, the long, rough journey of her spirit begins with the opening of her window at Thrushcross Grange and does not end until it is received by Lockwood, temporary tenant of her old bed, nearly twenty years later. The twenty-year roaming is an attempt to bridge the other gap in knowledge, the 'abyss' she describes here:

> "Supposing, at twelve years old, I had been wrenched from the Heights, and every early association, and my all in all, as Heathcliff was at that time, and been converted, at a stroke, into Mrs Linton, the lady of Thrushcross Grange, and the wife of a stranger; an exile, and outcast, thenceforth, from what had been my world — You may fancy a glimpse of the abyss where I grovelled!"

Now, her twelve-year-old ghost is 'exiled' from the Linton heaven where she is a 'stranger' and cast into a dark 'abyss', in words soon to be picked up by Heathcliff in unconscious sympathy: 'do not leave me in this abyss, where I cannot find you!' It is not Heathcliff, but Lockwood, who first recognises the ghost in the abyss, and allows it to 'come in'. Catherine tears her pillow 'with her teeth', creating a storm: 'The down is flying about like snow!', and Lockwood, years later, deciphers the 'hieroglyphics' of the 'white letters' into a recognisable image.

Catherine herself is trying to read her internal hieroglyphics, by means of 'plundering' the pillow (a kind of teething). Its white feathers derive from wild birds or spirits of the moor, echoing her past life and the spirits within her — her unborn child, and her own child-ghost — now associated with danger from Heathcliff, like the hanged dog:

> "This feather was picked up from the heath, the bird was not shot — we saw its nest in the winter, full of little skeletons. Heathcliff set a trap over it, and the old ones dare not come. I made him promise he'd never shoot a lapwing, after that, and he didn't. Yes, here are more! Did he shoot my lapwings, Nelly? Are they red, any of them?"

Her present fear and disturbance is associated with her own sacrifice of Isabella to Heathcliff, as she experiences it — putting a canary in the park on a winter's day. Her former power over Heathcliff has been challenged ('I made him promise') — she wonders if he broke his promise. Now that her own romance of 'foolish motherhood' is undermined, the reality of the nature of her internal children — the 'birds' and 'heifers' — is harder to determine and more complex. The whiteness is contaminated by blood, and she faces the frightening possibility of the live elements being a heap of 'little skeletons'. (In Shelley's image, life 'stains the white radiance of eternity'.) Nelly's condemnation of Catherine's activity as 'childish diversion' and 'baby-work' in fact illuminates her preoccupation with the baby within her — the actual baby and her internal spirit. In her confused endeavour to analyse her internal contents, she finds it hard to distinguish between creative and destructive penetration. The cave, the crag, the kirk, the bed, all coalesce into the image of what she later calls her 'shattered prison' (in particular the pelvis, the baby's 'narrow' escape route) — shattered or penetrated by Edgar, Heathcliff, Nelly, and herself in tearing open the pillow; each penetration being ambiguous. She sees Nelly as a kind of midwife disguised as a witch, a 'withered hag'. 'This bed is the fairy cave under Penistone Crag, and you are gathing elf-bolts to hurt our heifers'. She dares Heathcliff to find another way into her narrow home, though this be a grave twelve feet deep, with the church thrown down over it: 'Find a way, then! not through that Kirkyard ... You are slow! Be content, you always followed me!' She recoils from Edgar, with 'What you touch at present, you may have; but my soul will be on that hilltop before you lay hands on me again.' For the soul's release, or the baby's birth, is also ambiguous — will it be a dwelling secure from earthly contamination, the 'glorious world' imaged later, or lost in the dark 'abyss'. And ultimately, Catherine's process of self-analysis is ambiguous: it is a violent teething, marking the pillow with blood, which is the process of struggling to become 'moral', to achieve its own formal constriction or discipline, 'not through the Kirkyard'. Just as her diary was squeezed between the lines of a religious tome, and her earlier analysis of Edgar and Heathcliff was built around a dream (remaining partly untold in a mental situation not equipped to make sense of dreams), so now her self-expression is exiled into the form of delirium and 'brain fever', resulting in 'permanent alienation of intellect'. She cannot, within her own lifetime, arrange her internal hieroglyphics in an artistic structure; her utmost imaginative effort results in exposing the elements and casting them to the winds, in the hope that a 'stranger' may catch them.

Even at this stage, Catherine seems to imagine her death as coincident with the time of the baby's birth, 'before the spring is over': they are both in a sense a single action, a single change of state, a single inheritance. For Catherine's chaotic, lyrically expressed ideas, and her actions, are made on behalf of the Earnshaws and Lintons as much as herself: the time has come to seek an existence 'beyond herself'. In her death-birth she attempts to embody the transition from a primitive religion of Catherine (Lockwood's hieroglyphics) to a more mature, artistic one, which is aware of the ancient, internal signs, but able to organise them constructively. Like Isabella, she profits from Hindley's example: seeing the impossibility of bringing up a child in the context of the destruction of a fragile heaven (his and Frances's). The child — the generalised Earnshaw 'baby' — becomes a metaphor for the integrated, coherent structure of the personality; with the goddess Catherine as 'mother' to the internal elements. Whilst Isabella lives out and exposes the anti-romance (culminating in the false child of disguised hate), Catherine's develops from Hindley's (the child of love beset by illusion). Though physically she becomes 'a mere ruin of humanity', this is not Hindley's self-degradation and savage blindness, but preparation for a necessary transition outside herself. It is clear that Catherine envisages death as a real state of existence, and recognises when it is time for her to 'brave the ghosts' of the churchyard, no longer in childhood play with Heathcliff but in earnest, taking her place among the ancient deities or rather superseding them, the church thrown down over her. Her illness is self-destructive, and in that sense like Hindley's: thus Edgar, on his first sight of her in her delirium, says 'Catherine, what have you done?'; thus Heathcliff, 'I love my murderer — but *yours*! How can I?' And like Isabella, with 'I gave him my heart and he pinched it to death', she externalises it as 'You and Edgar have broken my heart, Heathcliff'. But, by contrast with Hindley's miserable departure ('He died true to himself, drunk as a lord') and Isabella's 'peevish, sickly' child, the progress of her final brain-fever ensures her underground power as director of the second Catherine's development: she begins a 'puny', 'moaning', 'unwelcomed infant', but soon takes root and 'grows like a larch'. Catherine, from her semi-conscious, alienated state, passively educates both Edgar and Heathcliff, in different ways, to carry on her story.

Firstly, her illness provides a more appropriate outlet for Edgar's service and attention to her, monitoring every variation of her 'irritable nerves and shaken reason'; nursing her, he learns the motherliness later directed toward Cathy: 'No mother could have nursed an only child more devotedly than Edgar tended her'. This is the point at which Nelly first mentions Catherine's pregnancy: giving a double meaning to the 'child' Edgar is nursing. The 'handful of golden crocuses' which he places on Catherine's pillow in March, to catch her eye as a 'gleam of pleasure' on awakening, prefigures the golden child, the second Catherine, who brings 'sunshine into a desolate house'. At this stage in the narrative, Lockwood also, in his parallel mental voyage, is looking forward to 'health, and spring!' and his own release from suffering. He is now educated enough for Nelly to hand over the narrative to his memory ('I'll continue it in her own words . . . I don't think I could improve her style'); and his first responsibility is a task for which, originally, he might have seemed peculiarly ill-fitted, namely the 'great occasion' of Heathcliff's final confrontation with Catherine. This is the meeting which brings on Catherine's final labour — the child born late that night, and her death two hours later; it takes place while Edgar is at church, his presence sensed in the distance through the open windows (after her death, Edgar ceases to attend church; he ritually lies on the mound of her grave, instead). The last day of her life recalls the mellow September of Heathcliff's return: 'the full, mellow flow of the beck in the valley came soothingly on the ear'; it occurs during a period of summer-within-winter, with the shining of a 'summer moon' (in Isabella's phrase), which closes with snow and renewed winter on the day of her funeral. As before, Heathcliff seems to emerge from the shadows skirting the house: this time, he has become a feature of the park round the Grange where, as Isabella makes us aware, he has been spending all his days and nights, 'fed by the angels'. Nelly, always sensitive to his presence, 'knew as well as if I saw him, that Mr Heathcliff was about the place'; she sets the house doors 'wide open' though she shuns 'going out'. Catherine sits 'in the recess of the open window . . . in a loose, white dress'. The window points to the fine balance of her existence between two worlds, her eyes no longer cognisant of 'material things' but looking 'beyond, and far beyond — you would have said out of this world', expressing in herself a change of 'unearthly beauty'. Her loose white dress emphasises her ethereal quality, about to metamorphose into ghost or spirit, a creature of another world — as does the book lying between her and the outside air: 'a scarcely perceptible wind fluttered its leaves at intervals'. The image reworks the twitching of Isabella's springer, from the sinister ugliness appropriate to her romance, into beauty. Catherine awaits her transition from 'shattered prison' to 'that glorious world', speaking not only for her spirit but for the baby to be born from her 'broken heart':

"The thing that irks me most is this shattered prison, after all. I'm tired, tired of being enclosed here. I'm wearying to escape into that glorious world, and to be always there; not seeing it dimly through tears, and yearning for it through the walls of an aching heart; but really with it, and in it."

Her 'escape' shadows Isabella's on one level; but more particularly the words of her daughter when she is imprisoned at the Heights and longing to be back at the Grange in her golden childhood: 'I'm tired, Hareton; I'm stalled.' The second Mrs

Heathcliff has to re-live aspects of the story of her mother and aunt, but in a changed context which changes their meaning.

Despite her pale, ethereal quality, Catherine's physical contact with Heathcliff figures their effort to grasp the reality of their final separation. Seizing his hair she 'kept him down', whilst he leaves 'four distinct impressions . . . blue in the colourless skin' (echoing Isabella's 'crescents of red' and Heathcliff's 'ghoulish' fantasy of painting the colours of the rainbow on her 'waxen' face). Again, echoing the embrace of Heathcliff and Hindley 'locked on the hearth': 'Catherine made a spring, and he caught her, and they were locked in an embrace from which I thought my mistress would never be released alive.' Their deathly embrace (Catherine's 'fight to the death' with Heathcliff, as well as Edgar) is a mutual teething: their attempt to come to knowledge of themselves and one another, their statuesque figures 'washed by each other's tears'. The tableau of Heathcliff with the 'lifeless-looking form' in his arms (which he hands over to Edgar) is repeated later with Edgar and Catherine, his features 'almost as deathlike as those of the form beside him'; and repeated, differently again, with Hareton and Heathcliff. Catherine and Heathcliff now, for the first time, try to speak honestly, to interpret their past separations and to make sense of the forthcoming separation which is inevitably expressed in Catherine's face and eyes. This contrasts with the separation of 'revenge' effected via Isabella, which was an attempt to escape from their own relationship, crushing the 'slaves beneath' rather than facing the 'tyrant'. Now Heathcliff faces the 'devil' which, on her death, he knows he must try to internalise:

> "Are you possessed with a devil . . . to talk in that manner to me, when you are dying? Do you reflect that all those words will be branded in my memory, and eating deeper eternally, after you have left me? . . . Is it not sufficient for your infernal selfishness, that while you are at peace I shall writhe in the torments of hell? . . . So much the worse for me, that I am strong. Do I want to live? What kind of living will it be when you — oh, God! would *you* like to live with your soul in the grave?"

For the first time, Heathcliff expresses verbally his feeling of her significance for him, taking over the expression of their relationship from the point where Catherine left it several years before ('I *am* Heathcliff'). In doing so, he approaches the 'unutterable':

> "Catherine Earnshaw, may you not rest as long as I am living! . . . Be with me always — take any form — drive me mad! only *do* not leave me in this abyss, where I cannot find you! Oh God! It is unutterable! I *cannot* live without my life! I *cannot* live without my soul!"

In measuring the 'abyss', and making the 'unutterable' thinkable, he begins to comprehend the long gap which began with their childhood separation and his degradation, when he 'ceased to express his fondness for her in words' and became 'dumb'. In facing the death within her eyes, while she is still alive, he symbolically takes on the emotional burden shelved by Hindley in relation to Frances. Catherine's reciprocal knowledge is that she will 'feel the same distress underground'; their attempt to cross the sense-barrier of death makes their intercommunication real, perhaps for the first time. With Catherine's death, Heathcliff's 'soul' becomes localised, and in a sense known, for the first time, though simultaneously removed from his possession and in that sense from his direct, easy knowledge.

Heathcliff's future actions take on the significance of a search for his soul, floundering in an 'abyss' and trying to interpret the 'forms' of Catherine available to him. Catherine's last meeting with him conveys, implicitly, a revision of the message voiced in her delirium — that he should 'follow' her and 'brave the ghosts': guided by reverberations from her, underground. She regains the tranquillity that was once associated with the silvery Linton heaven, dying in 'infinite calm': 'No angel in heaven could be more beautiful than she appeared'; now united with her dream of a home in the 'middle of the moor'. Lying in her coffin covered in scented leaves, in the premature spring, she already melts into her hillside position, 'on a green slope . . . where the wall is so low that heath and bilberry plants have climbed over it from the moor; and peat mould almost buries it.' Meanwhile Heathcliff, becoming the earthly agent for his own soul, merges with the landscape in a different way: marked with the livid colours of torment:

He had been standing a long time in that position, for I saw a pair of ousels passing and repassing, scarcely three feet from him, busy in building their nest, and regarding his proximity no more than that of a piece of timber . . .

I observed several splashes of blood about the bark of the tree, and his hands and forehead were both stained . . .

Like a 'piece of timber' himself, he requires the 'support' of a tree behind him, for 'he trembled, in spite of himself, to his very finger-ends'; dashing his head against the 'knotted trunk' he howls 'like a savage beast goaded to death with knives and spears'. The final image of Heathcliff's teething, against the teething-bark of the bloodstained tree, complements Catherine's change of state, her death-birth. As the earlier volcanic eruption of the storm that split the Heights, seems to settle temporarily, the 'rocks beneath' emerge in the form of the grey headstone set in the peatmould: the tooth achieved by the first generation.

# 4    The Fairy Cave
### (*Chapters 18 – 28*)

The lives of the second-generation children, with their contrasting education and upbringing, begin to interact in adolescence, when Cathy and Linton reach the significant age of twelve or thirteen, and Hareton is six years older. The story focusses on Cathy, who echoes and develops her mother's 'double nature' in her attraction to her two cousins and to her two fathers — Heathcliff again playing the anti-hero, or anti-father. In the exploratory, outward moves of her adolescence, she is simultaneously discovering the history of her forbears, and her own internal constitution: forming her present and future identity in the light of the past. The strands of the narrative interweave romance and anti-romance, education and anti-education, creative and destructive parenthood: all in a way which echoes the experience of the first generation, but without its rigid black and white alternatives. The picture becomes multi-tone, the texture varied, just as its single heroine is 'elastic as steel', made of resilient material, at home in different worlds. Cathy's explorations of the Heights, while still based at the Grange, begin with the Fairy Cave and end with her exit from 'her mother's window', suggesting the search for knowledge not only of her own body but also of her mother's body, her own first home. The 'moaning doll' of a baby who maintained a 'constant wail', later examines the 'mortal cells' (a phrase from the poems) of her mother: the passages, the exits and entrances of her mother's wailing child-ghost. The entire second-generation story seems governed by pulsing emanations from Catherine's grave in the moor, which localises the ancestral and unconscious emotional roots grafted via Heathcliff from Earnshaw's gift of God. Edgar, Heathcliff and the second Catherine each construct their interpretations of heaven by means of their individual imaginative links with Catherine's newly-forged heaven 'in the middle of the moor'.

    The second Catherine integrates and modifies the best qualities of Edgar and of Catherine: 'a real beauty in face — with the Earnshaws' handsome dark eyes, but the Lintons' fair skin and small features, and yellow curling hair'; and in terms of character, her 'capacity for intense attachments reminded me of her mother' but 'her anger was never furious, her love never fierce'. As a child, 'She was the most winning thing that ever brought sunshine into a desolate house'. Her first twelve years are 'the happiest' of Nelly's life; the radiant child exists in a Garden of Eden, enclosed by Thrushcross Park, a 'breeze-rocked cradle' in which Nelly's 'old songs — nursery lore' are complemented by Edgar's systematic care: 'He took her education entirely on himself, and made it an amusement':

> Till she reached the age of thirteen, she had not once been beyond the range of the park by herself. Mr Linton would take her with him, a mile or so outside, on rare occasions; but he trusted her to no one else . . . Wuthering Heights and Mr Heathcliff did not exist for her; she was a perfect recluse; and, apparently perfectly contented.

But now, on the threshold of adolescence, her imagination extends beyond her known world; her own 'sunshine' discovers features previously excluded from her mental geography: 'The abrupt descent of Penistone Crags particularly attracted her notice, especially when the setting sun shone on it, and the topmost heights; and the whole extent of landscape besides lay in shadow.' She is curious about 'those golden rocks', 'bright so long after it is evening here', and the 'Fairy Cave' beneath. The sexual significance of the rock formation — 'Penis' stone and the Cave already associated with the female body and pelvis by Catherine in her delirium — is brought out by Cathy's association of becoming 'a woman': 'Then I can go, too, when I am a woman. Has papa been, Ellen?' Ellen attempts to de-mystify and de-romanticise the picture: 'bare masses of stone, with hardly enough earth in their clefts to nourish a stunted tree', echoing Catherine's description of Heathcliff as 'an unreclaimed creature, without refinement, without cultivation; an arid wilderness of furze and whinstone'. But Cathy's 'head is turned' with the desire to explore the Cave; just as, in a sense, Heathcliff does 'exist for her' in the recesses of her imagination, soon to become visible in reality when she turns the light of her exploring 'sun' in his direction. Her own image of the 'rocks beneath' is one which transfigures them with radiance, rising majestically from the landscape and from the deep shadows and skulking corners to which they have been relegated hitherto. Her vision of the rocks prefigures the end of the novel, just as it echoes — and changes — the moonlit heaven of her parents before the re-appearance of Heathcliff from the shadow.

The Penistone Rocks are intimately associated with Wuthering Heights, topographically: 'The road thither wound close by Wuthering Heights. Edgar had not the heart to pass it'; they are an extension of the storm-swept house, already a semi-natural landmark. When Cathy does in fact 'break bounds' and embark alone on a voyage of discovery which is both a search for her mother and womanhood, it is no accident that she becomes embroiled in the life of the Heights, where Nelly finds her 'perfectly at home', 'rocking herself in a little chair that had been her mother's'. Before leaping the boundary on her pony, she got the gardener to cut her a 'hazel switch' — recalling the lost whip her mother had desired in lieu of Heathcliff, and foreshadowing the 'cut of my whip' given to Hareton on a later visit. It is no accident that it is Hareton, with whom she later falls in love, who emerges from the Heights 'to open the mysteries of the Fairy Cave, and twenty other queer places' associated with the mysterious life of the moor — without however exhausting its reserve stock of mysteries: 'I want to see where the goblin hunter rises in the marsh, and to hear about the fairishes . . .'. The 'goblin hunter' hints at Heathcliff, frequently called a 'goblin' and often seen hunting moor-game or grouse, particularly in the second half of the book; and ultimately to hunt Cathy herself. Cathy's relationship with Hareton is initiated by a bloody encounter between their respective dogs (Charlie and Phenix 'came limping, and hanging their heads'), symbolic as always of different shades of passion, and re-enacting with a difference, the entry of the first Catherine into Thrushcross Grange at the same age by means of the bulldog, 'his huge, purple tongue hanging half a foot out of his mouth': 'They had a smart battle, before the owners could separate them: that formed an introduction.' This 'introduction' recalls the quarrel which made Edgar and Catherine 'confess themselves lovers'; but in the case of the second generation, the physical violence is less grossly overpowering and the division between peace and trouble less marked. Cathy's bruising is essentially not physical, but mental, as is Hareton's; their respective feelings are hurt by mutual revelations about their own identities. Thus Hareton 'could not stand a steady gaze from her eyes, though they were just his own'; Cathy is not physically incapacitated in order to become 'queen' at the expense of an unbridgeable internal split; instead her queenship is ruffled by Hareton's recognition of the 'saucy witch' within her, which makes her disown him as 'cousin', 'upset at the bare notion of relationship with such a clown': 'She, who was always "love", and "darling", and "queen", and "angel", with everybody at the Grange, to be insulted so shockingly by a stranger!' Her equilibrium is upset by discoveries about herself (imaged in discovery about Hareton's status), which have hitherto been kept from her owing to Edgar's indulgence and his own inability to face them (he 'had not the heart' to pass Wuthering Heights). The golden girl has to face Hareton 'black as a thunder-cloud' (Heathcliff's colouring); but, though it takes years to reconcile the black and gold, neither of them is forced into a false position: the opposition between them, and within themselves, is exposed from the beginning, in preparation for a long period of adjustment.

The second Catherine's demotion from 'angelic' status, though it echoes her mother's, is quite different in its developmental function, hence in its meaning. In her childhood Eden, 'She was a happy creature, and an angel, in those days. It's a pity she could not be content'. Edgar advises her to 'think no more' about her new acquaintance at the Heights; but like Adam and Eve, 'happiest yet to know no more', her fall from Eden is a function of her search for further knowledge. Her early Eden is doomed, not owing to circumstances or external agents, but rather, owing to her own internal struggle for growth and identity, which in a sense invites contact with the Heathcliff story — Heathcliff's part in her history having been 'excluded from all her studies and all her ideas till now'. But whilst the first Catherine's heaven and angelic, queenly status was a fragile romance, only skin-deep and temporarily covering her tormented, split identity underneath, the second Catherine's remains a basis for her adult understanding of life; it is a heaven of innocence rather than of illusion, and consequently is capable of returning in a different form, after sustaining contact with experience. For although Edgar cannot himself face any direct contact with Heathcliff — symbolising aspects of intolerable knowledge of himself which remain forever shunned — yet the education he provides for his daughter, enables her to go beyond his own attainment of knowledge. Since his marriage he has been associated with books and self-contained reflection: partly it is suggested, as an antidote to his wife ('What has he to do with books, when I am dying?'). For him, the library is always, in part, a refuge. But the nature of his love for Cathy, who is his 'living hope' and his 'apt scholar', allows him to transcend his own limitations in relation to her. The library is now the most important room in Thrushcross Grange, and Cathy is brought up on a significant diet of books — not religious tomes, the 'lumber' thrust upon the first Cathy and Heathcliff, but ballads, poems, romances. (The library is also the source of some of Nelly's equanimity, as she tells Lockwood — 'You could not open a book in this library that I have not looked into'.) Thus when Cathy first breaks the bounds of her Grange nursery (Edgar's refuge), she goes accoutred as an 'Arabian merchant' crossing the desert, having no difficulty in leaping the 'low hedge' of the Park. She enacts a fantasy rooted in her range of reading matter, and stimulated by Nelly, who 'sent her on travels round the grounds'. Inevitably, the extension of her idyllic childhood into realms outside Edgar's imaginative control upsets her equilibrium at first and upsets her angelic status; her father 'never spoke a harsh word ' to her, but Hareton simply 'did not feel her threat' of 'I shall tell papa!' The Arabian merchant, trading her riches across the desert moor, is surprised at the hard bargaining price driven by a nature as proud and independent as her own — Hareton being 'a wealthy soil that might yield luxuriant crops', or 'gold put to the use of paving stones'. Later their relationship grows by means of their use of books, its character suggested by imagery of flowers and of gold: the books are Cathy's 'treasures'. She has her personal library within the Grange's library, and its contents seem inexhaustible: books are given to Linton ('his books are not as nice as mine'), to the groom Michael who assists her secret visits to the Heights (and is also in process of becoming independent, 'leaving to get married'); some books are later confiscated by Heathcliff, and others burnt by Hareton in a fit of rage, but there are still plenty left to carry the final development. Cathy's 'treasures' symbolise her internal richness and resilience. They are 'written on my brain and printed on my heart': an internalised fount of knowledge, not a superficial accomplishment, their meaning surviving even when their body is lost or destroyed. They are 'nicer' than Linton's because his represent the token education supplied by Heathcliff to fulfil the requirements of a gentleman's upbringing; they are a great improvement on her mother's 'misused' volumes, because they represent an inheritance not of dictatorial morality, but of love.

Meanwhile, the course of Cathy's adolescence does not run smooth, after her first excursion to the Fairy Cave, 'gay as a fairy'. Her relationship with Hareton goes underground while she develops the anti-romance of that with 'her "real" cousin', Linton, who arrives in her life almost simultaneously. Linton has her father's external form (looking like a 'younger brother'), without his or his sister's 'spirit'. He arrives wrapped in furs and closeted in a travelling coach, from which he refuses to look out, desiring only to go to bed. His heaven, as he later describes it, is one of 'peace'; while Cathy's is one of 'glorious jubilee'; thus they inherit contradictory states of the first Catherine: her unstable 'tranquillity' and the 'jubilee' (at the same time 'calamity') evoked by Heathcliff's renewed presence. Both the protected coach and the Cave have associations with Catherine and the closet of dreams in the 'old bed' of Wuthering Heights. The protected traveller is reminiscent of the Catherine who 'must not be crossed' but shielded from all mental disturbance; while the Cave displayed her vulnerable internal state during her brain fever, liable to attack by witches and Heathcliff. In this context, Hareton and Linton (both sons of Heathcliff in a sense) represent antithetical approaches to Heathcliff, both of which are experienced by the second Cathy. Recalling the old contrast between the dogs of passion and of sentimentality, the lively 'introduction' between herself and Hareton through a dog-fight, is transmuted into an unequal fantasy involving Linton as her 'pet': 'she had resolved to make a pet of her little cousin, as she would have him to be; and she commenced stroking his curls, and kissing his cheek, and offering him tea in her saucer, like a baby.' The fantasy is mutual; Linton is 'pleased' by her behaviour, 'for he was not much better' than a baby (Nelly later

calls their correspondence 'babyish trash', again echoing
Catherine's 'baby work'). Linton's ancestors are Isabella's
springer and the dog in the crimson room (where he is now),
both on one level aspects of Catherine. The picture recalls
Frances and Hindley ('like two babies') and its subsequent
recurrence in Catherine's making Isabella — only one year
younger than she — her 'child' or 'fondling'. Later Cathy
similarly magnifies the six-months' age difference between
herself and Linton, as if in reaction to the six years between
herself and Hareton:

> "And besides, I'm almost seventeen. I'm a woman — and
> I'm certain Linton would recover quickly if he had me to look
> after him — I'm older than he is, you know, and wiser, less
> childish, am I not? And he'll soon do as I direct him, with
> some slight coaxing — He's a pretty little darling when he's
> good. I'd make such a pet of him, if he were mine — We
> should never quarrel . . ."

Linton allows her to reinstate her sense of price, power and
virtue, bruised by Hareton; then, like her mother with Isabella,
she has to undergo the experience of her 'pet' child not 'doing as
she directs' (even with 'slight coaxing'), but betraying her; her
false adulthood is undermined. This justification of her
relationship is part of her defensive speech to Ellen beginning
'The Grange is not a prison, Ellen, and you are not my jailer'.
It is clear that leaping the boundaries of the Grange (practise for
Emily's 'final bound'), entails not a straight road to independence, but also the snare of self-delusion. Her original desire to
become 'a woman', awoken by the idea of the Fairy Cave,
involves also the illusion that already 'I'm a woman' — acted
out in relation to Linton. But Cathy, unlike her mother or any
of the first generation, later manages to integrate the experience
of illusion and inner 'death' within her total experience and
education, without its breaking her spirit.

The context of the false education which she practises on
Linton — and thereby, on herself — is clarified by her fear and
neglect of the educative relationship seeded between herself and
Hareton. On her sixteenth birthday, she visits the Heights for
the first time since the Fairy Cave: allowed to do so by her
mother's spirit, which occupies Edgar on his ritual day of

POETIC STRUCTURE OF WUTHERING HEIGHTS

mourning, leaving Cathy free to wander afield. As always, Linton has nothing of his own to offer Cathy in entertainment, 'not even a rabbit, or a weasel's nest' to show her; his inner life is empty. Instead it is Hareton who shows her round the yard, on Heathcliff's instigation, though with his tongue 'tied' by Heathcliff. In contrast to the Fairy Cave, Hareton proves a negative guide: 'Earnshaw had his countenance completely averted from his companion. He seemed to be studying the familiar landscape with a stranger's, and an artist's interest.' It becomes clear that his negativeness derives from the fact that in a sense he does not know what he is looking at — like Lockwood he has a stranger's interest in the landscape; his comprehension of life and nature is undermined. Underneath the comic irony, is the suggestion that Hareton, who on one level knows the moor intimately, is being made to review his knowledge in the light of Catherine's company, seeing it as an 'artist'. Deprived of the security of his previous understanding of life and himself, he becomes temporarily deranged and outcast, looking like an 'idiot': ' "Is he all as he should be?" asked Miss Cathy seriously.' For the tour of the guide-become-stranger ends up under the inscription over the front door ('Hareton Earnshaw: 1500'), being the overt statement of Hareton's own name, identity and inheritance:

> Hareton stared up, and scratched his head like a true clown. "It's some damnable writing", he answered. "I can't read it." "Can't read it?" cried Catherine. "I can read it . . . It's English . . . but I want to know, why it is there." Linton giggled . . .

For the first time, the 'use' of a new medium of verbal expression occurs to him and disturbs him: 'Why, where the devil is the use on 't?' And it is Heathcliff who is his 'master or guardian' in the affair, closely observing the interaction of the three cousins, and forcing Hareton for the first time to experience the nature of his degradation and 'tied' tongue. Up to this point, Heathcliff's anti-education of Hareton has had no sting in it, owing to the success of Hareton's contempt for 'book-larning', and to his being 'damnably fond' of his master/guardian. Now Heathcliff, by creating a situation of painful conflict, re-lives his own youthful suffering:

75

"Nelly, you recollect me at his age ... Did I ever look so stupid; so 'gaumless', as Joseph calls it? ... But he's no fool; and I can sympathise with all his feelings, having felt them myself — I know what he suffers now, for instance, exactly — it is merely a beginning of what he shall suffer, though.''

Already, the artificial context created for the purpose of 'revenge' on Hindley is being undermined, outside Heathcliff's consciousness, by his own feeling for and with Hareton — the 'damnable fondness' is mutual: 'do you know that, twenty times a day, I covet Hareton, with all his degradation? I'd have loved the lad had he been someone else. But I think he's safe from *her* love.' His observations also make him cognisant of Cathy's powers of judgement: 'I am afraid, Nelly, I shall lose my labour ... Miss Catherine, as the ninny [Linton] calls her, will discover his value, and send him to the devil.' All the elements for the ultimate 'thwarting of his revenge' are already present and at work within his mind and emotions; though many transformations are yet to occur before they become re-organised and lose the intended 'shape' of that revenge.

Catherine, meanwhile, in reaction to Hareton's and her own mutual confusion, immediately allies with the giggling Linton in a refuge of mockery, which shuts out the disturbance awoken in her by this paradoxical image of a quiescent, unacknowledged identity. The alliance of the 'flippant pair' is regarded with 'singular aversion' by Heathcliff. She feels safer with the cousin who is superficially educated — equipped with the machinery for expression, though he has nothing within him to express — than with the cousin whose inner life exists in untouched oblivion, its quality never tested. One relationship she regards as worked out; the other is confusing: 'I think he does not understand me; I can hardly understand *him*, I'm sure!' Later, when she narrates to Nelly her secret visits to the Heights, she explains how she 'shuddered at the thought of encountering Hareton'; she never encounters Heathcliff himself on these visits, and Hareton seems to take on some of his quality and significance. Thus on one occasion he 'suddenly issued from the shadow of the road-side' to intercept her departure and settle their understanding of an evening of violent events. But she cuts off his explanation: 'I gave him a cut with my whip, thinking,

76

perhaps he would murder me — He let go, thundering one of his horrid curses, and I galloped home more than half out of my senses.' Hareton is capable of driving her 'out of her senses', beyond the imaginative control she believes she can impose on Linton. The cut of the whip — her mother's weapon — contrasts with her petting of Linton in a written game of love: in Heathcliff's accusation, 'making love in play, eh? You deserved, both of you, flogging for that!' And the gallop over the moors brings a 'flush' to her cheeks whose source Nelly misinterprets as the 'library fire'. Yet at the same time, the 'cut' and the 'flogging' hint at the incipient violence, as yet denied, in her relation with Linton — who, as Heathcliff later says, will 'undertake to torture any number of cats, so long as their claws are pared', and who 'winks' to see his father 'strike a dog — he does it so hard'. For the sequence of violent events that evening had been initiated by Catherine herself, mocking Hareton's attempt to display his new prowess in reading (that is, to respond creatively, self-educatively, to her stimulus). She then saw her blow to education mirrored, first in Hareton's looks towards her (as if longing to 'knock her down'), then in his seizure of Linton bringing on a fit of coughing and gush of blood — after which he contritely carries him upstairs. The whole episode partly re-enacts the final scene between Heathcliff, Hindley and Isabella. As then with Heathcliff and Hindley, this is Hareton's first violence against Linton; and it is not only sparked off by Catherine, but it repeats her own 'little push' of an earlier occasion, which had resulted in a 'suffocating cough' and Linton's complaint: 'I wish *she* felt as I do ... spiteful, cruel thing! Hareton never touches me, he never struck me in his life'. The interaction between the three cousins touches the limits of their endurance and self-knowledge, unearthing forces outside their control. Just as Hareton cannot stand a 'steady gaze' from Cathy's eyes, so she fears the reciprocal emergence of his unpredictable, active potential: the newly-awakened desire for self-knowledge which mirrors her own (they have the same eyes). And in Hareton, now able to decipher the inscription of his name, the internal 'rocks beneath' are stirring — both his Earnshaw and his Heathcliff inheritance, aroused from their ancestral torpor.

Cathy, unlike her father, continues to make contact with the

77

hidden depths which she 'shudders' to confront; her knowledge of the family at the Heights develops through counterpointing romance and anti-romance. Her relationship with Linton begins as an anti-educational venture founded on a kind of innocent omnipotence; but, because her 'mothering' is never divorced from feeling, it progressively becomes educational in a way she had not intended, nor would have desired. Their first 'little romance' is imaged in the form of a forbidden corres- pondence kept in a locked drawer in the library, formerly used for 'playthings and trinkets', and now 'transmuted into bits of folded paper'; and though, when accused, she cries indignantly 'We don't send playthings!', it is clear that — as Heathcliff asserts — their 'love' is in effect another plaything. It is defined by Nelly, who has looked into every book in the library, as 'a fine bundle of trash . . . good enough to be printed!' Cathy's drawer of treasures parodies her mother's plundered pillow and nest of lapwings: 'Never did any bird flying back to a plundered nest which it had left brim-full of chirping young ones, express more complete despair in its anguished cries and flutterings'. Cathy, pursuing a fiction of a romance rather than a real one, is unable to distinguish the fake quality of the rhetoric in the letters, described by Nelly as 'singularly odd compounds of ardour and flatness . . . foolish as the age of the writer rendered natural, yet with touches . . . borrowed from a more experienced source'. That is, she is unable to detect the false presence of Heathcliff projected in the joint compositions — the Heathcliff of Isabella's 'hero of romance', Lockwood's 'misanthrope', or Nelly's Gothic 'incarnate demon' or 'goblin' of superstition. In her experience, Catherine partly retraces the footsteps of her aunt's romance, and in doing so comes to learn from experience of her father's own area of blindness and ostracised knowledge (the disowning not only of Heathcliff but of his sister). For Edgar, also, is oblivious of the overruling presence of Heathcliff, in the later batch of letters received with his consent: 'He had a fixed idea . . . that as his nephew resembled him in person, he would resemble him in mind; for Linton's letters bore few or no indications of his defective character'. The 'fixed idea' is his own romance, his own library of sheltered refuge, the blind spot in his literary education. Linton's contrived, artificial letters embody the false conjunction of 'Linton Heathcliff'; they are an assortment of dead elements, Catherine's 'pile of little skeletons', not a nest of living fledgelings. Cathy had originally accepted her aunt's romance in the terms of a bookish fiction suggested by Heathcliff — 'he thought me too poor to wed his sister'; and this is not fully dispelled by Edgar's 'too timid' explanatory history; Cathy has to learn about it through her own experience — and in doing so, she revises the meaning of the original romance. The educational status of her relationship with Linton contrasts with the primitive but genuine attempt which Hareton begins to make, to express himself in words, and to expand his identity through 'book-larning'. The Heathcliff within Linton is associated with the deceptive or superficial use of words and writing, with superstition and stereotypes — 'pretty' in externals but hollow within. The Heathcliff within Hareton is the natural 'goblin hunter' arising from the depths of emotional experience, but not as yet contained in verbal expression or thought: a fertile landscape requiring the fresh vertex of a 'stranger' and the organisation of an 'artist'. Heathcliff, observing his two sons, sees his false or destructive and his true or creative self mirrored; and Cathy, in her experiential reconstruction of her mother's history, needs the knowledge of both sides, first of all exorcising the destructiveness of a false education.

Unlike Edgar, Cathy is not long bound by a 'fixed idea' of Linton — the idea of Linton as 'pet', with herself as mistress-mother. Her relationship with him begins to change in the context of her apprehension of death: when firstly her father falls ill, and secondly she is disturbed by Heathcliff's accusation that Linton is 'dying for love' of her, which leaves her 'clouded in double darkness'. When she and Nelly visit Linton after the chance meeting with Heathcliff, Cathy entertains him by reciting ballads (an extension of feeding him tea from a saucer), allowing him to lean on her knee 'as mamma used to do, whole afternoons together'; this is their reconciliation after Linton's throwing of a fit, caricaturing the manner of his mother and his aunt as a child: he 'lay writhing in the mere perverseness of an indulged plague of a child'. But already her mothering begins to take on a new flavour, of disturbance at the nature of his illness, which seems to reflect that of her father: 'He's younger than I ... and he ought to

79

live the longest, he will — he must live as long as I do . . . It's
only a cold that ails him, the same as papa has — You say papa
will get better, and why shouldn't he?' Nelly is caught in the
rationale of her own misguided efforts to soothe Cathy's anxiety
for Edgar; Cathy has no alternative but to discover the reality for
herself, which involves her temporarily casting an involuntary
spell on Nelly such that she becomes bedridden, for the only time
in her life, for three weeks. Cathy is the cause of her 'sitting such
a while at the Heights' in 'soaked shoes and stockings' (herself
being on horseback); this is her version of 'witchery' ('see how
far I have progressed in the Black Art', she torments Joseph),
the other side to her angelic quality: 'My mistress behaved like
an angel in coming to wait on me, and cheer my solitude'. But
her witch-angel double nature contrasts with the first
generation's in its unselfishness, though prompted by the same
sense of necessity. She becomes nurse to not two but three
invalids — 'her day divided between' Edgar and Ellen, and her
dark evenings spent in investigating the other life, at the Heights
— not in itself an experience of pleasure: 'It was not to amuse
myself that I went; I was often wretched all the time.' Earlier,
her pleasurable illusion of motherhood had begun to be undermined by mutual revelations between herself and Linton about
their family background: her 'pet' opening of 'Pretty Linton! I
wish you were my brother' was soon transformed, via her information that his father had an 'aversion to her aunt':

> "Well, I'll tell you something!" said Linton. "Your
> mother hated your father, now then . . . And she loved
> mine!"
> "You little liar! I hate you now", she panted, and her face
> grew red with passion.

Later, their discovery of their forbears' cupboard of toys,
including the balls marked 'C' and, ambiguously, 'H', also
symbolises their examination, though the re-enaction of 'play',
of a tortuous family inheritance which is not only historical but
also internal to themselves.

Their relationship is clinched, on the visit after the violent
encounter with Hareton, by a single moment of sincerity, which
seals their future marriage by rendering their fates inextricable.
Catherine goes to Linton in order to say 'goodbye', feeling as if

she were 'doing a duty' in visiting him. But Linton, prompted by the reality of her intention to part, makes the unexpected confession:

> "I am worthless, and bad in temper, and bad in spirit, almost always — and if you choose, you may say good-bye — you'll get rid of an annoyance — Only, Catherine, do me this justice; believe that if I might be as sweet, and as kind, and as good as you are, I would be, as willingly, and more so, than as happy and healthy. And, believe that your kindness has made me love you deeper than if I deserved your love, and though I couldn't, and cannot help showing my nature to you, I regret and repent it, and shall regret, and repent it, till I die!"

Catherine's reaction is that 'I felt he spoke the truth; and I felt I must forgive him; and, though he should quarrel the next moment, I must forgive him again.' Their mutual acknowledgement of Linton's 'distorted nature' is a statement of knowledge achieved between them: the strange nature of a negative, yet genuine, 'love' which exorcises the illusory quality of the presence of false love within the first generation (such as Isabella's, also present within the fragile egocentricity of the others). Linton's decaying physical condition is symbolic of his mental 'bad nature', and in a sense he is dying for the sins of the forbears, a 'feeble tool to his father' (in Edgar's words). Yet that single moment of reality between him and Catherine, places the 'feebleness' within a new context. With her new knowledge, Catherine takes on responsibility for his bad nature, and for seeing him through to his death, 'leaning on her shoulder'. It is a new kind of motherhood; she knows that she 'must forgive him, and forgive him again', whatever his future treachery. Their joint approach to the reality of 'death' exorcises the first generation's 'fight to the death'. Her final marriage to Linton is not essentially an event forced on her by plot and circumstance, despite the surrounding charade of imprisonment; rather, it is the inevitable fruit of her acknowledgement of 'bad nature' as part of the ancestral human constellation to which she, also, is committed, and which she, also, carries within her. It is this move toward the integration of 'badness' in the form of Linton, which eventually gives her the strength to face up to Heathcliff

directly, in his 'bad' aspect: 'I know he has a bad nature — he's
your son'. Through Linton, she understands one aspect of
Heathcliff's significance; just as through Hareton, she comes to
understand another; and contain both within her revised double
nature. Only the experience of her marriage to 'death' enables
her to face Hareton honestly, acknowledging the 'witchery'
which he had first brought out in her. Cathy epitomises the life-
preserving quality of the second generation, which is flexibility
— the ability to turn 'bad' experience to good account, creating
a fibre 'elastic as steel'. Despite temporary magnetic repulsions
during her indirect encounters with Heathcliff, their overall
movement is integratory, as she reworks the brittle constitution
of the first generation through their original 'gift of God'.

Through her cousins at the Heights, Cathy extends and
strengthens the knowledge passed on to her by her father, who
in himself finds the subject of Heathcliff unapproachable: 'He
could not bear to discourse long upon the topic, for though he
spoke little of it, he still felt the same horror and detestation of his
ancient enemy that had occupied his heart ever since Mrs
Linton's death.' Though Heathcliff is excluded from Edgar's
educational system, the 'ancient enemy' still 'occupies his
heart'; he leaves it to his daughter to investigate the forbidden
emotional knot and experience the 'occupation' from another
vertex: taking on the name of the 'nameless man' (the 'contemptible, degrading title of Mrs Heathcliff'), but balancing the
experience of her aunt against that of her mother. From the
moment of Cathy's first independent departures from the
Grange, for the Fairy Cave and her double life, she begins to
separate from her father: not in the sense of distancing or
deterioration, but in the sense of each responding in their
different ways to the emanations from Catherine's grave. The
gradual release of Edgar's hold on life is simultaneous with
Cathy's growing involvement with Heathcliff — her
investigation of her other father, apparently an anti-father. It is
marked by a series of encounters: the first being an extension of
Cathy's search for the nests of 'moor-game', still in her 'angelic'
days, 'her eyes radiant with cloudless pleasure'. She believes she
has 'gone very near with papa'; but inevitably, her hunt, though
founded on her 'walks' with him, outstrips his range as it does
Nelly's breathless expostulations, and her internal search pulls

her across the boundary between Grange and Heights land, 'scampering round the brow at full speed', where she encounters Heathcliff. The 'moor-game' recall the feathers in her mother's pillow, the wild spiritual elements of the moor in some way scattered like an invisible snow-storm by her mother's spirit; and Cathy herself is, as her mother imagined, one of the creatures of the moor, like the lapwings, destined to come face to face with Heathcliff, the goblin hunter. (Both Heathcliff and Hareton are fond of shooting — hence Lockwood's 'gift of grouse'.) Cathy's childhood invulnerability, cradled in affection and indulgence, is exposed by her own internal urge for development, to the twin apprehension of her father's death and Heathcliff's ascendance. The sunshine associated with her childhood becomes the variable, moist weather of her adolescence, echoed in the alternating sun and shadow flitting across her face at one point, 'like the landscape'. Edgar catches the cold which becomes his slow, consuming fever, one evening when he and his daughter stay out late at the end of a late harvest to watch 'the carrying of the last sheaves' (imaging the limits of Edgar's own education of his daughter, and a premonition of his own death). During the subsequent 'watery' season, brimful with tears, 'the cold, blue sky was half hidden by clouds, dark grey streamers, rapidly mounting from the west, and boding abundant rain', Catherine has her next encounter with Heathcliff. On a walk with Nelly, a vignette of her early 'breeze-rocked cradle' is described, now represented only by a 'lonely blossom trembling in its earthly shelter', left over from the July flowering, 'looking melancholy': suggesting that in her present sadness and isolation, the loss of her early heaven is inseparable from her foreknowledge of her father's death: 'And what shall I do when papa and you leave me, and I am by myself?' It is in this context that she climbs over the Grange wall, as if trying to regain her old spirit, clambering after colourful rose-hips that only the 'birds' can reach: only to find that her exploration traps her outside her old cradle, like the young moor-game, exposed to the presence of Heathcliff:

An approaching sound arrested me. It was the trot of a horse; Cathy's dance stopped; and in a minute the horse stopped also . . .

"Ho, Miss Linton!" cried a deep voice (the rider's), "I'm glad to meet you."

Their mutual hunt is a kind of pas-de-deux, the horse's trot paralleling Cathy's dance in unconscious unison. The accidental meeting has a sense of inevitability, with Heathcliff emerging as an active presence in the landscape, heralded by horses' hooves, as though continually skirting the boundaries of Cathy's childhood, waiting to respond to her slightest move outward.

As the two Lintons approach death at either end of the landscape, both incapacitated and unable to reach the mid-point (the milestone), the central drama focusses more obviously on the active Cathy and Heathcliff, mediating: both engaged in their own moor-game, a search for Catherine, and driven relentlessly from within. Linton, after the confession of his 'worthlessness', his energies exhausted, abandons any further attempt to establish a genuine relationship with Cathy; her 'good' nature, he knows, will take the burden of his death and 'bad nature' from him. Beginning with the doctored letters, he becomes a mere mouthpiece for Heathcliff's bad nature, evincing his father's superficial traits without their profound motivation of love and hate. He becomes a caricature of the false 'baby' whom Cathy fed from a saucer: as Nelly describes him on the morning of her release, when Catherine is still imprisoned: 'Linton lay on the settle, sole tenant, sucking a stick of sugar-candy, and pursuing my movements with apathetic eyes . . . He sucked on like an innocent.' Linton finally achieves his personal elysium of sugar-coated innocence and 'peace' (meaning apathy), at the cost of Cathy's torment; the two are inseparable. He parodies his aunt's peaceful death (which resulted in Heathcliff's torment), and her physical collapse prior to death. Thus, during the final meetings with Cathy on the moor, in which he is used as bait by Heathcliff to trap Cathy, his grovelling, jerky movements ('abject reptile — 'convulsed with exquisite terror' — 'nerveless frame' — 'prostrate in a paroxysm') parody the tantrums of his mother and aunt, and the self-laceration of his father dashing his head against the trunk; they also contrast with the nervous thrilling of Heathcliff's body before his death. In effect these are Linton's death-throes: the paroxysms of a puppet whose movements are controlled by Heathcliff from behind the nab:

> "I thought I heard my father", he gasped, glancing up to the frowning nab above us . . . And, still under the spell of the imaginary voice, his gaze wandered up and down to detect its owner . . . so absorbed was he in anticipating his father's approach.
> . . . hearing a rustle among the ling, I looked up, and saw Mr Heathcliff almost close upon us, descending the Heights.

The pet becomes puppet, serving Heathcliff's omnipotent control, twitching like Isabella's hanged dog (though, as Heathcliff points out afterwards, he has never physically beaten Linton). And Catherine accepts the bait of the disgorged pet-turned-traitor, not through gullibility, but through her sense of responsibility for the Linton whom she once wanted to make 'good' through being 'mine'. In accepting the thing of darkness endowed by her predecessors, she exorcises the harm embodied in the lapdog emotional fallacy. She does this not, however, in saintly manner, but with a bitterness which redounds acerbically on Lockwood when he misconstrues the heap of dead rabbits: 'A strange choice of favourites!' She pays the price for her mother's feared 'little skeletons', through her own 'plundered nest'. When Cathy goes to live at the Heights, Heathcliff gives her the option of watching Linton's death herself, or leaving him alone: 'None here care what becomes of him; if you do, act the nurse; if you do not, lock him up and leave him.' She does not 'lock him up' or banish him from her thoughts, but accepts the burden of absorbing in isolation the black emptiness of a meaningless death. This is her real service to the House divided since Earnshaw's 'gift of God'; and Heathcliff insistently requires to know how she 'feels':

> "Now — Catherine", he said, "how do you feel?"
> She was dumb.
> "How do you feel, Catherine?" he repeated.
> "He's safe, and I'm free", she answered, "I should feel well — but," she continued with a bitterness she couldn't conceal, "you have left me so long to struggle against death, alone, that I feel and see only death! I feel like death!"

He presses her to verbalise her 'feeling', not out of mere sadism, but because it is felt partly on his behalf (as father to Linton, and in particular, as the black sheep in the Earnshaw fold); consequently, it is essential to him to know the feeling.

In Linton's death-scene there is no sense of another world; he leaves no ghost and enters no peat-mould; the emptiness of his life is sealed by an empty death. Yet Catherine's ability to sustain 'death' itself, is founded partly on the nature of her participation in her father's recent, antithetical, death scene. Though she appears, through Linton, to become Heathcliff's prisoner, it is clear that, when it is necessary, she can escape. After the imprisonment of her marriage, it is no accident that she escapes from the Heights in time to reach Edgar's deathbed (in spite of Heathcliff's apparently impermeable locks and bolts): not though the agency of Ellen, nor through the Grange's four servants equipped with 'serviceable weapons', but — with some help from Linton — through her mother's window: 'Luckily, lighting on her mother's, she got easily out of its lattice'. This is her second 'birth' from the confines of her mother's body, following the route led by her mother's spirit. Not only the Grange's territorial power, but also Heathcliff's usurpation of its force (in his recent legal dealings as well as the physical imprisonment), prove ineffective beside the emotional force which drives Cathy to become part of the tableau of reunion imagined by Edgar.

Edgar's death is seen as given from the moment of his wife's; delayed only by the necessity of conveying his own understanding of life, now deepened by his knowledge of death, to his 'living hope' on earth. The central pull of his existence has always been his 'wishing, yearning' for her mother's grave:

"I thought the memory of the hour I came down that glen a bridegroom, would be less sweet than the anticipation that I was soon, in a few months, or possibly weeks, to be carried up, and laid in its lonely hollow! Ellen, I've been very happy with my little Cathy. Through winter nights and summer days she was a living hope at my side — but I've been as happy musing by myself among those stones, under that old church — lying, through the long June evenings, on the green mound of her mother's grave, and wishing, yearning, for the time I might lie beneath it."

His nurturing of a 'living hope' parallels his living image of Catherine's spirit, and is at the root of his turning increasingly from external to internal preoccupations, forsaking his public life as master of Thrushcross Grange, chief landowner and magistrate. By contrast Heathcliff, who establishes himself from being a 'nameless' dependant to being the active force in the country, is later to describe himself as ceaselessly tormented by 'a spectre of a hope', a ghost-without-spirit, whose life or reality slips from his grasp. Unlike Edgar, increasingly confined to his bed or library, Heathcliff is generally seen out on business, on foot or horseback, busy securing to himself the two estates and with them the force of law itself — as transpires when Edgar cannot alter his will because Mr Green, the lawyer, has 'sold himself to Heathcliff'. But Edgar does not even notice Mr Green's absence, once Cathy returns in his place ('It was not the attorney. My own sweet little mistress sprung on my neck'). Edgar's ultimate legacy to his daughter is not the inheritance of Thrushcross Grange or its traditional values, not the sense of being 'the first lady in the neighbourhood' for which Catherine married him, but an idea of love, based on his internal image of Catherine, in which their child is also included:

> The harvest moon shone clear outside . . .
> Catherine's despair was as silent as her father's joy. She supported him calmly, in appearance; and he fixed on her features his raised eyes that seemed dilating with ecstasy.
> He died blissfully, Mr Lockwood; he died so. Kissing her cheek, he murmured —
> "I am going to her, and you, darling child, shall come to us;" and never stirred or spoke again, but continued that rapt, radiant gaze, till his pulse imperceptibly stopped, and his soul departed.

Edgar's death is a re-writing of the deceptive peace, the summer-in-winter, surrounding Catherine's. It recalls their first moonlit heaven (again the 'harvest moon' associated with Heathcliff); but this time it is the ecstatic radiance emanating from Edgar's eyes which seems to melt outward into the moonlight, not merely reflecting light from without. The reality of his soul's existence seems born from the intensity of his gaze at Catherine, who seems partly to metamorphose (through their identical eyes) into her mother. Thus the exit of Edgar's 'soul' is made through his daughter's 'features'; his certainty of their reunion is a function of a 'living hope'. By staying on earth with his living hope, Edgar has in a sense internally re-written his original fragile happiness in his marriage, to convey an idea of harmony to the second Catherine; hence his conviction of his family's mutual love is not a delusion, as it might have been, had he in fact followed his wife straight to the grave; rather, it is an emotional reality. Cathy is then able to survive, not only Linton's death, but the desecration of her locket, containing the images of her parents (one crushed, one stolen by Heathcliff), because her resilience is in fact based on an internal not an external manifestation of love. The first Catherine, as in a sense she divined during her delirium, proves a better mother dead than alive; offering herself not in the form of an earthly 'shattered prison', but in the form of a moorland heaven or Fairy Cave, full of spirits derived from her own original dream-chamber with its window on the moor.

# 5      A Strange Way of Killing
(*Chapters 29 – 34*)

The first four acts of *Wuthering Heights'* drama, then, have brought us to a point at which the internalisation of images becomes possible. The internal 'story' of mental evolution has reached a stage at which transcendence and metamorphosis is in the air, rather than acting-out and breakdown, as with the first generation. The explosive confrontations which erupted when the initial ossified Linton-Earnshaw stability was disturbed by recognition of Heathcliff and the 'rocks beneath', are ready to have their energies transmuted on to a new level of mental reality. During the final stage of the narrative, which takes place between September 1801 and September 1802, Lockwood's time begins to correspond with that of the inner story. The Lockwood-Heathcliff tension which has sustained the drama, struggles to resolve. The two main strands of the drama, Catherine's protracted 'strange way of killing' Heathcliff, and her strange upbringing of her daughter, converge with Lockwood's dawning consciousness in a single or total story, which culminates in an image of internal metamorphosis or creative thought.

To review the narrative of events carrying this final development: we remember that Lockwood leaves the moor in early spring; in September 1802, he finds himself as if by accident, in the neighbourhood of Gimmerton, and is seized by a 'sudden impulse' to revisit Thrushcross Grange. But he finds his source, Nelly, is at the Heights, and has been since his own departure — as if to continue with the reception of the story in his absence, on his behalf. Approaching the Heights on foot, he spies and overhears Cathy and Hareton reading a book at a window, and is immediately cognisant of their changed relationship. 'Skulking' in envy, he creeps to the back entrance, where Nelly (while the lovers go for a moonlight ramble) describes to him Heathcliff's 'queer' end three months before, simultaneous with the blossoming of the young people's relationship and the bypassing of Joseph's rule. This final inset narrative contains Heathcliff's description of 'strange change'

89

approaching, and his gradual concentration on 'one univeral idea', which it becomes clear is a vision of Catherine, and which ultimately draws him from the process of everyday life back into the panelled bed from which he felt 'beaten out' after her death. Here he is discovered dead one rainy morning, with the window 'flapping open'; and is buried beside Catherine and Edgar in the hillside, mourned by Hareton's 'streaming' tears. Though superstition insists that the ghosts 'walk', Lockwood sees that the lovers are 'afraid of nothing', and on his way back to the Grange, observes the peacefulness of the three headstones in the landscape.

To the reader who has incompletely identified with Lockwood throughout the drama, and who has relegated his spiritual journey to the realms of 'irony', nothing is more uncomfortable than the ending of *Wuthering Heights*. This is regarded (sometimes with approval) as romanticised, watered-down, domesticated, or tongue-in-cheek. But the inability to face the emotional revelation presented during this final act, is due to a failure to follow-through Lockwood's story and to allow this structural figure to absorb and work through, on one's behalf, the more painful and humiliating aspects of replacing false romance with real romance. We remember that the main part of Nelly's narrative corresponds with Lockwood's mysterious binding illness; these come to an end simultaneously, as Lockwood surfaces first via Zillah's narrative and then via his own visit to the Heights; his own release, and the death of his romantic delusions, coinciding with the mind's ability to internalise images (on an overall view of the drama). After this the main action is no longer past, but present, though subconscious. Lockwood leaves Nelly as an agent of perception, whilst he becomes absent in body and allows the region of Gimmerton to become 'dim and dreamy' in his mind; then events take place from which he is in one sense distant, and in another sense intimate. He no longer imposes 'fairytale' matches on a mental configuration (as when he dreamed of eloping with Catherine to the town). Instead his return to hear the end of the action suggests his experience of a new kind of dream, founded on his first dream of reality in Catherine's closet-bed, yet quite different in quality. The desire to settle his 'business' with his landlord, Heathcliff, indicates his compulsion to understand his previous shattering experience in the isolated, mysterious regions of understanding represented by the valley of Gimmerton. Inevitably his preconception of that 'business' is undermined; he finds that instead of settling his rent, his function is to receive the twin stories of Heathcliff's queer end, and of the first real romance between Cathy and Hareton. This 'dreamy' knowledge has to be juxtaposed to the 'busy world'. Parallel with Lockwood's dreaminess, Heathcliff retires into a new 'misanthropy', from which — by contrast with his previous dependence on action — he begins to 'account' verbally for his internal state. Then in the series of Shakespearian semi-soliloquies which bear the weight of the final stage of the narrative, Heathcliff relates, expresses, reviews his internal history, in the terms of his relationship with Catherine's ghost, during the eighteen years since her death. The history of her 'strange way of killing' him is mirrored in his relationship with his adopted 'children'; and his final metamorphosis into the death which is his achievement of 'heaven', is similarly reflected in their catastrophic reversal between 'hate' and 'love'. Both stories, in their interaction and mutual dependence, enact the 'strange way of killing' which provides Lockwood with a new dream of his 'unknown Catherine', finally 'known' in her moor-heaven. And the turning-out of Heathcliff's dream, corresponds with the inward-looking of Lockwood's; a final act of tension between the misanthropes setting the pattern for the reader's own internalisation of a beautiful but uncomfortable revelation.

The end of what Heathcliff calls his 'long fight', begins when after Edgar's funeral he comes to collect Catherine from the Grange, leaving a 'tenancy' vacant which is shortly to be filled by Lockwood: 'I've come to fetch you home ... I'm seeking a tenant for the Grange ... and I want my children about me, to be sure'. The timespan of eighteen years is repeatedly stressed — being the lifespan of the second Catherine, from conception onwards. Heathcliff's entry into the Grange as a 'guest' under a harvest moon corresponded with the time of her conception; now his return under 'the same' harvest moon this time without 'ceremony', as 'master' to claim her as his child, has more than a legal reality:

It was the same room into which he had been ushered, as a guest, eighteen years before: the same moon shone through the window; and the same autumn landscape lay outside. We had not yet lighted a candle, but all the apartment was visible, even to the portraits on the wall — the splendid head of Mrs Linton and the graceful one of her husband.

Heathcliff advanced to the hearth. Time had little altered his person either. There was the same man; his dark face rather sallower . . .

The same room, the same moon, the same landscape, the same man; but this time, Mr and Mrs Linton have been transposed from their picture-like position of mutual peace, framed within the open lattice, to the literal moon-lit portraits on the wall, suggesting their latent yet 'passionless' presence (as Heathcliff later describes Catherine's features in the grave). Their pictures form the background to the living, passionate, second Catherine whom Heathcliff has come to take to her other 'home'. As a family group, they indicate different aspects of the 'image' of Catherine with which Heathcliff is struggling, in a process which echoes Lockwood's deciphering of Catherine's 'hieroglyphics' into a dream-image. Earlier, Heathcliff had seized Cathy's locket portrait of her mother, while crushing that of her father and striking her so that her mouth 'filled with blood'. Now, he orders Catherine's portrait to be removed to the Heights: but is conscious of a certain confusion in his motivation: 'I shall have that home. Not because I need it, but —'. He can only attempt to explain himself by giving Nelly an account of his two desecrations of Catherine's grave, eighteen years apart: during which it becomes clear that the false images of Catherine, violently possessed, merely add to what he later describes as his already existing 'dreadful collection of memoranda — that she did exist, and that I have lost her'. What he really covets in Cathy (as he 'covets' Hareton) is her capacity for internalisation of her mother's image (never seen, yet relayed through Edgar): the ability to hold her 'treasure' like the content of her books, 'written on the brain and printed in the heart'. He does not need a portrait, but an internal, ghostly image. His obsessional takeover of lands, wealth and heirs, represents his misconception of the way to Catherine: while at the same time camouflaging an emotional development that is followed, unacknowledged, in spite of his will — figured in his departure with his latest 'possession', down the tree-lined alley: 'I watched them, from the window, walk down the garden. Heathcliff fixed Catherine's arm under his, though she disputed the act at first, evidently; and with rapid strides, he hurried her into the alley, whose trees concealed them.' Tormented through eighteen years by 'the spectre of a hope', he now adopts Edgar Linton's 'living hope'. And despite their mutual repulsion (Heathcliff would 'rather be hugged by a snake'), the two figures are 'fixed' together, their destinies interlinked and ultimately guiding one another in the same direction.

Heathcliff transports the second Catherine to his 'home' at Wuthering Heights in order that she may unlock the associations of the first Catherine which, he feels, are present in the house, yet barred from him, beating him out of his own dream-chamber. This exclusion from access to his own dreams, his 'soul' (as he calls Catherine), his inner self, dates from his confrontation with Isabella and Hindley on the night after Catherine's funeral which led to Isabella's taunt about the 'dead' quality of his 'love' (a 'deity' now 'senseless dust and ashes'), and then to her escape from the Heights. Now, as if trying to re-form past history, Heathcliff takes a second eighteen-year-old Linton girl whom he suspects has knowledge of a 'live' Catherine. She, also, taunts him about his misery in love: 'You are miserable, are you not? Lonely, like the devil, and envious like him? *Nobody* loves you —'; but this time the taunt is the prelude to a fixing together, not a separation; and this time, instead of physical violence, Heathcliff orders the 'witch' out of the room, and uses her words as a stimulus to verbalise to Nelly the source of his misery, in the form of descriptions of his encounters with Catherine at either end of this period of torment:

> "I'll tell you what I did yesterday! I got the sexton, who was digging Linton's grave, to remove the earth off her coffin lid, and I opened it . . . I struck one side of the coffin loose . . . and I bribed the sexton to pull it away, when I'm laid there, and slide mine out too. I'll have it made so, and then, by the time Linton gets to us, he'll not know which is which!"

With Edgar's death, and the consequent shift in relationships, Heathcliff senses the possibility of a new integration: a mutual 'dissolving into earth' which also includes Linton, in a negative way; it is significant that Heathcliff, despite his power over law and church officials, does not press his threat to have Edgar's grave moved (according to Nelly, because 'the will' prevented him). Edgar's death reawakens the possibility of *seeing* Catherine again, of lifting 'the lid' on buried memory to receive 'a distinct impression of her passionless features' — a vision which leaves him 'tranquil' for the first time in eighteen years:

> "Disturbed her? No, she has disturbed me, night and day, through eighteen years — incessantly — remorselessly — till yesternight — and yesternight, I was tranquil. I dreamt I was sleeping the last sleep, by that sleeper, with my heart stopped, and my cheek frozen against hers."

The Biblical expression of his dream of the 'last sleep' recalls the circular rhythm of Edgar's life-cycle framed round Catherine, from 'the hour I came down that glen a bridegroom' to his premonition of being 'carried up, and laid in its lonely hollow!' Heathcliff's vision of a frozen, timeless dissolving forms an earthly counterpart to Edgar's gaze 'dilating with ecstasy'. The religion of Catherine, based in her moorland grave, takes on an 'existence beyond herself' through the 'dreams' of Edgar and Heathcliff, now both related to the second Catherine.

Heathcliff's first desecration of Catherine's grave (now related to Nelly) had resulted in a positive and a negative kind of knowledge. Thus he gained the conviction of her spirit's life and its existence somewhere in his 'house'; but at the same time, realised its inaccessibility and apparent loss: barred from him by the dead ghosts of Catherine in the form of Hindley and Isabella, who at the same time imaged his own internal imprisonment:

> "I got a spade from the toolhouse, and began to delve with all my might — it scraped the coffin; I fell to work with my hands; the wood commenced cracking about the screws, I was on the point of attaining my object, when it seemed that I heard a sigh from some one above, close at the edge of the grave, and bending down. 'If I can only get this off', I muttered, 'I wish they may shovel in the earth over us both!'

94

POETIC STRUCTURE OF *WUTHERING HEIGHTS*

and I wrenched more desperately still. There was another
sigh, close at my ear. I appeared to feel the warm breath of it
displacing the sleet-laden wind. I knew no other living thing
in flesh and blood was by — but as certainly as you perceive
the approach to some substantial body in the dark, though it
cannot be discerned, so certainly I felt that Cathy was there,
not under me, but on the earth.

A sudden sense of relief flowed, from my heart, through
every limb. I relinquished my labour of agony, and turned
consoled at once, unspeakably consoled. Her presence was
with me; it remained while I re-filled the grave, and led me
home.''

The sensuous reality of the spirit, with its 'warm breath ...
close at my ear', overtaking the natural reality of the weather
with its 'sleet-laden wind', is more powerful than the other
physical reality stressed in the context: the violent active verbs
('delve — cracking —wrenched') and solidity of the coffin in the
earth with its wood splitting. One reality 'displaces' the other; in
the displacing darkness, the sensuous spirit takes on 'substantial
body'. The passage conveys Heathcliff's most intimate
communion with Cathy: the internal conviction of 'presence'
that is more sensuously real than any earthly reality. His sense
of Catherine's presence is more vivid than his physical attack on
the coffin, and takes over the guidance of his physical actions:
'Her presence ... led me home'. The inseparable identity of
Cathy's 'I am Heathcliff' here develops into a separation which
is yet closer than the original adhesiveness. The spirit rising
from the grave images Heathcliff's own soul testing the confines
of his body ('How would *you* like to live with your soul in the
grave?' he had asked her): and in this way, becoming known to
him for the first time. The barrier of death, the dark 'abyss' in
which 'I cannot find you' — symbolic of all separations past and
future — is transformed into a tool for new perception; just as in
*Paradise Lost* Milton finds normal sight 'expunged and razed'
before Light can 'shine inward'. This catastrophic change in
Heathcliff's knowledge of himself prefigures his ultimate
'ghostly' union with Catherine, the attainment of his 'heaven'
through death. It is this experience which shows him that
immediate death, suicide, constitutes a false solution to his

95

agony; the spirit leads him in another direction initially — to deal with the problems of his 'home'. For before Heathcliff can 'see' the Catherine whose presence he 'feels', and before he himself can metamorphose into spirit, he has to achieve a self-knowledge which increases in substantiality in proportion to the slow destruction of his body which he feels is occurring. This he expresses as Catherine's 'strange way of killing' him, a process spun over eighteen years rather than achieved by an immediate death: 'It was a strange way of killing, not by inches, but by fractions of hair-breadths, to beguile me with the spectre of a hope, through eighteen years!' He has to subsume the false images, the 'spectres' left by their relationship on earth, before he can gain access to the true image, the living hope, the spirit of Catherine.

As soon as Heathcliff reaches 'home', on that evening after the funeral, he finds the live spirit is invisible. Catherine has led him back to the Heights to confront, not herself, but the false or deformed images of herself in the persons of Hindley and Isabella — her destroyed 'eyes' and her crushed romantic spirit. They represent the destructive aspects of Heathcliff's relationship with Catherine: his indirect 'revenge' on her and thereby on his own soul. These demand resolution before any 'heavenly' union can become viable. The dead images bar him from his spirit's house; and the beating he inflicts on Hindley — of which he is virtually unconscious — later recoils on himself when he feels himself 'beaten out of' 'my room and hers', the old dream-chamber:

"I remember stopping to kick the breath out of [Hindley], and then hurrying upstairs, to my room, and hers — I looked round impatiently — I felt her by me — I could *almost* see her, and yet I could not! I felt I ought to have sweat blood then, from the anguish of my yearning, from the fervour of my supplications to have but one glimpse! I had not one. She showed herself, as she often was in life, a devil to me! And, since then, sometimes more and sometimes less, I've been the sport of that intolerable torture! Infernal — keeping my nerves at such a stretch, that, if they had not resembled cat-gut, they would, long ago, have relaxed to the feebleness of Linton's.''

Heathcliff's attempted break-in to the coffin had been displaced by his awareness that the spirit was not there, but somewhere else; now, in breaking-in to the house and Hindley, he reasserts the destructive penetration from which Catherine had kept him then. The action epitomises the nature of his general 'revenge' tactics, like the 'levers and mattocks' he has assembled to 'demolish the two houses'. And it now becomes clear that these tactics are related to a false image of Catherine, a misconception of her way of presenting herself to him — which, in turn, makes her appear a 'devil' barring him from 'heaven'. Thus, Heathcliff is unable to sleep in the dream-chamber because he is unable to dream; and he is unable to dream owing to his misconception of what 'seeing' Catherine's spirit is, or would be, like:

> "And when I slept in her chamber — I was beaten out of that — I couldn't lie there; for the moment I closed my eyes, she was either outside the window, or sliding back the panels, or entering the room, or even resting her darling head on the same pillow as she did when a child. And I must open my lids to see. And so I opened and closed them a hundred times a night — to be always disappointed!"

Catherine's image evades him, because his mind is not prepared to receive it; the emotional and the aesthetic aspects of this mental preparation are inextricable. It is this deadlock which is penetrated, first by the second Catherine in her move to the Heights, and then by Lockwood who revives the function of the dream-chamber, allowing the child-ghost of 'Catherine Linton' to present her image. The image, even then, is still barred from Heathcliff despite his wrenching of lattices — remaining a 'spectre' with 'an ordinary spectre's caprice; it gave no sign of being, but the wind and snow whirled wildly through'. Nevertheless, Lockwood has, innocently, released the frozen deadlock at the Heights, paving the way for the second Cathy to revivify Heathcliff's internal knowledge of Catherine. She sustains the weight of internal death, symbolised for Heathcliff and the entire household by Linton Heathcliff (whose father's presence is 'as potent on his nerves, as a ghost'); and lights the dark 'abyss' in which Catherine's image is 'lost'.

Lockwood's 'rapid recovery' of strength is simultaneous with

97

the ending of Mrs Dean's story, and brings the reader's concept of time back to the single present. This momentarily simple perspective is the hinge between the past and the future 'dream': for just as the main narrative to date has filled in the background history to Lockwood's actual experienced dream, while he is bedridden, so the final stage of the story is in a sense another dream, transporting Lockwood's mind out of the context of its normal home, the 'busy world', to the inaccessible 'dim and dreamy' Gimmerton, now a heavenly landscape: 'In winter, nothing more dreary, in summer, nothing more divine, than those glens shut in by hills, and those bluff, bold swells of heath'. Lockwood's departure from the district, abandoning his false romance, underlines the revelatory quality of the catastrophic change in the network of relationships at the Heights, as 'infernal' winter becomes 'divine' summer. His need for a six-months' break in the outside world, suggests the absence of conscious awareness or regulation, while the story's denouement works itself out distanced from his active interference; the digestion of the first dream results in the new dream. And, although the catastrophic action takes place during his absence (on one level of mental operation), it is nevertheless stimulated by him, on the earthly as well as the ghostly level.

Lockwood's last reflection on life at the Heights, after his farewell visit, is 'How dreary life gets over in that house! . . . What a realization of something more romantic than a fairy tale it would have been for Mrs Linton Heathcliff, had she and I struck up an attachment, as her good nurse desired, and migrated together, into the stirring atmosphere of the town!' In one sense, he remains a 'stranger'; never fulfilling his bond with the story in Mrs Dean's terms ('who knows how long you'll be a stranger?'). But despite his personal escape into an ironically-termed 'stirring atmosphere', it is he who does stir and release the latent passion in a situation which has reached its nadir. Thus, he finds Catherine echoing her mother's desire for death, as 'gazing towards the hills', she murmurs, 'I should like to be riding Minny down there! I should like to be climbing up there — Oh! I'm tired — I'm *stalled*, Hareton!' From the time when 'the frost set in' in the context of Linton's death, the family have been driven together by cold, not heat: Catherine, 'chill as an icicle, and high as a princess', feeling like a personification of death, announced she had been 'driven down here by the cold, not . . . to enjoy your society'. And after her experience with Linton, she is prey to no more false letter-romances; so now, she immediately 'chucks off' Lockwood's 'adroit' planting of Nelly's missive in her lap, as if she imagined it 'a missive of his own'. Her action symbolises the exposure and death of the false romance, the 'fairy tale' concocted between himself and Nelly. But the end of this romance allows Lockwood to speak plainly to Catherine for the first time, rebuking her and also stating his genuine 'intimacy' with her story: 'Mrs Heathcliff . . . you are not aware that I am an acquaintance of yours? So intimate, that I think it strange you won't come and speak to me.' He awakens Cathy from her 'tiredness'; she 'wonders' at his speech and begins to examine her sulky lethargy, her depression, in terms of the 'treasures' which have been 'robbed by Mr Heathcliff' (her books) and, in a different way, by Hareton, who she knows has a 'secret stock' in his room, gathered 'as a magpie gathers silver spoons, for the mere love of stealing!' Though she has 'most of them written on my brain and printed in my heart', she still experiences the loss as a kind of inner death, echoing Heathcliff's loss of the image of Catherine. Lockwood, 'remembering Mrs Dean's anecdotes of his first attempt at enlightening the darkness in which he had been reared', is able to identify with Hareton's experience of Cathy, and to defend his motives. This has the effect of provoking her to expose the real problem which separates her from her 'treasure' — the degradation from queen or angel status: 'he has no right to appropriate what is mine, and make it ridiculous to me with his vile mistakes and mispronunciations! Those books, both prose and verse, were consecrated to me by other associations, and I hate to have them debased and profaned in his mouth!' (Her language recalls Milton's Samson, before his catastrophe: 'how vile, contemptible, ridiculous,/What act more execrably unclean, profane?') But Cathy's self-protective religion, unlike her mother's, is not founded on the need to feel universally 'loved'. Rather, it is a temporary 'consecration' of the idea of her father, whose death still represents an unabsorbed pain, not yet worked out in the context of continuing life. Her golden childhood and the wealth of books inherited from him (the 'other associations') seem 'consecrated', hence vulnerable to pollution from other influences — 'profaned in the mouth' of Hareton. Rather than face the trauma of trying to integrate Edgar and Hareton, the Grange and the Heights in her mind, she would prefer to sacrifice the books themselves: 'I shall connect them with you, and hate them'. So, the books are burned — a 'sacrifice' also for Hareton, as Lockwood (who 'fancied, guessed the incitement to his secret studies') is sympathetically aware.

The 'conflagration' of the books, though it appears to represent the death of learning at the Heights, is in fact the foundation for a new life 'stirred up' by Lockwood and re-born phoenix-like from the ashes, 'something more romantic than a fairy tale'. In the fire, the quality of Cathy and Hareton's resilience is tempered and tested — Cathy 'elastic as steel', Hareton 'tough as tempered steel'. The conflagration echoes the dog-fight of their first encounter, preceding the Fairy Cave, and the subsequent recriminations evoking Cathy's 'witch' and Hareton's 'clown' quality. The development of their future relationship is founded on the ability to survive mutual painful attacks on 'self-love' (as Lockwood terms it). On Catherine's first descent after Linton's death, wearing a black dress, Hareton had touched her yellow ringlets, 'attracted like a child by a candle', and she had recoiled 'as if a knife had been stuck in her neck' — suggesting her ancestral recollection of the knife flung by Heathcliff at Isabella, or the 'stab of a knife' which Edgar declared he felt on seeing 'his lady vexed'. The emotional events of Cathy and Hareton's past are neither denied, nor repeated with a vengeance, but rather, sensed on a different plane — the plane of thought-or dream-symbols rather than of literal action; their destructiveness is known, yet contained without an irrevocable explosion. Cathy, who as a child brought 'sunshine into a desolate house', now wears her golden colouring surrounded by blackness, her internal 'treasures' sensitive to the feel of 'death', like a candle in darkness. The emergence of her inner light from its state of death corresponds to the radiance she lights within Hareton, replacing the dark, smoky colours associated with his relationship with Joseph, by those of white, yellow and silver — a new kind of fire. What Nelly calls 'the clouds of his ignorance' are figured in the smoky clouds associated with his refuge behind Joseph: 'instead of snatching at her bait, in wet weather he took to smoking with

100

Joseph, and they sat like automatons, one on each side of the fire'. One day when Joseph is absent, and Hareton is nursing a gunshot wound, Cathy 'abstracts' the pipe from his mouth:

> "Let me take that pipe," she said, cautiously advancing her hand, and abstracting it from his mouth.
> Before he could attempt to recover it, it was broken, and behind the fire. He swore at her and seized another.
> "Stop," she cried, "you must listen to me, first; and I can't speak while those clouds are floating in my face."

Her seduction of Hareton consists of abstracting Joseph's influence, replacing the pipe with her 'treasure', in the first instance a book wrapped in white paper — no longer 'profaned' by the association with his 'mouth'. It is a new kind of witchery: in Joseph's words, 'It's yon flaysome, graceless quean, ut's witched ahr lad'. She dispels the veil of 'mucky pride, and damned, mocking tricks' through which Hareton sees her, and which acted as a smoky barrier between them. After his initial reaction, to 'blacken and scowl like a thunder-cloud', 'his face glowed'. The white paper, like the yellow primroses she sticks in his porridge (lightening Joseph's cookery), contrasts with Joseph's 'dirty bank-notes', the true content of his piety, revealed in reaction to the 'two radiant countenances bent over the page of the accepted book': 'His emotion was only revealed by the immense sighs he drew, as he solemnly spread his large Bible on the table, and overlaid it with dirty bank-notes from his pocket-book'. The two kinds of reading, or education, available to Hareton, are those of Catherine and of Joseph ('Mr Heathcliff never reads'), and they are mutually exclusive — just as he finds himself making a flower-bed on her directions in the midst of Joseph's currant-bushes, 'forgetting' they were Joseph's. Hareton's 'clouds of ignorance' disperse before his 'brightening mind' and 'brightening features', revising the picture of the young Heathcliff like a 'prince in disguise', just as the new fire lit between the lovers suggests a reconstruction of the hearth over the rocks beneath, long ago split by stones and soot. Cathy's decision to emerge from her darkness, is made because she felt 'tired of living, her life was useless' — echoing her mother's desire to find a 'use' for her 'creation'. Her new comfort at the Heights, now that Nelly is back, has no lasting

101

effect on her happiness until she finds a 'use' for her 'treasure'. Moreover, the new relationship between herself and Hareton is founded in the kitchen, repairing the explosive quarrel in the Grange kitchen before she was born, and indicating a new concept of love as work: 'While I admired, and they laboured, dusk drew on . . .'. And it is the unexpected sight of his children 'labouring' together, which leads Heathcliff to the reality of the spirit of Catherine.

The same sight presents itself to Lockwood, who likewise makes an unexpected return one dusk. He returns to hear the end of Mr Heathcliff's story on one of his ungovernable 'sudden impulses', reaching beyond the bounds of his everyday curiosity, as if unconsciously drawn by new sensuous emanations from the Heights:

> 1802. This September, I was invited to devastate the moors of a friend, in the North; and, on my journey to his abode, I un-expectedly came within fifteen miles of Gimmerton . . . my residence in that locality had already grown dim and dreamy.

He arrives as if by magical coincidence, in time to witness the conclusion of that other 'moor game' between Heathcliff and the ghost of Catherine, now played out by their earthly descendants, Hareton and the second Catherine. As if by chance, Gimmerton's 'late harvest' is thrown in his path in the shape of 'a cart of very green oats', and 'a sudden impulse seized me to visit Thrushcross Grange'. As on his first visit, he finds that the Grange is not the centre of the action (again there is no fire):

> So I turned away and made my exit, rambling leisurely along, with the glow of a sinking sun behind, and the mild glory of a rising moon in front; one fading, and the other brightening, as I quitted the park, and climbed the stony by-road branching off to Mr Heathcliff's dwelling.
>
> Before I arrived in sight of it, all that remained of day was a beamless, amber light along the west; but I could see every pebble on the path, and every blade of grass, by that splendid moon.

The melting landscape, infused by subtly changing lights, recalls the heralding of earlier changes of state — Heathcliff's return, the deaths of Catherine and Edgar; and the evidence of

Gimmerton's 'harvest' outside the valley indicates the fulfilment of the harvest which began long ago with the importation
of Heathcliff under Earnshaw's cloak, 'at the beginning of
harvest'. Lockwood's original dream was forced upon him
through a soldered lattice and a closeted bed in which he felt
secure; this new kind of dream, growing out of a 'divine'
landscape and illuminated by moonlight, appears full of
sensuous invitation: the gate yields to his hand, the doors and
lattices are open, a 'fragrance of stocks and wall flowers' wafts
outwards to his 'nostrils'. But this time, Lockwood finds himself
excluded in a different way: the centre of the picture creates its
own boundary, which relegates him to the background shadow.
Thus he perceives from outside, the lovers stationed at the open
window, as if equally related to the 'fine, red fire' at the centre
of the house (even in August, this is 'usually the case in a coal
district'), and the moor landscape with its changing lights. Envy
'grew as I lingered':

> "Con-*trary*!" said a voice, as sweet as a silver bell — "That
> for the third time, you dunce! I'm not going to tell you, again
> — Recollect, or I pull your hair!"
> "Contrary, then," answered another, in deep, but
> softened tones, "And now, kiss me, for minding so well."

The second-generation lovers have integrated the 'contrary'
tones which split their forebears — the kiss, sweet voice, angel,
with the hair-pulling, knife-throwing, devil. The 'smiting
beauty' of the new Catherine makes constructive both aspects of
the ambiguous gift of God. Their own radiance — Cathy's
'silver' tones, 'light shining ringlets', Hareton's 'handsome
features glowed with pleasure' — is derived from their dual
experience of the moor's magical fairy lights, and the coal fire
which tempers their steel: the Fairy Cave and the volcanic
energy of the 'rocks beneath'. By contrast Lockwood, as if
taking on the discarded chaff of Heathcliff's duskiness, stripped
of its glamour, senses his overshadowed condition: 'feeling very
mean and malignant, I skulked round to seek refuge in the
kitchen' — a 'refuge' which (like his first dream-shelter)
reinforces his discomfort. He experiences the infernal aspect of
even a divine dream, as he becomes the shadowy recipient of the
intertwined histories of Cathy's and Hareton's love, and of

Heathcliff's 'queer end', the metamorphosis which achieved 'heaven' for his partner in misanthropy.

In Heathcliff's catastrophe, also, Lockwood had been the stimulatory factor. His return to the 'busy world' has a mysterious connection with Heathcliff's gradual retirement into himself during the last months of his life, growing 'more and more disinclined to society', his mind 'occupied with other subjects than the present company'. They pursue contrasting notions of 'business' which both, however, have the effect of encouraging the relationship between Cathy and Hareton. On Lockwood's farewell visit, Heathcliff volunteers an uncharacteristic expression of warmth: he is 'glad to see' him 'from selfish motives partly; I don't think I could readily supply your loss in this desolation'. Learning of Lockwood's intention to leave, he retracts again; but both the warmth and the coldness indicate a turning-point within him: acknowledging his debt to Lockwood in his 'desolation' (Lockwood's own phrase), while recognising that his usefulness is over. One of Lockwood's parting functions is to record the concept of Heathcliff 'thwarting' himself, already in the air at this apparently most 'dreary' time at the Heights. The context is Hareton's distress (this time, over the conflagration of the books), just as the concept arose originally in the description of Heathcliff rescuing him as a baby:

> "It will be odd, if I thwart myself!" he muttered, unconscious that I was behind him. "But, when I look for his father in his face, I find *her* every day more! How the devil is he so like? I can hardly bear to see him!"

Hareton, for him, is already becoming progressively like the live image of Catherine, rather than the dead one. And Lockwood's position, 'behind' Heathcliff's conscious, wilful status, is to record his 'unconscious' mutterings, as he did at the beginning of their acquaintance when, his candle blown out, he became 'involuntary witness' to Heathcliff's passionate plea to Cathy's ghost. Heathcliff then replaces the 'loss' of Lockwood with Nelly, who is recalled to the Heights to oversee the development of those who are 'in a measure, my children'; his 'taking a new mind' about her coming is related in psychological, as well as practical, terms to his farewell to Lockwood. He requires to work out the process of unconscious 'thwarting' — the 'queer end' to his 'long fight', which has been 'more than flesh and blood can bear, even mine'.

The death of Heathcliff is recounted to Lockwood between the picture of Cathy and Hareton departing from the house, and returning to 'take one last look at each other' by the moon's light, suggesting the new integration and ease of movement between contrasting worlds, and indicating how their growing relationship embodies an internal revision of Heathcliff's image of Catherine — a new kind of internal communication. The progressive real-isation of that image is marked by a series of catastrophic shocks which shake his frame, as the energy of external 'revenge' is diverted inwards in a process of 'disarma-ment', a 'strange way of killing'. Heathcliff is torn between the impulse to end his inner struggle through explosive violence, and the compulsion to see it through to the end — expressed in terms of an external force taking over the guidance of his actions at moments of crisis. This force, by the end, is clearly recognisable as Catherine's ghost, the spirit which had guided him away from suicide and from the linked desecration of her image, eighteen years before. One such crisis point is provoked by the 'devastation' of Joseph's flower bed, which signals the open manifestation of Cathy and Hareton's new alliance, and which Nelly warns will result in a 'fine explosion':

> "Accursed witch! This time she has provoked me, when I could not bear it ..." His black eyes flashed, he seemed ready to tear Catherine in pieces, and I was just worked up to risk coming to the rescue, when of a sudden, his fingers relaxed, he shifted his grasp from her head, to her arm, and gazed intently in her face ...
>
> "You must learn to avoid putting me in a passion, or I shall really murder you, some time!"

As always, no external pressure is powerful enough to change his mind or action for him: hence the comic inset about Nelly working up to come to the rescue; while Hareton himself is bound to Heathcliff by 'ties, stronger than reason could break' (this is the point at which Cathy accepts that Heathcliff is his 'father', and stops trying to 'raise a bad spirit' between them). It is an internal force which shifts his grasp and relaxes his fingers, and leads him to the struggle of recognition suggested by

105

his 'gazing intently in her face': facing the 'devil' within her, the tormenting ghost of Catherine ('a devil to me'): 'What fiend possesses you to stare back at me, continually, with those infernal eyes? Down with them! and don't remind me of your existence again.' Heathcliff finds the existence of both Cathy and Hareton, separately, a torment in different ways, as different aspects of the live image of Catherine begin to show through them, particularly through their eyes. But it is when he accidentally encounters their eyes moving in unison, that an ultimate crisis of recognition and self-knowledge is forced upon him. This occurs on his return 'quite unexpectedly' one evening, to find them reading before the fire: 'They lifted their eyes together, to encounter Mr Heathcliff — perhaps, you have never remarked that their eyes are precisely similar, and they are those of Catherine Earnshaw.' Clearly, Heathcliff has always known this 'similarity' intellectually; but it is the unexpected movement 'together' which awakens within him the emotional recognition of the identity of Catherine Earnshaw, expressing a flash of insight within him.

As before, instead of venting his disturbance in vengeful wrath, Heathcliff orders the couple out of his sight and proceeds instead to analyse his feelings to Nelly, turning his mind out: 'you'll not talk of what I tell you, and my mind is so eternally secluded in itself, it is tempting, at last, to turn it out to another.' This turning-out measures a conversion of energy, a chemical change, from action into thought: his mind suffers a catastrophic reversal. In the process, he re-lives and catharsizes his internal history. First of all, as Nelly observes acutely, the 'resemblance' in the eyes 'disarmed Mr Heathcliff': a disarmament paralleling his previous intent gaze on Cathy's face; and again, beyond his conscious or deliberate design:

"It is a poor conclusion, is it not," he observed, having brooded a while on the scene he had just witnessed. "An absurd termination to my violent exertions? I get levers and mattocks to demolish the two houses, and train myself to be capable of working like Hercules, and when everything is ready, and in my power, I find the will to lift a slate off either roof has vanished! My old enemies have not beaten me — now would be the precise time to revenge myself on their representatives — I could do it; and none could hinder me — But where is the use? I don't care for striking, I can't take the trouble to raise my hand! That sounds as if I had been labouring the whole time only to exhibit a fine trait of magnanimity. It is far from being the case — I have lost the faculty of enjoying their destruction, and I am too idle to destroy for nothing!''

Heathcliff's 'Herculean' labours (he laboured like 'Hercules' for Isabella's hatred), have brought him to the peak of his strength and the height of his powers over the 'representatives' of his old Linton and Earnshaw oppressors; now is the 'precise time' for revenge. Like Catherine, he takes on some of the significance of an ancient god, Charlotte's 'giant' — Nelly later describes the activity of his last days as enough 'to knock up a Titan'. But, like Samson, he can find no 'use' for his strength: 'where is the use?'; like Prospero, when through magic art all his enemies are gathered under his control, he finds the concept of 'revenge' irrelevant to his labours. Heathcliff's momentary loss of direction, his 'idleness', represents the turn of the tide; the drama is poised on a knife-edge with Heathcliff on the point of a metamorphosis, a turning-out of 'mind', ready to convert the energies compounded in material power, into spiritual knowledge. He recognises that a 'strange change' is imminent: 'Nelly, there is a strange change approaching — I'm in its shadow at present — I take so little interest in my daily life, that I hardly remember to eat, and drink —'. The nature of the change is itself unknown: 'I shall not know that till it comes . . . I'm only half conscious of it now'; and it is not, literally 'death': for as Heathcliff says, 'I have neither a fear, nor a presentiment, nor a hope of death' — words which underline the metaphorical significance of Heathcliff's death when it does occur. It is less a death, than a metamorphosis from body into spirit, imaging the transformation from physical action, events, existence, into mental action or thought: the 'strange change' leads to a 'strange way of killing'.

Heathcliff's language begins to echo Catherine's metaphysical speech about the 'existence beyond herself', the speech which first separated them. And as at that time, the 'strange talk' evokes catastrophic anxiety in Nelly, who refuses to listen

107

to him after this occasion, becoming prey to her old superstitious fears about the 'little dark thing', the alien entity in everyday life. Although the nature of the final catastrophe is not yet 'known', what is clear is the growing intimacy of Heathcliff's communion with Catherine's spirit which takes place through his internal digestion of external 'resemblances', sorting out the true from the false and in the process re-writing his internal history, re-forming the inhabitants of his mind. Thus Heathcliff describes how what 'moved' him in Hareton was not the literal, physical 'startling likeness' to Catherine, which he in any case sees everywhere and which merely tantalises and persecutes him with its dead quality:

> "what does not recall her? I cannot look down to this floor, but her features are shaped on the flags! In every cloud, in every tree — filling the air at night, and caught by glimpses in every object, by day I am surrounded by her image! The most ordinary faces of men, and women — my own features mock me with a resemblance. The entire world is a dreadful collection of memoranda that she did exist, and that I have lost her!''

This is the mocking, false Catherine — his and her own 'murderer' — as she appeared in Hindley's destroyed eyes, or with death in her own eyes: a concept now expressed in aesthetic terms as a kind of false art, as external imitation without spirit. Heathcliff's long struggle with her ghost, consists of his endeavour to find her true image, her essential spirit, amidst the dead 'collection of memoranda', the 'mocking' resemblance, the Gothic spectre or bizarre object comprised by waxwork bits and pieces, the nest of 'little skeletons' associated with the destructive aspect of their relationship. All these false resemblances still leave her, and his own 'soul', lost in the dark 'abyss', as from the time of her death: '*do* not leave me in this abyss, where I cannot find you! ... I *cannot* live without my soul!' But, in contrast, the movement of Cathy's and Hareton's eyes in unison, now guide him to a different image: whose reality is felt, first of all, as an internal revision, a new idea of the young man (represented by Hareton) within him:

> "Five minutes ago, Hareton seemed a personification of my

youth, not a human being — I felt to him in such a variety of ways, that it would have been impossible to have accosted him rationally . . . Hareton's aspect was the ghost of my immortal love, of my wild endeavours to hold my right, my degradation, my pride, my happiness, and my anguish —''

Echoing the first Catherine's attempt to give Nelly 'a feeling of how I feel' through her dreams, Heathcliff describes a kind of dream of Hareton, an internal image in the process of becoming a 'personification', less an actual person than an embodiment of meaning:

> "If I could do it without seeming insane, I'd never see him again! You'll perhaps think me rather inclined to become so," he added, making an effort to smile, "if I try to describe the thousand forms of past associations, and ideas he awakens, or embodies . . ."

Through the spirit of Catherine contacted through Hareton, Heathcliff becomes able to re-discover and organise historical emotional associations, through the 'thousand forms' and 'ideas' of symbol-formation; for the first time, thought — about her and himself — becomes possible; as opposed to the primitive cries of emotion evacuated straight into action.

It is this reversal of Heathcliff's idea of the nature of reality itself, which results, during the first stage of his metamorphosis when he is still in the 'shadow' of change, in Cathy and Hareton becoming 'the only objects which retain a distinct material appearance to me' (echoing his 'distinct impression of [Catherine's] passionless features'). Through them, he perceives a coherent, integrated image of Catherine, rather than a conglomeration of dismembered features: the real idea of Catherine emerges as spirit from its grave-like blockade, 'bursting the fetters and breaking the bars' (in the words of Emily Brontë's poem). In the love of the second generation, which is in a sense his creation despite himself, Heathcliff begins to see an existence of Catherine 'beyond herself', the ultimate goal toward which her spirit led him 'home' eighteen years before. Alone of external appearances, Heathcliff 'notices' them because they provide a means for perception of 'one universal idea':

"I cannot continue in this condition! I have to remind myself
to breathe — almost to remind my heart to beat! And it is like
bending back a stiff spring . . . it is by compulsion, that I do
the slightest act, not prompted by one thought, and by
compulsion, that I notice anything alive or dead, which is not
associated with one universal idea . . . I have a single wish,
and my whole being and faculties are yearning to attain it.
They have yearned towards it so long, and so unwaveringly,
that I'm convinced it *will* be reached — and *soon* — because it
has devoured my existence — I am swallowed in the
anticipation of its fulfilment.''

In the process of real-ising that 'universal idea', Heathcliff
revises the past 'associations' of his youth, and — through the
intent awareness of his 'condition' at the present moment —
changes his mind's direction. This is far from a romantic 'trait
of magnanimity' (a notion he himself dispels); rather, it is a
turning-out of mind, a complete mental revolution which
'swallows' his physical existence: 'My soul's bliss kills my
body'. His 'whole being and faculties', body and mind, are
overtaken by the force of the 'idea'. The drawing-power of the
new reality is measured against the 'compulsion' with which his
physical existence continues, 'like bending back a stiff spring',
as if (in terms of the poem) his body were 'measuring the gulf',
gathering energy for the 'final bound', 'its home, its harbour
found' — later he sees himself as 'swimming to the shore'. He
prepares his entire self, in 'anticipation', for the catastrophic
reversal from 'revenge' to 'disarmament'; mediating between
Catherine's inspiring wind-spirit (which disturbs his own ability
to 'breathe') and the earthly manifestation of creativity figured
in Cathy and Hareton's new world. Like Edgar, he dismisses
the question of his will ('never mind Mr Green'), to leave a
different legacy: his mind, turned out to a 'stranger' (via Nelly
who, far from 'not talking' of his experience, tells Lockwood
everything); he beomes an artist.

In the final stage of his story, Heathcliff emerges from the
'shadow' to participate in 'strange change' itself. He ceases to
express himself verbally (no-one will listen to his 'strange talk'),
and turns to a negative kind of action, in which his body —
instead of initiating action — becomes a vehicle for his mind,

expressing an internal process of change. Symbolically, Catherine herself is now the only being who remains in communication with him, the rest of the universe having become (as in her terms) a 'mighty stranger', with even Cathy and Hareton now subsiding into the background: 'Well, there is *one* who won't shrink from my company! By God; she's relentless. Oh, damn it! It's unutterably too much for flesh and blood to bear, even mine.' Heathcliff's 'flesh and blood' now 'utters' his metamorphosis, shuddering with successive shocks as the 'idea' progressively takes over his everyday functioning. With a strange 'joyful glitter in his eyes', he breathes 'fast as a cat', his soul spun out from the web of his 'catgut nerves'; 'his frame shivering, not as one shivers with chill or weakness, but as a tight-stretched cord vibrates — a strong thrilling, rather than trembling.' His ability to eat, to subsist on earth, is denied him: by no intention of his own, but by the 'idea' which itself devours him: 'He took the knife and fork, and was going to commence eating, when the inclination appeared to become extinct . . . if he stretched out his hand to get a piece of bread, his fingers clenched, before they reached it, and remained on the table, forgetful of their aim.' His everyday existence is eaten away by the new image of Catherine (the same force that prevented him tearing Cathy to pieces): 'whatever it was, it communicated, apparently, both pleasure and pain, in exquisite extremes . . . The fancied object was not fixed, either; his eyes pursued it with unwearied vigilance; and, even in speaking to me, were never weaned away.' His 'unearthly vision' is seen as 'three feet' or 'two yards' distant from him; and he reaches for it like a drowning man, 'struggling in the water within arm's reach of the shore'. Catherine's 'strange way of killing' is in fact a kind of salvation, rescuing him from the 'abyss' into which he fell at her death, surrounded by images of illusion which slipped from his grasp: 'I have nearly attained my heaven — and that of others is altogether unvalued, and uncoveted by me!' Our last two images of Heathcliff are window-images (like the door and window images which enclose Cathy and Hareton's 'moonlight ramble'); they picture his imminent change of state, the departure for 'heaven' from the confines of the dream-chamber, to which he is finally able to return during his last days. The first picture shows Heathcliff 'leaning against the ledge of an open lattice', between the 'interior gloom' and the damp 'cloudy evening' in which the murmur and gurgling of the beck are clearly distinguishable. The sound of the stream links Wuthering Heights with Thrushcross Grange, through its passage down the valley; it was heard from the Grange during the trance-like time of Catherine's death and Heathcliff's farewell, and suggests mobility between the two houses and the wild moor. Heathcliff himself seems to partake of the dusky atmosphere: as in the past, merging with the shadows of house and landscape. Yet, when Nelly approaches him, he seems to leap out from that shadow, with an unearthly brilliance: 'The light flashed on his features, as I spoke. Oh, Mr Lockwood, I cannot express what a terrible start I got, by the momentary view! Those deep black eyes! That smile, and ghastly paleness! It appeared to me, not Mr Heathcliff, but a goblin'. Nelly had brought a candle into the Grange's moonlit parlour long ago, to help her announce the disturbing presence of Heathcliff below; now again she brings a 'candle' (of everyday, common sense) which goes out, leaving her 'in darkness', as Heathcliff, embedded in naturalistic description and speaking in his 'familiar voice', seems to undergo an inexplicable reversal, a terrifying illumination. The transformation of Heathcliff's features images the 'final bound' which he is about to make into the unknown — fulfilling the 'shape of a prophecy', the 'fearful catastrophe' heralded for Nelly by Catherine's metaphysical speech. In her disturbed dream that night, Nelly realises that the meaning of Heathcliff cannot be encompassed within conventional social or religious confines; despite 'tracking his existence' over in her mind, she cannot 'dictate an inscription' for his tombstone — only 'the single word, Heathcliff'. The truth expressed by his mental action, remains for her a kind of madness, a 'monomania', indigestible.

In the same way, endeavouring to rationalise his behaviour, she conjectures that Heathcliff's return to his old chamber indicates his intention to make physical 'midnight excursions, — rather than, as in fact, mental ones. The window is 'wide enough for anybody to get through' (the last body to 'get through' being the second Cathy, followed not long afterwards by the hands of Lockwood and her mother's child-spirit). However it is not Heathcliff's body but his soul which departs through the open window:

112

> I could not think him dead — but his face and throat were washed with rain; the bed-clothes dripped, and he was perfectly still. The lattice, flapping to and fro, had grazed one hand that rested on the sill — no blood trickled from the broken skin ... I tried to close his eyes — to extinguish, if possible, that frightful, life-like gaze of exultation, before any one else beheld it. They would not shut — they seemed to sneer at my attempts, and his parted lips, and sharp, white teeth sneered too!

The eyes and teeth staring out, revise the earlier image of Heathcliff stuck in the window of Wuthering Heights, barred out by Hindley and Isabella — then coated in snow, now drenched in rain. His grazed hand links his exit with the child-ghost, though this time there is 'no blood'; instead, Heathcliff's soaked body suggests the beginning of his dissolution beneath the earth, following the murmur of the beck towards the churchyard, and 'dissolving with' Catherine. The ritual washing is aided further by Hareton's bath of tears:

> He sat by the corpse all night, weeping in bitter earnest. He pressed its hand, and kissed the sarcastic, savage face that every one else shrank from contemplating; and bemoaned him with that strong grief which springs naturally from a generous heart, though it be tough as tempered steel.

Then, 'with a streaming face', Hareton 'dug green sods, and laid them over the brown mould himself, at present it is as smooth and verdant as its companion mounds'. He exorcises Cathy's curse of Heathcliff that 'Nobody loves you — nobody will cry for you, when you die!', the only one able to 'face' Heathcliff with love. Hareton's 'strong' grief serves to harmonise the image of Heathcliff's grave (the earthly home of his heaven), with those of Catherine and Edgar: uniting his 'life-like gaze of exultation' with their angelic 'peace' and 'radiant ecstasy'. With the aid of Hareton's tears, Heathcliff has 'swum to the shore'; and it is on 'rainy nights' that his ghost walks with Catherine's.

Emily Brontë's ghosts are not 'laid' in the usual sense; this does not mean that her final paragraph is ironic or ambivalent. It is spoken by Lockwood not because he is ignorant, but on the

113

contrary, because he has earned his understanding of the story, and completed his 'tenancy' in these mysterious 'dreamy' regions of knowledge. The old ghosts are not 'at peace' in the sense that Nelly would have it; they still 'walk', are still part of the life of the living. But while popular superstition is frightened of the unknown depths they represent (the 'country folks' and the little boy with the sheep), Cathy and Hareton, for whom the ghosts are part of their blood and their education and their relationship — the inheritance more important than either Thrushcross Grange or Wuthering Heights — are not afraid:

> "*They* are afraid of nothing", I grumbled, watching them approach through the window. "Together they would brave satan and all his legions."

Their 'last look' under the inscribed lintel of the house (where their reading of 'Hareton Earnshaw' and, through him, of Heathcliff, began) symbolises their farewell to the old Earnshaw tradition. Heathcliff's story is at the core of their own, just as the telling of his death — or metamorphosis — images the new life which includes their internal recognition of his alien spirit, though they will no longer inhabit the external shell of 'this grim house', which is left to encompass the withering but indestructible Joseph. Joseph remains with the ghosts of the house, but his power is de-fused, and his interpretation of Hareton's ancient rights superseded by Catherine's; like an ancient superstition, he is content with a visitor's occasional bribery. And though the ghosts in one sense 'inhabit' the house (as Lockwood observes), in another sense they are free to roam the moor, to 'walk': their real home firmly established in the image of the three headstones, the heaven in the middle of the moor. Catherine's ghost has 'come home' to rest between Edgar and Heathcliff, forming a chapel outside both the Lintons' and the Earnshaws' traditional homes, and outside the rigid guidance of the established church.

It is the union of the dead and the living, the earthly and the ghostly, the different levels of consciousness, the past and the future, that lies behind the peace of the last paragraph: a peace different from any of the single, partial 'heavens' adumbrated in the book. The alien 'gift of God or the devil' introduced by old Earnshaw has become a creative rather than a destructive force:

the bloody 'teething' which won the first headstone, now integrated under turf and moss with the aid of tears which represent 'strong grief' rather than weakness or terror:

> I sought, and soon discovered, the three head-stones on the slope next the moor — the middle one grey, and half buried in heath — Edgar Linton's only harmonized by the turf and moss, creeping up its foot — Heathcliff's still bare.
> I lingered round them, under that benign sky; watched the moths fluttering among the heath and hare-bells; listened to the soft wind breathing through the grass; and wondered how anyone could ever imagine unquiet slumbers for the sleepers in that quiet earth.

The violent wind-spirit containing Cathy's ghost, that shattered first Lockwood's defences, and then Heathcliff's during his last fight, is now the 'soft wind breathing'; the disparate elements of the snow-storm (Cathy's haphazard hieroglyphics) settle into the steady, quiet animation of the 'moths fluttering': their brightness, like Heathcliff's 'sharp, white teeth' against the blackness, being transmuted into the moonlit flowers set among the grass — the flowers of the second-generation love story. Heathcliff's 'last sleep' is not the 'frozen' one he had imagined, but a fluid dissolution into universal elements studding the weather and landscape: exhaled both in the form of ghosts walking the earth on a rainy night, and of the lovers in the moonlight, who are 'afraid of nothing'. Despite leaving no blood-descendants, he has changed for ever the nature of the Linton-Earnshaw inheritance, imaged in the triple grave. The second marriage between the families is founded on the elements of the first, revised and dissolving into a new form underground, and marked by the progressively harmonising fossilised 'teeth' above ground. It suggests the integration of body and soul into an 'existence beyond oneself': the creation of a new 'universal idea' or idea of the universe, which is not abstracted from life, but rather is continued, reformed, newly enacted by the earthly generations of the future. When Lockwood notes that 'decay had made progress' in the churchyard, he is emphasising the development inherent in apparent destruction; and though 'coming autumn storms' will work the slates off the church roof, the 'contrary' fusion of the lovers — since Heathcliff lost 'the

115

will to lift a slate off either roof' and joined his 'universal idea' — is resilient to turbulence, since it is in fact founded on the 'storms' of their ancestors. They emerge from the 'shadow' which haunted their predecessors, to partake of the lights of change, both external and internal, related to their own luminosity: more subtle and varied than Catherine's 'glorious world' or Nelly's 'shadowless hereafter'. Their spiritual life is not tied to the values of Wuthering Heights, nor of Thrushcross Grange, nor of the church; it cannot be demolished by 'levers and mattocks' since it is fed by the 'wind' in the grass and the 'rocks beneath'. The second generation are equipped to face the unknown catastrophes and revolutions of the future.

Lockwood, then, returns to Gimmerton from the 'busy world' only to discover the worthlessness of its currency, by comparison with the richness of the 'late harvest' from the 'desolate' region which he now sees as embodying a 'divine' dream. He returns to record the end of his own year of tenancy, and to announce the beginning of the 'New Year' of Cathy and Hareton, who will move to the Grange when they are married on New Year's Day. His footing in both worlds — the everyday and the imaginative, the conventional and the prophetic — is represented by his slipping a coin to Joseph on the one hand (to appease the dirty story rising in his mind), and on the other hand, by committing to words the dream of Catherine and the history of Mr Heathcliff, which at last coalesce into a new unified reality in his mind. Excluded from the brave new world in one sense, in another sense the 'universal idea' of an earthly-ghostly love becomes part of his knowledge and therefore of his internal development. Like the artist-critic, he becomes equipped to mediate between a vision of truth or reality whose boundaries by nature exclude him, yet which is mirrored in his subjective experience. So Lockwood, by virtue of his very amphibiousness, remains alone to record the new divinity of the 'misanthropist's heaven'.

# II
# *WUTHERING HEIGHTS* AND CATASTROPHIC CHANGE

# 1    A Psychoanalytic Viewpoint

*Wuthering Heights* has always been recognised as an enigmatic, mysterious and therefore in a sense inaccessible work, peculiarly unresponsive to reductive interpretations of its content or its structure. For example, although it appears an attractive candidate for psychoanalytic interpretation, yet the revelatory nature of its symbolic drama means that its total movement cannot be encompassed by a scheme which views the work as an attempt — successful or otherwise — to cure a disturbed personality and achieve a balanced normality. If the characters are regarded as case-histories, or even as internal objects or part-objects, the reality of the *poetic* quality is lost; consequently the essential meaning of the whole process is altered, since this is knowable only within the poetic form of its being, not as any allegorical abstraction. And any substantial study which is neither an interpretation within specific limits, nor an excursion 'round' the novel in terms of source, literary genre, contemporary context, is liable to be assumed to be a 'paraphrase'. But it is possible to make a constructive use of a psychoanalytic viewpoint which concentrates on the essentially aesthetic nature of the mind's organisation in the process of coming to knowledge — the process of creative thought, not discursive 'thinking about'. The concept of 'catastrophic change' is fundamental to the understanding of learning from experience, a process applicable to both author and reader, in which the structure of the mind itself becomes as it were poetic, responsive to a principle of beauty.

It is this, rather than any extravagant notion of virtue, which lies behind an ideal such as Milton's of 'becoming a true Poem'.[1] And recent developments in psychoanalytic practice, have been concerned less with establishing the validity of interpretation, and more with the analyst's problem of observing and knowing the nature and significance of the patient's impact on himself. It is a switch of orientation from a somewhat aggressive omnipotent activity (associated with viewing psychoanalysis as a science), to an aesthetic quest, focussing on how a received symbolic pattern can constitute self-knowledge and become poetic. An emotional cloud is evolved between the analyst and analysand, somewhere 'in the air' through a clash or interaction, like Forster's 'thundercloud' emotions of *Wuthering Heights*; the analyst's temptation may be to interpret back at the patient in a way which soothes his own anxiety; but his artistic problem is to allow the emotional disturbance to reorganise the pre-existing constituents of his mind in such a way that a new symbolic pattern is formed. This is the process of 'catastrophic change', a movement towards aesthetic understanding. It is a concept which can be applied to suggest how the revelatory process manifest in *Wuthering Heights*, can itself assist a reader who is struggling towards self-knowledge, through an attempt to contain and organise the disturbing flashes of illumination evoked by the book's emotional impact on his mind.

The concept of catastrophic change was introduced into psychoanalytic thought by Wilfred Bion; he describes its action through a metaphorical system centred on the image of the catastrophic moment of birth, and the consequent prototypal war between prenatal and postnatal reality, with the difficulty of making aesthetic sense of disorienting emotional pressures. All evolutionary transitions in the development of the mind are activated at points of catastrophic change, when during intensified internal contact the mind's symbolic structure re-forms under the pressure of a new idea. [2] The moor in *Wuthering Heights* consists of a whole network of adjacent but non-interacting worlds, marked by separations in time and space. These include: the boundary between life and death, earthly and ghostly; Linton and Earnshaw; latency and adolescence (the key age of twelve); Lockwood and romance; the window between the house and the wild moor; and the relations between individual characters, as well as the underlying balance between first and second generations. The dialectical texture of the book traverses vertical and horizontal dimensions simultaneously, creating at crossing points the emotional 'explosions' which reverberate throughout. Tensions are set up; for initially, even the separateness of these different spheres of existence goes without recognition; the Lintons and Earnshaws feel no hostility because they feel no proximity; Cathy and Heathcliff's

120

separation is 'not practicable' (as she says) because it is not thinkable. Awareness of separation itself constitutes a first primitive knowledge. This is the kind of intuitive knowledge expressed by Catherine when she parts the adhesive alliance between herself and Heathcliff, even though the emotional cost is more than she can bear and her heart 'breaks'. There was no possibility of creative interaction in the existing form of their relationship; they have to cross into another sphere of existence (rebirth via death) before they can 'walk' together; and that relationship is itself dependent upon the creative use which the second generation have made of their various separations. Thus, the first Cathy's dreams 'change the colour' of her mind. But they cannot find external resonance; there is no canvas to receive the changing colours in creative form; Nelly refuses — that is, feels unable — to listen to her dreams. In consequence, these dreams rebound destructively, shattering Cathy's own mind. Only when Catherine herself becomes a kind of dream, in the minds of Edgar and her daughter, and ultimately in the mind of Heathcliff (via Lockwood), can her image be received artistically and her ghost become 'soul' as opposed to an assemblage of dead, disparate elements — a 'collection of memoranda' which proves only that she is 'lost'. The reincarnation of her soul, her re-entry into the home of her birth and her reunion with Heathcliff, is an interpenetration of realities, resulting in the formation of a new symbolic language.

This is the process of catastrophic change; a tension between previously non-reacting worlds is set up, studded with explosions of feeling which at first threaten only chaos; and resolved only when a symbolic language of some sort is formed which is capable of receiving them aesthetically, as a complete new mental state. This essential, universal creative process is the guide and model for the reader who wants the book fully to penetrate his mind and become part of his life-experience. The interpenetration of realities is not achieved through any automatic or natural growth process. On the contrary, each time a boundary between non-reacting or 'commensal' realms is brought to notice, and each time a separateness is felt, there is an impulsive move to turn it back into a 'parasitic' mode of communication — the false, deathly romance, or self-destroying revenge. It is the alien outsider Heathcliff who initially sets up the tensions in *Wuthering Heights*, threatening the disintegration of the moor-mind. Likewise it is Heathcliff who — as Charlotte said, embodying the 'spirit' of the whole narrative, haunting 'every moor and glen' and beckoning in 'every fir-tree of the Heights' — is at the forefront of our emotional contact with the book. His entry into a previously stable, secluded, non-developing world with which he nevertheless has some deep, ancient, primitive affinity, threatens to fragment the mental landscape, and brings with it a 'catastrophic anxiety'. The central section of the book, in which the onus of the action is transferred from first to second generation, is consequently pre-occupied with the theme of moral teething, in a kind of purgatory. The painful, destructive, false action is concentrated here, while the generations change over and some become ghostly, in preparation for a different kind of recognition of his existence (through metamorphosis). This is a new idea altogether, unforeseen by any single participant in the drama, and unspoken because the language to speak it is formed simultaneously with the mind's capacity to receive it. Heathcliff does not 'die' according to any of his enemies' wishes or intentions; still less according to his own preconceived notion. These preconceptions were part of a primitive revenge structure which is superseded as its violent conflicts become conceivable on the plane of thought. The shell of worn-out values, the House of Earnshaw, is superseded before its over-perpetuation can result in the loss of its traditional preservative function and a rigid stranglehold over the life within. Mr Earnshaw's parting gift 'from God or the devil' was a chance for his descendants to develop, continuing their spiritual life, in ways which he could not fulfil or imagine for himself, since he was the representative of a previous evolutionary state of mind.

The action reaches its climax when Heathcliff struggles to dispel the false image expressed by his collection of memoranda of Catherine — the pieces of a jigsaw puzzle which seem to fit yet do not speak the mystery. It is the ultimate point of catastrophic change built upon a succession of previous attempts to demarcate reality from its false shadows — illusory romance, self-idealisation, the tyranny of omnipotence. When he finally 'sees' the eyes of Catherine Earnshaw in those of the second Catherine and Hareton, he embodies a transformation from the state of common-sense 'knowing about', to that of 'knowing' itself. This is the essential process of creative thought, inseparable from the artistic language of its expression; in which the mind expands beyond its previous boundaries. It is what poets have called 'inspiration': the means by which poetic language, embodying infinitely more meaning than a lexical paraphrase would appear to allow, pulls forwards the mental state of the surrounding culture from which it has sprung. Heathcliff, acquiring heroic status, receives the idea of truth in the spirit of Catherine, which transforms his conception of reality and results in his metamorphosis. By this point he has the weight of the foregoing action upon his shoulders, as the only protagonist to have traversed the two generations; and the crux of the reader's ability to follow the author's overall thought-process lies in his ability to observe Heathcliff's strange way of dying, in such a way that it makes aesthetic sense even if at first it appears puzzling to the interpretative sense. The irrevocable shift in mental structure attendant upon inspired knowledge, was described by Emily Brontë as a 'final bound' which feels its roots back in earthly form: 'The soul to feel the flesh and the flesh to feel the chain'. Its transcendent awareness brings a past and future state of mind into a present one (Byron's 'Former world and a Future'). It expresses the very principle of thought-formation. The idea or spirit of truth re-forms the flesh of the mind. Recognition of the inherent, essential sexuality of the inspired mind helps dislodge speculation about Emily Brontë's sexual knowledge: such as, how she could 'know about' sex, pregnancy or childbirth when she had never 'experienced' them. She did not know *about* them, in common-sense terms; she *knew* them, in the sense of essential, inspired knowledge — Milton's 'Bright effluence of bright essence increate'. The bright essence is attained, not through abstraction nor through conquering, but through a strenuous passivity, with the soul feeling the flesh. In *Wuthering Heights* the live ghosts hover round the consciousness of the living, pregnant with new metaphor, and still part of present life rather than an entombed memory. In Bion's terms, the thought has shaped the thinker.

Susanne Langer, in *Philosophy in a New Key*, describes the relation of symbolization to thought — creative not discursive thought:

... if the material of thought is symbolism, then the thinking organism must be forever furnishing symbolic versions of its experiences, in order to let thinking proceed. As a matter of fact, it is not the essential act of thought that is symbolization, but an act ESSENTIAL TO THOUGHT, and prior to it. Symbolization is the essential act of mind; and mind takes in more than what is commonly called thought.[3]

*Wuthering Heights* embodies and presents an 'essential act of mind', focussed on its hero's achievement of symbol-formation. After his metamorphosis, 'thinking' can 'proceed'; the society of the moor-mind can develop. Emily Brontë's experience of catastrophic change, far from being a kind of vestigial intrusion on the artistic form of her work (as the presence of the author is often regarded, in modern criticism), governs and directs the response of the reader who in his turn observes form with a strenuous passivity. Observation of the art form cannot be effected with detached objectivity; it results in, and is *dependent* on, sparks, explosions and disturbing insights evoked by the proximity of a new idea (that is, in the reader who has got *close* to the book in the first place, and not approached it as a purely academic or reductive exercise). In one sense the book makes an immediate and accurate impact on the reader, and its whole structure is seen feelingly, upon the pulses. The essence of poetry, as Milton said, is to be 'simple, sensuous and passionate'.[4] But this immediate impact tends to become lost when one tries to think 'about' the book by means of what is commonly called 'thought'. This is because the mysterious essence of the book cannot be captured and contained in discursive terms. In fact, thinking about it is liable to result in distancing one from the heart of the book and filling the space between with a lot of substitute information — Forster's seeing 'round' the novel.

Part of the problem is that what is commonly called thought provides no equipment for dealing creatively with the 'catastrophic anxiety' aroused by quiescent emotions springing to life and disorienting the mental status quo. On the contrary, it is equipped for the authoritarian repression of the rebellion. I. A. Richards, in *Practical Criticism*, observed that the reader who has been deprived of the preconceptions which protect him from observing the true form of a poem, 'feels like a friendless man deprived of weapons and left naked at the mercy of a treacherous beast'.[5] One's immediate, instinctive, impulsive reaction is to set up a network of defences in the form of false identifications; then, perhaps (if engaged in the business of academic criticism), to categorise and rationalise those defences into standpoints of judgement and evaluation against which to measure the author's achievement. False identifications consist in, for example, choosing characters who one assumes are most like oneself to represent a form of self-idealisation, or correspondingly black-marking others — making Heathcliff, or Nelly, or Edgar, the villain of the piece. Once a character is labelled or interpreted, his contribution to the evolving web of the book's knowledge becomes sealed off, in a way that also curtails all the direction lines which use him as a reference point. He becomes a fixed item in an allegory, not an element of fluid significance capable of attaining metaphorical or symbolic status. In modern criticism, in the struggle between contraries, the second-generation story is most frequently seen as a watered-down version of the first, with Heathcliff correspondingly de-natured. The artistic achievement of *Wuthering Heights* is measured according to whether it ultimately manages to achieve, or manages to avoid, the expression of 'compromise'. This compromise or domestication may be considered a good or a bad thing depending on the initial viewpoint. But the search for compromise is itself an inevitable result of interpreting the factors in the drama beforehand: a false move when the values in the dialectic change continually with a series of 'explosions' of emotion, working towards a new state of mind altogether, not towards supremacy or compromise between the original constituents. The barrier of a premature interpretation has the effect of blocking observational routes, so that the ultimate picture is of a substitute structure, resting upon gaps in observation of the book's actual phenomena and juxtapositions. Thus once Heathcliff has been labelled in a moral or interpretative sense, it become impossible to observe what actually happens to him as he strangely dies; the whole sequence is so puzzling that it is often ignored in criticism, or dismissed as showing that both Heathcliff and Emily Brontë had got fed up with the story. Similarly, if Lockwood is categorised — as he usually is — as merely a function of the author's irony, we do not notice what happens to him during his final strange dream of a death and a marriage. What does not make sense, in the terms of our preconceptions, automatically becomes unobservable.

In order to allow the mind to receive the imprint of catastrophic change — to think *with* the book's own thought-process, not about it — an artistic criticism is necessary, itself founded on the flexible qualities of symbolic language and metaphoric structure. An artistic criticism lets the mystery speak. It acts as a containing structure for the inexplicable and emotionally disturbing elements of the book, holding them in solution so that they do not attack the mind too painfully, whilst a wider pattern gradually takes shape that in its totality evokes a sense of 'beauty'. Once through beauty the mystery has become known — that is, has become a part of one's own mind — then it is legitimate to add appendices to one's knowledge in the form of discursive thought. The essential process of criticism, before any application of judgement, evaluation or interpretation, is to create through semi-symbolic language a vehicle flexible enough to receive the poetic facts, tensions and juxtapositions which emanate from the book's symbolic structure. The beginning of this essential process, is exemplified in an interesting way by Charlotte Brontë in her criticism of *Wuthering Heights*. In her 1850 Preface to Emily's novel, she wondered whether it was 'right or advisable to create beings like Heathcliff', and declared him as 'unredeemed' villain: 'never once swerving in his arrow-straight course to perdition'. Yet after another paragraph, in which she defiantly asserts her own experience of inspiration — the 'creative gift' which 'strangely wills and works for itself' — her attitude changes:

> *Wuthering Heights* was hewn in a wild workshop, with simple tools, out of homely materials. The statuary found a granite block on a solitary moor; gazing thereon, he saw how from the crag might be elicited a head, savage, swart, sinister; a form moulded with at least one element of grandeur — power. He wrought with a rude chisel, and from no model but the vision of his meditations. With time and labour, the crag took human shape; and there it stands colossal, dark, and frowning, half statue, half rock: in the former sense, terrible

and goblin-like; in the latter, almost beautiful, for its colouring is of mellow grey, and moorland moss clothes it; and
heath, with its blooming bells and balmy fragrance, grows
faithfully close to the giant's foot. [6]

Charlotte does not change her *opinion* of the book or its hero; her
opinion, being something which has to be discursively formulated, remains bound with the values of her moral consciousness. Instead she adopts another approach to the book altogether
which is founded on her own artistic experience. She enters the
realms of symbolic language, and through this attains a
sympathetic, negative-capability type of identification with
Emily's mind. By echoing Emily's language in a way which is
nevertheless her own, she came to understand the structural
importance of the 'giant' Heathcliff, the inextricability of the
landscape and 'human shape'; and the essential process of integration undertaken by the story, as symbolised by the raw,
crude rock mellowing and overgrown by flowers, like
Heathcliff's headstone as last seen by Lockwood. In this brief
but evocative commentary Charlotte's own mind can be seen
taking the imprint of Emily's, through Heathcliff, the character
whom she morally abhorred and whose proximity filled her with
catastrophic anxiety: yet who she came to realise as 'almost
beautiful'.

Charlotte pioneers for *Wuthering Heights* the road to criticism
as aesthetic containment of what is, at first, felt as alien,
disturbing and ugly owing to the frightening depth of its
revelation. She begins to show how, through the use of a
symbolic language based on that of the book itself, the reader as
critic can play a creative part in allowing the text to come alive
in his mind, without resorting to the illusion that through
'freeplay' and 'deconstruction' he must substitute his
preconceptions for the author's creative thought. Artistic
reading involves, as well as initial talent, an active negation of
the self with its preconceptions and idealisations; holding fast to
the disagreeable or frighteningly inexplicable aspects of the text
until they become suspended within a receptive pattern,
matching the structural lines of emotional tension present in the
book. Just as Heathcliff sticks to the proximity of the second
Cathy though it is like being 'hugged by a snake', so one must

stick to Heathcliff though he is so repugnant, to Nelly though she is so treacherous, to Catherine though she is so egocentric, to Lockwood though he is so foolish, to Linton though he is so weak, to Hareton though he is so uncouth, to Joseph though he is so sinister. As these fluid points of reference trace and retrace their movements across the moor-mind, a picture of a total emotional constellation evolves, from within the book itself. Certain key, puzzling phrases revolve against one another and against one's previous experience and vocabulary until they find a place in an aesthetic pattern founded upon the primary symbolic language of the author. Thus Heathcliff's 'moral teething' loses its appearance of mania or perverted taste and takes its place as one of his moments of blindingly accurate self-analysis, as soon as the link between the complementary processes of birth and death in the purgatorial section, becomes perceivable. If one suspends disbelief and takes literally the strange rhetoric of his powerful soliloquies — mind 'turned out', 'strange way of killing' — they cease to become mere virtuoso expositions and their part in a wider pattern of mental action allows meaning to shine through them. The early partial or false identifications are not so much denied as subsumed in the form of compost to the final vegetation, remaining part of the total texture of knowledge like the critic's own version of Lockwood's romance. Instead, a more genuine kind of 'love' evolves, which is not directed at any of the characters in isolation but responds to the reverberations between them — the emotion which is externalised like thunderclouds and fills the air with its electrical charges.

*Wuthering Heights* is one of those great poetic works which impresses its form and being on our language and culture, dominating and changing pre-existing attitudes and values, not expressing or conforming to them. It cannot be understood or properly assimilated by means of reductive formulations, which by their nature only express society's preconceptions and prejudices, whether explicit or unacknowledged. It has what Shelley called 'legislative' quality, poets being the 'unacknowledged legislators of the world';[7] it shows how a state of mind (be this individual or collective) is brought, by alien forces seeking recognition, to a point at which it must either fragment destructively (fulfilling the revenge cycle) or re-orient itself and

128

expand its horizons of knowledge, 'in order to let thinking proceed'. One sees how Emily Brontë recognised, through a kind of prophetic science fiction, the violent confrontations of the years immediately following the book: the imminent revolutions in Europe and the Empire, including the type of totalitarian or revenge revolution — the revenge which Heathcliff does not take. Standing disharmoniously against the main current of Victorian optimism and complacent paternalism, she explored the possibilities of a state of mind expanding and changing form, making change catastrophic in the aesthetic rather than the disastrous sense; in Yeats's words, 'Myself must I remake'.[8] The power of the book lies in its dramatisation of the very process of creative thought, a mystical attainment of knowledge or reality worked through into concrete artistic form. But its very originality and power make it difficult to apprehend: firstly because of the emotional trauma involved in allowing 'catastrophic change' to take place in one's mind as an image which is more than an image but a figment of reality; secondly because the ordinary process of reading-through a novel does not automatically provide the aesthetic containment which can take the poison out of this catastrophic anxiety and allow the organic form of the work to become 'almost beautiful' in the mind's eye. Just as artistic psycho-analysis concentrates on modelling a process of self-knowledge rather than interpreting from a standpoint of superior 'scientific' knowledge, so do artistic forms of criticism show *how* to think with the book, not *what* to think about it. They do not stand between the book and the reader, but enable him to read it again, for himself and with himself; so making it easier for the book to fulfil its 'legislative' function in the mind of the world.

\* \* \* \* \*

# III
# EVOLUTION OF THE POETIC
# SPIRIT

# 1      The Final Bound from Gondal: Emily Brontë's Poetry

Emily Brontë, according to Charlotte, did not 'draw well' with Monsieur Heger, their teacher in Brussels. Yet he was a pioneer in his own field and made some intuitive comments about her mind. He described her to Mrs Gaskell as, potentially, 'a great navigator. Her powerful reason would have deduced new spheres of discovery from the knowledge of the old'; adding that if she had written a 'history', her view would have 'dominated over the reader', whatever his 'cooler perceptions of its truth'.[1] *Wuthering Heights*, in fact, can be seen as that dominating history, that new sphere of discovery, deduced from the old sphere of her knowledge and imagination, as it was expressed in her poems. The final bound between the world of the poems and that of the novel, is not solely literary and technical, but also emotional and psychological. She was no longer content to be the omnipotent controller of her material, and became instead a 'navigator', explorer and discoverer. At a key point in her development, which I would locate around the time of writing the famous lines known as 'The Prisoner' (H.190),[2] the visionary mystic within her emerged from its protective daydreamer's chrysalis. As in the lines

> Let us part, the time is over
> When I thought and felt like thee
> I will be an Ocean rover
> I will sail the desert sea, (H.113)

she parts from her earlier self. And here, as throughout her poems, there is no essential distinction between Gondal and non-Gondal subjects, in so far as they are all 'personal' to her imaginative experience. None of Emily Brontë's prose juvenilia remain, though she was writing the 'Life of the Emperor Julius' up to the point of beginning *Wuthering Heights*. But in any case, it is the emerging poetic quality of her mind, more than the content of her fantasy world, which is most relevant to her novel.

In Gondal, with her sister Anne, she evolved an epic-heroic fantasy in verse and prose. *Wuthering Heights* certainly has roots in the permutations and combinations of the Gondal characters and Gondal situations (imprisonment, betrayal, revenge); in the transposition of metaphysical themes; and in the significance of landscape and natural phenomena. Most of the characters have some kind of prototype in the Gondal saga: Heathcliff, for example, derives on one level from Gondal's dark 'melancholy boy' potentially redeemable by love; the 'accursed man' watched by guardian angels; the stranger whose eyes with 'basilisk charm' flash 'lightning all unearthly' from beneath his ordinary 'mantle grey', and wither hospitality with their 'spectre's look' (H.107). As in the novel, this figure becomes generalised, in a reiterated picture of adolescence itself as a shadow thrown over golden childhood, the entry of an alien 'spectre' within the confines of an innocent consciousness. In the novel, the familiar themes and modes of expression belonging to Gondal become the basis for a drama which explores mental reality rather than make-believe. Yet the medium of poetry itself was always for Emily Bronte a focus for inner struggle and intellectual development; she expressed in an early poem (H.27) her frustration at not being able to 'speak the feeling', 'The glorious gift to many given/To speak their thoughts in poetry'; and in 1836 she appended to some lines she was writing the self-castigating note: 'I am more terrifically and idiotically and brutally STUPID than ever I was in the whole course of my incarnate existence.'[3] And within the poetry itself, particularly that of 1844-45 leading up to the writing of *Wuthering Heights*, one can trace the signs which herald a major development. This chapter concentrates, not on the way the content of Gondal prefigures that of *Wuthering Heights*, but on the development of Emily Brontë's creative spirit: the spirit which 'springs elate ... to anticipate/Rewarding Destiny', as 'Measuring the gulf it stoops and dares the final bound'.

In the early poems, there is a division between a direct response to nature's interplay of wind and calm, light and shade, and the thematic basis for crude allegory, describing the dialogue between different voices or characters (human and non-human or 'spectral'), which still has a tinge of the 'Islander' games enacted by the Brontë children in earlier years. But later, these elements become integrated into a preoccupation with the nature and action of the mind or imagination itself: the 'spectre', for example, becomes that aspect of the imagination felt as a 'sterner power'. The potential for drama within the natural scene is captured vividly in one of the early poems, describing the effect of the wind on the moors:

> High waving heather, 'neath stormy blasts bending,
> Midnight and moonlight and bright shining stars;
> Darkness and glory rejoicingly blending,
> Earth rising to heaven and heaven descending,
> Bursting the fetters and breaking the bars. (H.31)

The poem's imagery of sensuous contrast is developed time and again in later poems, forming the basis for the different 'heavens' depicted in *Wuthering Heights*, and for the different quality of its two houses: one a house of 'wind', the other of 'earth' enclosed by foliage. A 'glorious wind', she says in another poem, can 'sweep the world aside'; becoming 'a principle of life ... Lost to mortality', a 'spirit':

> And thou art now a spirit pouring
> Thy presence into all —
> The essence of the Tempest's roaring
> And of the Tempest's fall — (H.148)

In another key, the same night wind awakens the senses to an earth 'instinct with spirit':

> The thick leaves in my murmur
> Are rustling like a dream,
> And all their myriad voices
> Instinct with spirit seem. (H.140)

The earth and natural phenomena are brimful of life which verges on 'spirit': the sensuous pressing into the supra-sensuous. Whilst by contrast, the idea of conventional heaven, the 'sweet land of light', lacks spirit; its 'children' are ignorant of mortal and mental knowledge, of 'What tenants haunt each mortal cell,/What gloomy guests we hold within' (H.149). Emily Bronte's personal religion is founded on the earth as 'mother':

> Our last dear longings blend with thine;
> And struggle still and strive to trace

With clouded gaze, thy darling face.
We would not leave our native home
For *any* world beyond the Tomb.

And the earth-religion with consists of 'tracing' the 'darling
face' of the earth-mother (prefiguring the function of the dead
Catherine), represents the foundation for the process of
'speaking thoughts in poetry'. The earth exists in light and
shade, with recesses that correspond to 'mortal cells', capable of
housing those 'gloomy guests' the mind's internal 'children' or
'tenants'; it provides the stage for their play.

It is earth's capacity for drama that gradually begins to link
the nature poetry with the heroic, romantic, semi-allegorical
tales of the inhabitants of Gondal, who live under 'Another
clime, another sky'. These two parallel structural features of
Emily Brontë's poetry begin to coalesce in her descriptions of
imaginative activity itself, which form the core of her later
poetry. Thus, the Gondal characters communicate, or at least
direct their thoughts, across normally impenetrable barriers
such as the grave or thick dungeon walls, with the aim of
exposing a dialogue of 'real feeling' rather than everyday social
interaction. Likewise, in an early 'personal' poem, spoken from
the point of view of an alien power, Emily Brontë writes:

I'll come when the heart's real feeling
Has entire, unbiassed sway,
And my influence o'er thee stealing,
Grief deepening, joy congealing,
Shall bear thy soul away.

Listen, 'tis just the hour,
The awful time for thee;
Dost thou not feel upon thy soul
A flood of strange sensations roll,
Forerunners of a sterner power,
Heralds of me? (H.37)

The 'awful' (awe-ful) time for the reception of dark or alien
knowledge occurs when the daylight of 'careless childhood's
sunny time' is overshadowed, or the superficial light and noise
of social intercourse peels away to reveal the disregarded,
sleeping unconscious:

136

The organ swells, the trumpets sound,
The lamps in triumph glow;
And none of all those thousands round
Regards who sleeps below. (H.28)

Later in the poetry, as Emily Brontë concentrates these themes
within descriptions of visionary experience, conflicting ideas of
the function of the imagination appear with increasing urgency.
She speaks of restless, 'useless roving', as if searching for a new
kind of poetic expression: 'Shall Earth no more inspire thee,/
Thou lonely dreamer now?' (H.147). Neither the wilful
imagination, 'Where thou and I and Liberty/Have undisputed
sovereignty', nor the escapist 'day dream' imagination ('a
vision dear, though false'), provide sufficient scope for her
developing mind and her dramatic powers. In 1844 Emily writes
a poem 'To Imagination' (H.174) which confirms the breach
between 'Truth' and 'Fancy' (the protective, daydream
imagination). This is followed a few weeks later, in October, by
'O thy bright eyes must answer now' (H.176), a poem which
suggests a new, wholehearted commitment to the power of
imagination — a different kind of imagination. Instead of the
first poem's negative reasoning ('So hopeless is the world
without,/The world within I doubly prize'), there is the
energetic commitment of the conclusion:

And am I wrong to worship where
Faith cannot doubt nor Hope despair
Since my own soul can grant my prayer?
Speak, God of Visions, plead for me
And tell why I have chosen thee!

Instead of Fancy or Imagination she addresses a personified
God of Visions, whose 'bright eyes' are encountered face to face.
The reality of the 'phantom thing' now asserts itself in this
image of a direct communion; in the progression 'My slave, my
comrade, and my King!', the King is paramount. Emily Brontë
images a kind of imagination which instead of serving the will
and its circumscribed preconceptions (here seen as 'Stern
Reason'), overthrows the previous condition of mind which has
ventured on a 'strange road'. The new God requires committed
choice at the expense of other values — first Wealth, Power,

Glory and Pleasure (who 'once indeed seemed Beings divine' but by now are temptations long-past); and now, Reason itself, the last powerful temptation or obstacle to inspiration. In the face of the 'mockery' of Reason, the God's advocacy is essential, to support the integrity of the mind in process of revolution:

> Stern Reason is to judgement come
> Arrayed in all her forms of gloom:
> Wilt thou my advocate be dumb?
> No, radiant angel, speak and say
> Why I did cast the world away;

and *Wuthering Heights*, begun a year later, may be seen as the formal speech of the 'radiant angel', the work of art heralded by this poem.

From this point, the imagination ceases to provide solace or escape from 'Nature's sad reality'; instead there is imaged a clash, or interaction. The vivid, intense poem of 1845 known as 'Stars' (H.184) describes the struggle between the starlit and sunlit worlds at their point of changeover — the process of awakening. At this point the 'peace' of the lunar dreams is disturbed by fear of the 'blinding reign' of the sun:

> Blood-red he rose, and arrow-straight
> His fierce beams struck my brow:
> The soul of Nature sprang elate,
> But mine sank sad and low!
> . . .
> . . . the pillow glowed
> And glowed both roof and floor,
> The birds sang loudly in the wood,
> And fresh winds shook the door.

The moment of disorientation has the effect of intensifying sense — and, with it, sensitivity to mankind's suffering. Although the dreamer wishes to have only the single, starlit vision (the solacing imagination), yet with the 'blood-red' sun's rays which wound the dreamer's brow, pours in the image 'drains the blood of suffering men:/Drinks tears, instead of dew'. The sun is blamed for bloodthirstiness; but the artistic effect of the poem suggests rather that the sun brings the knowledge of blood; and that this knowledge is also dependent on the dreamer's previous

138

immersion in the stars' aqueous 'worlds of solemn light'. The painful truth is born from the conflict itself, becoming a dream which, instead of fading with the dawn, colours the flow of total experience, like those described by Catherine as running 'through and through me, like wine through water, changing the colour of my mind'. The new, and frightening, imagination, is not a 'sure solacer of human cares' as earlier: but on the contrary, a fierce God of Visions whose relentless human knowledge imposes a 'blinding reign': a revelation, rather than a refuge from reality. In the poems of these months, the 'lonely dreamer' has a new sense of direction, no longer engaged in 'useless roving'; and that direction is associated with a sense of steeling and energising in anticipation of Destiny's burden: 'make me strong to undergo/What I am born to bear'.

Years before, she had written that 'in the days of ardent youth/I would have given my life for truth', but that now, though

> My soul still chafes at every tone
> Of selfish or self-blinded error;
> My breast still braves the world alone,
> Steeled as it ever was to terror;
> Only I know, however I frown,
> The same world will go rolling on. (H.119)

She had always had a keen sense of humanity's suffering, and the world's injustice; Ellen Nussey said she 'invited confidence in her moral power', and remembered her playing with the tadpoles, 'moralizing on the strong and the weak, the brave and the cowardly'.[4] Then she came to accept the impossibility of doing anything about it simply by 'frowning'; and the uselessness of worldly ambition and worldly fulfilment gave her a sense of self-sufficient quietude, by comparison with her brother and sisters. As she wrote in her birthday diary note of 30 July 1845:

> I am quite contented for myself ... merely desiring that everybody could be as comfortable as myself and as un-desponding, and then we should have a very tolerable world of it.[5]

She decided to cast her 'anchor of Desire/Deep in unknown Eternity', herself 'Held backward from the tempting race'

139

which had fruitlessly dissipated the hopeful morning of her 'own compeers' (H.188). But now, engagement with Eternity begins to assume the significance of a life of action rather than of contemplation:

> The more unjust seems present fate
> The more my Spirit springs elate
> Strong in thy strength, to anticipate
> Rewarding Destiny! (H.188)

Suggesting a development from 'Stars', the phrase 'springs elate' here refers to the condition of the poet, not just of nature — whose resilience she has inherited. Her new sense of commitment to the Imagination points towards the writing of *Wuthering Heights*, more significantly than does her refining of the content of the Gondal legend.

In fact, Emily adhered to Gondal as an indulgent game or daydream, up to the last moment. The content of Gondal, as distinct from its poetic expression, was a contrary force pulling her away from *Wuthering Heights*. Her strong insistence on continuing to play the game of the 'fighting gentry'[6] is a measure of her wish to escape from the subversive Spirit of Destiny threatening to overwhelm her. Thus in the diary notes of 1845, Anne expresses her boredom with the Gondals, while Emily declares they 'flourish bright as ever', and how she and Anne made a trip to York:

> And during our excursion we were, Ronald Macalgin, Henry Angora, Juliet Angusteena, ... [etc.] escaping from the palaces of instruction to join the Royalists ...[7]

At some point during the late summer of 1845, the struggle between the escapist daydreamer and the visionary mystic within her was resolved, and she made the 'final bound' from Gondal to *Wuthering Heights*. The turning-point seems to be associated with her attitude to the general misery of the others at home — Branwell drugged and debilitated, Anne and Charlotte suffering from unfulfilled love-affairs and from the failure of their plan to start a school at Haworth. In the midst of the general gloom and lack of direction, an external event occurred which it is hard not to see as on some deep level engineered by Emily: she allowed Charlotte to 'discover' the manuscript of her poems. This episode is generally accepted by Brontë scholars as the 'accident' which it was at face value. But the entire context of the discovery — in terms of family relations, career structure and above all, internal development — indicates otherwise. Not just the Brontës' writing careers, but also the frontiers of Emily's imagination, awaited a critical push forwards. One aspect of Emily's mind responded to this double need; though another aspect, inevitably, withdrew in anger and disgust, and she was certainly not prepared to take responsibility for the business. For years she had kept her poems secret from everyone but Anne. Then one day, she left the manuscript open and unguarded long enough for Charlotte to read the whole of it. Charlotte saw, as Emily must have known, that these poems could represent a realistic beginning to their publishing ventures; and seized on them as an opportunity to alter their worldly lot. The new impetus would also involve a change in the quality of their writing, a confrontation with a real world of some kind. Yet the violence of Emily's reaction indicates how much it cost her not only to make public her private dreams, but also to commit herself to a new kind of writing which in effect knocked Gondal off the map. *Wuthering Heights* meant the end of the Gondal fantasy for ever; after writing it, Emily's mind was changed. She seems never to have forgiven Charlotte for this rupture of her 'comfortable' and 'undesponding' tranquillity, which dragged her into the world's tide — not in the sense of worldly ambition as with Charlotte, but in the sense of experiencing a new and disturbing functioning of her imagination, and a new meaning of her concept of 'giving life for truth'. In writing *Wuthering Heights*, she took sufferings greater than her own upon her shoulders, after the prototypal pattern of all great poets.

It cannot be known for sure which particular poem was left by Emily 'accidentally' open after just writing or transcribing it, in the late autumn of 1845, and which immediately struck Charlotte as having 'a peculiar music — wild, melancholy, and elevating'.[8] Winifred Gérin takes it to be the one known as 'The Prisoner' (H.190), since Emily copied it on 9 October, and it is the only poem entered since August.[9] Certainly internal evidence also would make this one poetically appropriate. The poem as a whole is a long and typical Gondal narrative, whose theme may be read as a kind of allegory. Julian, the 'master' at

141

the height of his power, looks inside the 'dungeons' of his own heart apparently on a whim of idle curiosity; but his Joseph-like 'sullen guide' is replaced by his knowledge at second-hand of the 'messenger of Hope' springing out of the prison from inside the golden-haired Rochelle, his soul. (In terms of figures and allegory, the parallel with *Wuthering Heights* is evident.) But the central section of the story-within-a-story, beginning 'He comes with western winds', far exceeds the rest of the narrative in poetic power. It describes the moment of direct mystical vision or communion with truth, reality, knowledge unknown:

> He comes with western winds, with evening's wandering airs,
> With that clear dusk of heaven that brings the thickest stars;
> Winds take a pensive tone, and stars a tender fire,
> And visions rise and change which kill me with desire —
>
> Desire for nothing known in my maturer years
> When joy grew mad with awe at counting future tears;
> When, if my spirit's sky was full of flashes warm,
> I knew not whence they came, from sun or thunderstorm;
>
> But first a hush of peace, a soundless calm descends;
> The struggle of distress and fierce impatience ends;
> Mute music soothes my breast — unuttered harmony
> That I could never dream till earth was lost to me.
>
> Then dawns the Invisible, the Unseen its truth reveals;
> My outward sense is gone, my inward essence feels —
> Its wings are almost free, its home, its harbour found;
> Measuring the gulf it stoops and dares the final bound!
>
> Oh, dreadful is the check, — intense the agony
> When the ear begins to hear and the eye begins to see;
> When the pulse begins to throb, the brain to think again,
> The soul to feel the flesh and the flesh to feel the chain!

The 'messenger of Hope' never appears in personified form, but is sensed first through the spirit's sky's sensuous interchange ('pensive tone', 'tender fire'), which is in turn transposed into the speaking silence of 'mute music', 'soundless calm', 'unuttered harmony'. The habitual alignment of sense-experience is loosened, so that although earth-knowledge (such as that in 'High waving heather') is the basis, earth as hitherto known becomes 'lost'. Earth in the sense of natural observation, and in the sense of the earth-mother of Emily Brontë's poems, fades before the Invisible, the Unseen. The balanced line 'My outward sense is gone, my inward essence feels', summarises the double movement of going outwards through looking inwards; negation of the egocentric self leading to its antithesis — 'real feeling' (as in H.37). Immediately after the moment of greatest abstraction, the statement of 'essence', is the startlingly concrete figure of the bird or winged wild beast which 'stoops and dares the final bound'. The sudden re-emergence of the sensuous in one 'bound' suggests the magnified awareness of a single heartbeat. And the ultimate result of the 'loss' of earth is in fact an agonising intensification of experience, 'When the ear begins to hear and the eye begins to see'. This hearing and seeing is not a return to the situation of the enchained body before the vision, any more than the 'blinding reign' of the sun in 'Stars' is ordinary daylight. It represents the injection of meaning into form, spirit into flesh, essence into chains. Symbolically, afterwards, the master Julian expresses his new identification with the prisoner by twisting his own fingers in 'the links of that iron hard and chill': the prerequisite for earning an 'equal love'.

Emily Brontë, like Julian, was grappling with the comfortable self-mastery which was in a sense imprisoning her soul's flight or development. Like Catherine, she was trying to extend an egocentric or at least self-sufficient concept of 'heaven' into an 'existence beyond herself': where her mind, stretched to its limit, could 'become useful'. The tremors of the mental earthquake, the 'forerunners' of the 'sterner power', are felt 'When the pulse begins to throb' in 'The Prisoner'. Emily left her work open at this point to await an external thrust from Charlotte which would help dislocate her from the sterile fantasy world of Gondal. Charlotte had always been her guide to the outside world — dragging her to Brussels, where she worked fiercely 'like a horse', extending her formal and rhetorical education; [10] likewise it was mainly Charlotte who purveyed in graphic detail accounts of their neighbours' lives and conversations — for *with* them, she 'rarely exchanged a word', [11] saying that Charlotte would bring it all home to her. At this point of crisis, the movement outward also had the symbolic significance of a movement inward, toward an assimilation of

143

the family 'ghosts' — the deaths of their mother and sisters, the fall of Branwell, all represented or prefigured in their childhood games and juvenile writings. Thus Lockwood's flight from the possibility of his seaside romance being reciprocated, seems to begin with Branwell's recoil from the real interest of Mary Taylor[12] and escape into a delusory romance with Mrs Robinson — which was itself an acting-out of a false relationship with literature, dramatised in his letters in similar language. A measure of the distance between Gondal and *Wuthering Heights* is Emily's ability to identify with a narrator as unlike herself as Lockwood: rather as Milton, in *Samson Agonistes*, chooses a hero with values and opinions antithetical to his own. In both cases, the point is not to gain an ironic distance, but to empathise with a position of ignorance from which a genuine learning from experience can evolve. Emily, whose failures in the outside world had to some extent paralleled Branwell's (before the turning-point at Brussels where she conquered them in herself), seemed to take responsibility for Branwell physically — waiting up for him at night and dragging him to bed — and also symbolically, as the exemplum of the Brontë mind's inability to confront reality. When she wrote *Wuthering Heights* she overcame that temptation in herself.

Her achievement in *Wuthering Heights* was so radical, however, that not even Charlotte or Anne, still less Branwell, could understand it. Charlotte distinguished between the poetry, which presented an image of Emily's mind she could recognise, and the novel, which alienated her:

> Ellis has a strong, original mind, full of strange though sombre power. When he writes poetry that power speaks in language at once condensed, elaborated, and refined, but in prose it breaks forth in scenes which shock more than they attract.[13]

For Charlotte, the work which accurately epitomised Emily, was the poem which, after Emily's death, she presented as her 'last' (though it was not, quite):

> No coward soul is mine
> No trembler in the world's storm-troubled sphere
> I see Heaven's glories shine
> And Faith shines equal arming me from Fear

O God within my breast
Almighty ever-present Deity
Life, that in me has rest
As I Undying Life, have power in Thee

Vain are the thousand creeds
That move men's hearts, unutterably vain,
Worthless as withered weeds
Or idlest froth amid the boundless main

To waken doubt in one
Holding so fast by thy infinity
So surely anchored on
The steadfast rock of Immortality

With wide-embracing love
Thy spirit animates eternal years
Pervades and broods above,
Changes, sustains, dissolves, creates and rears

Though Earth and moon were gone
And suns and universes ceased to be
And thou wert left alone
Every Existence would exist in thee

There is not room for Death
Nor atom that his might could render void
Since thou art Being and Breath
And what thou art may never be destroyed.

It is Emily Brontë's finest poem, clinching the link with the God of Visions she had earlier asked to plead for her, with a finality which states unequivocally her position as the writer of *Wuthering Heights* (she had by this point written much, perhaps all, of the novel). It describes her triumph over the fears which beset her in the break from Gondal romancing and the venture into 'the world's storm-troubled sphere', sustained by the infinitely distant yet internal presence of a creative principle — Catherine's 'being beyond yourself', a Being with the Breath of Immortality. The sense of present self and of infinity heighten one another, instead of being mutually exclusive as in her previous poems rejecting worldly values. The two poles contain without loss of balance a voyage across a vast gulf of a mental

145

universe infinitely extended, in a unity so complete that 'There is not room for Death'. The final movement of *Wuthering Heights* is echoed in the ghostly, brooding, dissolving aspect of the spirit, and in the anchorage to the 'rock of Immortality' like the fossilised headstones. Emily's creative spirit recalls Milton's 'dove-like spirit' 'brooding over the vast abyss' in one stanza, and his 'co-eternal beam', the 'bright effluence of bright essence increate' in the next. Yet the poem is a polished statement of an achieved position: as Charlotte said, 'at once condensed, elaborated and refined'. It compels the reader's admiration and acceptance of the author's personal credo, but does not force any disturbing involvement upon him, unlike *Wuthering Heights*, which is a complex exploration taking the reader with it. Charlotte could wholeheartedly admire the refined language of the poem for the very reason that it allowed her to relax into a detached idealisation of the nature which 'Stronger than a man, simpler than a child . . . stood alone.'[14]

Emily's two-generation story in *Wuthering Heights* could be said to image the stages of her own transition between poems and novel: the mystic in her emerging from self-absorption into art and an existence beyond herself. The inevitable death-throes of the fantasy world of Gondal which this necessitated, are expressed in a fiercely un-refined Gondal narrative which is (to our knowledge) the only thing she wrote during the two years of her life which remained after *Wuthering Heights*. It exists in two versions, spanning that period, showing that its theme obsessed her and could not be brought to a satisfactory aesthetic conclusion. The first version begins:

Why ask to know the date, the clime?
More than mere words they cannot be:
Men knelt to God and worshipped crime,
And crushed the helpless, even as we.

The theme — the unthinking oppression of vulnerable humanity by ourselves — is familiar in her work; but the bitter, sarcastic, committed expression, is new. There is a world of difference in commitment between the Gothic horror of early Gondal, seen in verses of the 1830's such as:

And truly at my side
I saw a shadowy thing
Most dim, and yet its presence there
Curdled my blood with ghastly fear
And ghastlier wondering, (H.12)

or:

I flung myself upon the stone,
I howled and tore my tangled hair,
And then, when the first gush had flown,
Lay in unspeakable despair, (H.15)

and the prophetic, apocalyptic vision of a self-destroyed world found in H.192:

A red fire on a distant hill —
A line of fires, and deep below
Another dusker, drearier glow —
Charred beams, and lime, and blackened stones
Self-piled in cairns o'er burning bones . . .

Let street and suburb smoulder there —
Smoke-hidden in the winding glen
They lay too far to vex my ken.

The key to the difference between these early and late horror-stories lies in the attitude of the hero, or rather anti-hero, of the latter, whom Emily designates an 'Enthusiast'. He is not the usual amoral avenger careless of sacrifice, but a type of Everyman who has merely lost his imagination — the implication is, 'even as we'. His crusade is propelled by jargon, 'in a name delighting'; and the gory destruction which he wreaks is in a sense unintentional, done 'with unregarding eyes'; he literally cannot see what he is doing. He is a slogan-wielder; convinced that he is fighting for 'Loyalty and Liberty', he ultimately discovers uncomprehendingly that his own child is on the point of being sacrificed. What had been 'too far to vex my ken' only becomes real when his imagination, his mind-child, is awoken, but then it is too late.

This pessimistic allegory could not be fitted satisfactorily, which any degree of aesthetic finish, into the Gondal framework. The short second version ends, flat and ugly, with a straight condemnation of the 'enthusiasm' of the crusader:

I, doubly cursed on foreign sod,
Fought neither for my home nor God. (H.193)

And behind the allegory, is an implicit condemnation or ultimate total disinterest in the entire romanticisation pervading the Gondal fantasy. Emily Brontë is in a sense completing her picture of the true poet, the 'Believer' of 'No coward soul', by contrasting it with the false poet or Enthusiast, who in his self-delusion is ultimately responsible for the world's miseries. And the false poet is no distant totalitarian but the aspect of Everyman which shuts him off from 'home and God' and destroys his 'child'. Emily Brontë's experience of creation in *Wuthering Heights* made her realise, sharply, its antithesis; and it destroyed her equanimity. She could no longer 'cast the world away' and play with the 'fighting Gentry' under 'Another clime, another sky'. When she became a 'navigator' of the internal world, Gondal itself became 'foreign sod', and the indulgence of 'mere words' and enthusiasm which it had offered, became meaningless. In this sense, her last poem, which she could not complete, is as much as 'No coward soul' a commentary on the 'new spheres of discovery' which, fulfilling Monsieur Heger's report, she had entered.

# 2    Charlotte Brontë and Emily: The Juvenilia and *Jane Eyre*

When Charlotte Brontë was thirteen, she wrote 'The History of the year' 1829, which begins:

> Once papa lent my sister Maria a book. It was an old geography book; she wrote on its blank leaf, 'Papa lent me this book.' This book is a hundred and twenty years old; it is at this moment lying before me. While I write this I am in the kitchen of the Parsonage, Haworth . . . [15]

She wrote an account of the 'Origin' of the 'Islanders Play' and from this period dates the Brontë children's collective compulsion to express and record their childhood fantasy games in writing. The content of their fantasy is not so remarkable as the necessity of putting it into words, and words in the form of imitation printed books. The concept of a 'book' seems to have contained for them a sense of finding their family history, of being automatically an appropriate vehicle for the story of their lives. They perused their father's printed volumes (such as, the *Cottage Poems*, or *The Maid of Killarney*), and undoubtedly their obsession with writing was encouraged by the sense of social and intellectual ambition, and strong partisanship, emanating from Patrick Brontë. As Mrs Gaskell said, he was 'silently cognisant' of their activities; [16] he invented a mask-game to detect the 'signs of rising talent' in his children, and through his somewhat eccentric mode of education gave the impression — with regard to Branwell at least — that he was nurturing genius. He was fanatically if fondly possessive of Charlotte in the years of her fame. The 'old geography book' lent by him to Maria his eldest daughter (who died in 1826 aged eleven), somehow symbolises the function of 'the book' in placing the children's identities; they were all fond of drawing and later of music as well, but writing was a necessity. Before Emily could write, Charlotte occasionally wrote down pieces for her, such as 'A Day at Parry's Palace', and allowed her influence to speak in records of their 'bed plays' ('Emily and me one stormy night were going through the wood . . .'). [17] Charlotte's very first book was for and about Anne ('There was a little girl and her name was Ane').[18] A characteristic of her juvenilia is, amidst the tedious extravagance, sharp and satirical observations of her family, especially Branwell. Charlotte later wrote, with slightly idealised nostalgia, of 'minds cast in the same mould' with 'no disputes to divide them',[19] and of the fantasy world born 'out of [their] own brain' peopled with 'Melchisedics — without father, without mother'.[20] In fact, as her own juvenilia attest, their 'web of sunny air'[21] consisted mainly of incessant warfare, in which they would 'maul and mangle each other in the most horrible way';[22] the parsonage echoing to 'the horrible howl of their war-cry'. But in a sense they created their own 'father and mother', through eroticising and dramatising their own relationships, and through erecting their parental figures into household gods, partly deified and partly defied. To Ellen Nussey, Charlotte described Maria as 'a little mother among the rest, superhuman in goodness and cleverness', 'Christ-like' in fortitude.[23] Images of Maria hover throughout, ending for Charlotte in Helen Burns of *Jane Eyre* and for Emily in the child-ghost of the married 'Catherine Linton' wailing in *Wuthering Heights*. Thrown in on themselves 'like growing potatoes in a cellar' (as Mary Taylor saw them),[24] they explored what Charlotte called 'the world below', the 'infernal regions', both emulating and reversing the power-balance of adults and children.

Maria's geography book, which Charlotte carefully places in its homely realistic setting of the table in the Parsonage, Haworth, was the symbolic predecessor of a more modern work, *Goldsmith's Geography*; this contained maps and information used to give the imaginary countries of Angria and Gondal a local habitation and a name. These two countries (different in climate and in principles of government) embodied an aesthetic division used to give substantiality to the different identities of the two rival groups — Emily and Anne 'like twins' headed by Emily;[25] Charlotte and Branwell ostensibly headed by Branwell who provided the territorial plots, but really by Charlotte the stronger personality. Gondal and Angria were offshoots of the original Arabian Nights 'Country of the Genii'; as Branwell described their activities:

I see, I see appear
  Awful Brannii, gloomy giant,
Shaking o'er earth his blazing air,
Brooding on blood with drear and vengeful soul
He sits enthroned in clouds to hear his thunders roll.
  Dread Tallii next like a dire eagle flies
And on our mortal miseries feasts her bloody eyes.
  Emii and Annii last with boding cry,
Famine and war foretell and mortal misery. [26]

The four Genii are all-powerful and all-pervasive, inhabiting a country whose ancestral skeletons, gigantic Britons and Gauls, are kept chained in the desert under mountains of red sand. [27] Branwell describes their 'meddling' in graves — 'For Genii come with spades/To dig you up'; [28] and Charlotte uses their violent omnipotence linguistically, in a passage cited by Mrs Gaskell as evidence of 'language run riot': [29]

It is well known that the Genii have declared that unless they perform certain arduous duties every year, of a mysterious nature, all the worlds in the firmament will be burnt up, and gathered together in one mightly globe, which will roll in solitary grandeur through the vast wilderness of space, inhabited only by the four high princes of the Genii, till time shall be succeeded by Eternity; ...

In this apocalyptic vision the end of the world is in the hands of the Genii, who are capable of reducing it to a 'desert' for the very purpose of erecting their palace in greater contrast:

... in the midst of this desolation the palace of the Chief Genii shall rise sparkling in the wilderness, and the horrible howl of their war-cry shall spread over the land at morning, at noontide and night; ... they shall have their annual feast over the bones of the dead, and shall yearly rejoice with the joy of victors.

In a sense the 'palace of the Genii' in this passage is the rhetorical construction itself, the powerful energy of her own words assuming the position of God; Charlotte is apologising for this as much as for the content when she characteristically appends a qualifying moral note: 'the horrible wickedness of this

151

needs no remark'. Writing itself is an underlying subject of their warlike activities, and vehicle of their magical powers. At will they can create and destroy visions; indeed the most fascinating images, for her, evoking her most fluent language, focus on life-death catastrophes or reality-unreality boundaries, as in her vision of the destruction of Glasstown and the Genii world:

> 'Twas the Ruler of Spirits that sent forth the sound
> To call his dread legions in myriads around . . .
> The Hall where they sat was the heart of the sky,
> And the stars to give light stooped their lamps from on high
> . . .
> The secrets of Genii my tongue may not tell,
> But hoarsely they murmured: 'Bright city, farewell!'
> Then melted away like a dream of the night . . .
> For at midnight passed o'er them the Angel of Death! [30]

Charlotte is fascinated by the imaginative power which both creates and destroys simultaneously; by the fiction of Glasstown seeming more real at the point of its dissolution by herself, the 'Ruler of Spirits'. To the inhabitants of 'that little isle' England, the African Glasstown 'bore the character of a dream or gorgeous fiction', [31] its qualities enhanced by its unbelievability.

The vision of herself and the children as both diminutive and huge, fairies and Genii, at the mercy of their fantasies yet omnipotently controlling them, is dramatised in the early story 'Strange Events' (1830), where one of her characters, like the toy soldier he was originally, is lifted up by a giant hand to confront the immense blue eyes of his creator — 'a huge personification of myself, hundreds of feet high'. [32] This convinces him of his 'non-existence' except as 'the mere idea of some other creature's brain', in 'another corporeal frame which dwelt in the real world, for ours I thought was nothing but idea'. The character, Lord Charles Wellesley — who is to become Charlotte's chief narrator throughout the juvenilia — undergoes this experience whilst in a daydream in the Public Library, exploring the alternative of literature to 'razor, rope and arsenic' as a solution to dullness. He is looking, as it were, for a different kind of Angel of Death to intensify vision. Charles Wellesley is small not only because he is a toy, but by virtue of his character. Prying, cynical and peeping, he looks on the real-unreal world of the Verdopolitan (Glasstown) aristocracy as a voyeur without significance of his own. Yet his apparently unprepossessing characteristics also represent necessary aspects of the novelist: 'My eye is quick, my fingers are light'. [33] His function is to record and disapprove of the glamorous actions of his brother Arthur Augustus Adrian Wellesley, Marquis of Douro and Duke of Zamorna, Charlotte's 'Byronic' hero. Throughout her juvenilia she separates her own identity as writer between these two poles or 'brothers': king and outcast, protagonist and voyeur, giant and puny powerless being. Eventually in *Jane Eyre*, her two major roles find expression in the romance between Zamorna-like Rochester and Charles-like Jane, though in a way which evolves a more creative struggle between them, rather than the sour deadlock which eventually results in Angria.

Competition was fierce amongst the Brontë children in their writing, particularly between Charlotte and Branwell, despite — or because of — their mutual dependence in the story of Angria. To some extent Branwell became the butt of Charlotte's satire, representing a kind of false Zamorna, whose genius she partly believes in and partly mocks, by comparison with her own more real powers; and whose privileges as the only boy in a Victorian household she cannot help resenting and ridiculing. This 'false genius' aspect of their relationship finds repeated expression in her portrayals of how magic is distributed in the book world. More significantly, Branwell seems also to have come to represent irritating aspects of herself as a writer and a type of false poet. Charlotte uses images of Branwell for the projection of certain features of authorship which are alternately exalted and despised. In 'Characters of Celebrated Men' (December 1829), heavy-handed scholarship is embodied in Captain Bud, the 'ablest political writer' in Glasstown, who makes one 'fall asleep over his best works'. This is Branwell with his obsessionally detailed and solemn catalogues of wars and political struggles in Angria, and also Charlotte with her reliance on obsessional detail: a characteristic seen most clearly in her copying of engravings which she later lamented had nearly made her 'blind'. This type of heaviness goes with internal lightness; Bud is a 'heatherbell apt to be blown away at every blast of the wind'. [34] In the same series Charlotte portrays

Young Soult the Rhymer (another of Branwell's pseudonyms), as the Romantic poet caricatured, aping the external characteristics without the inner strength: 'The expression of his countenance is wild and haggard, and he is eternally twisting his mouth to one side'. In *The Poetaster* (1830), Charlotte has Henry Rhymer tremble in his efforts to capture 'the inspiration of genius', which he is unable to dissociate from the effects of alcohol:

> I'm certainly in a consumption brought on by excessive drinki-st-study I mean. Or was it only the effect of those fervid flashes from one of the Muse's flames that just then passed through my mind? [35]

Then, awaiting the death which the savage Verdopolitan literary society prescribes for his pretensions, Rhymer remembers how on a 'tempestuous night',

> I stood alone in the midst of a mighty desert, entranced, en-wrapped, enfolded with the mantle of my own glorious thoughts and broodings. The yellings of a hundred ghosts arose on each successive blast that swept over the heath with wild, maniacal moaning. Oh, in that sublime solitude, how my heart beat, and my brain throbbed ... (p.493)

Charlotte's rhetoric is an excellent example as well as parody of Gothic suspense; equivalent to the horror-stories with which she frightened the schoolgirls at Roe Head, [36] and not so different from the hallucinatory visions which assailed her during her second period there. Thus in her 'Roe Head Journal' of 1836, she writes repeatedly about the dream-bearing rushing wind:

> Glorious! that blast was mighty it reminded me of Northangerland, there was something so merciless in the heavier rush, that made the very house groan as if it could scarce bear this acceleration of impetus. O it has wakened a feeling that I cannot satisfy — a thousand wishes rose at its call which must die with me for they will never be fulfilled. Now I should be agonised if I had not the dream to repose on — [37]

The correspondence between such passages makes it clear that it is primarily an aspect of herself, more than just Branwell, which she is satirising. They focus on a problematic point in her entire

EVOLUTION OF THE POETIC SPIRIT

vision of literature. Moreover it is essentially characteristic of Charlotte (in contrast to Emily and Anne) that problems about the nature of imaginative vision are intertwined with problems of worldly literary ambition. The prospect of fame, or the unlikelihood of it, intensifies her obsession with the dichotomy between imagination and reality, and increasingly leads her into a situation of imaginative sterility during the later juvenilia.

One of Rhymer's pretensions had been to convert his name to Remeër, rather as Patrick Brontë had quietly allowed his to change from its Irish peasant form Brunty (or Prunty, or Branty). Although it has been questioned whether the Brontë children in fact knew of this change, one suspects an awareness of it, given their romantic loyalty to their Celtic heritage, and a strong sense of what it meant to rise in the world; moreover Patrick always maintained some contact with his family. The name-change took place while he was at Cambridge; and Charlotte's identification with her father at this point in his history is shown in the letter of September 1841 to her aunt, converting her to the Brussels project: 'Who ever rose in the world without ambition? When he [Papa] left Ireland to go to Cambridge University, he was as ambitious as I am now'.[38] Rhymer-Remeër, in Charlotte's parody, represents the overweening ambition of the misfit in an aristocratic literary society: represented in turn or simultaneously, in Charlotte's writings, by being small, ugly, of low origins, female, a child. Rhymer is freed on condition that he write no more and 'take some useful employment'; the Verdopolitan bookseller fears the prospect of 'every child that walks the streets, bearing its manuscripts in its hand, going to the printers for publication'.[39] Charlotte herself both identifies with the aristocratic ambition, and is contemptuous of it: on the one hand it is the only reality; on the other, it denies all reality. Charles Wellesley is punished for his 'peeping' into the aristocratic 'Picture Book' by being forced to study 'The Cook's Guide', through which 'my sin was soon washed away' (May 1834).[40] In 'My Angria and the Angrians' (October 1834), she describes Branwell's pretensions by the side of his 'sempstress' sisters:

My mind was always looking above my station. I was not satisfied with being a sign-painter at Howard [Haworth], as

155

Charlotte and them things were with being sempstresses. I set before myself the Grand Plain of Africa, and I traced a path for my own feet through it, which terminated at the door of a splendid Palace situated on Cock-hill, whose portal bore inscribed 'Residence of the Duke of Thorncliffe'.[41]

A mark of his arrogance is his toadying, to even the creatures of his own imagination: falling 'flat on his face' in obeisance as one of his Angrian heroes passes by.[42] Although only satirised through the figure of Branwell, this is an attitude which has its equivalent within Charlotte herself. In her poem of January 1836, 'But once again, but once again', she presents herself like countless heroines of her juvenilia who fall prostrate before Zamorna: 'grovelling in the dust I fall/Where Adrian's shrine lamps dazzling glow'.[43] Likewise she partly identifies with and partly ridicules those male characters who, like Lord Charles, cannot find an entry into the 'rising sun' of Zamorna's influence, in the social or the literary sense.

Lord Lofty, in 'The Tragedy and the Essay' (1833), is another of those crushed for his pretensions. In this case, to complete the picture of tyranny and futility, he is mocked not for his aspirations to inspiration (like Rhymer) but for his pedantic research. Lofty desires to partake of 'the brilliant wit, the exhaustless knowledge, and the varied information' of Zamorna's literary aristocracy, 'the feast of reason and the flow of soul'.[44] We see Marian, listening rapt, exclaiming 'I wish I had written a book!' This 'feast' is available only to the 'brighter children of fashion'. Lofty has just ridiculed and caused to be hissed off stage a Tragedy written by one of Zamorna's protégés, who (in Rhymer-fashion) immediately offers to die: 'All hope of fame is gone and I desire to live no longer'. His literary merit *per se* is clearly no greater than Rhymer's; but the object-lesson here is that any protégé of Zamorna will succeed and any rival will fail. Through his mode of revenge, Zamorna clearly reveals his nature as a patron of the arts and god of aesthetic activity. He sets Lofty the task of achieving 'originality' in a literary project, in a speech in which Charlotte displays her keen satiric awareness of the conventional view of what women should think about. She parodies in anticipation the advice which she was to receive from Southey three years later, about the 'distempering' effect of daydreams and how 'literature cannot be the business of a woman's life, and it ought not to be'.[45] Zamorna instructs Lofty:

> Let me briefly define to you the meaning of originality. It consists in raising from obscurity some theme, topic, employment, or existence which has hitherto never been thought of by the great mass of men, or thought of only to be despised; in pouring around it the light of genius, proving its claim to admiration by the subtle tools of logic, clothing it with all the bright hues of a lively imagination, and presenting it thus adorned to the astonished world.

It is advice which Charlotte follows herself in choosing a plain heroine who is a governess; but as always, she ridicules and stamps on her own aspirations in advance, before anyone else can do so. So Lofty is counselled by Zamorna to take the subject of 'washing, starching and ironing'; and he immerses himself 'day and night . . . in the solitude of his study' until his thesis is completed. (One recalls the sketches in which Charlotte has herself and her sisters as sempstresses or washerwomen, tongues clicking incessantly while Branwell lies on his back idling.)[46] Through the fall of Lofty, Charlotte images as a warning to herself the likely fall of her own hopes of literary fame, given the nature of the ruler of her literary world. The conclusion of her little parable is that Lofty is publicly ridiculed by Zamorna. At last 'the light of truth burst on him with almost annihilating splendour' — the truth that Zamorna is god in the field of literature, which is really just a field of status and power-politics.

Zamorna for Charlotte is not just king of Angria, but king of literature. While dispensing fame in Verdopolis, that 'gigantic emporium of God-like wisdom',[47] he is also the ruler of spirits and conferrer of reality. Without Zamorna, neither enthusiasm nor dutiful labour can flourish; he confers magic on the book. He is her 'mental king',[48] 'principle of life' and principle of poetry:

> He's moved the principle of life
> Through all I've written or sung or said,
> The war-song routing to the strife,
> The life-wind wakening up the dead.

In Charlotte's version of the Brontë history and the Book, the search for internal identity and for public acceptance go hand in hand. Yet no real creative link between the beggar and the king is possible. The 'Cook's Guide' and the 'Picture Book', the washerwoman and the prince, remain in separate spheres of unreality, serving to satirise and undermine, but not to transform one another. What began as an inspiring dialectic, offering different perspectives on the nature of the book's life or magic, degenerates into a hardened repetition: in effect a stranglehold over her imagination. Gradually her phantasy world becomes less humorous, even when satirical; more bitter, and even deluded. This hardening of internal attitudes seems to be intimately connected with the question of what part literature could play in her getting a 'stake in life' (as she later phrased it), [49] the primary preoccupation of her later adolescence. For Charlotte this preoccupation was inseparable from, and confused with, the parallel need to evolve a new kind of writing *in itself*. During the years 1836 – 40 Charlotte's writing improved in technique and sophistication, but not in imaginative outlook. Her obsession with the Zamorna principle led her into a situation of deadlock. She veers between extremes of Calvinistic self-castigation ('If the Doctrine of Calvin be true I am already an outcast'), [50] and self-indulgent erotic daydream, in which she is also an outcast. For Zamorna's aristocratic world of literature as gratification, is more tantalizingly unattainable than ever. By the time of her second period at Roe Head, as a teacher or 'drudge', her 'dreams' have taken on a persistently two-dimensional, hallucinatory quality:

> I hear them speak . . . I see distinctly their figures — and though alone, I experience all the feelings of one admitted for the first time into a grand circle of classic beings . . . transcendantly fair and inaccessible sacred beings . . . [51]

Time and again the hallucinatory images are 'broken' by those of actuality: Miss Wooler with a plate of butter, a 'dolt' with a lesson, the girls with their curl-papers; Charlotte ends one entry with 'I thought I should have vomited'. Her book-world loses its realism and character perception and three-dimensional potential; the only alternatives are admission or exclusion from hallucination; there is no mental space for any miniature

Charles Wellesley to consider the reality of his creator's 'idea', or vice versa. Charlotte's relationship with her co-author Branwell deteriorated, whilst she also became more dependent on him for this species of substitute reality — such as wondering whether he had 'really killed' the Duchess. As she explained to Miss Wooler at a later date, 'Hypochondria' made her life a 'continual waking Nightmare', and left her 'a stalking ghost'. [52] For as she wrote in a poem of May 1837, a 'cold destroying finger' had passed over the sacred images of 'My dreams, the Gods of my religion', [53] making them dead images. The 'stalking ghost' aptly describes Charlotte's literary or imaginative identity at this time, when she was obsessively fixated on a bygone world and unable to develop.

Charlotte gradually came to feel that her writing was getting her nowhere, not in terms of worldly status but in terms of ultimate knowledge. Its early richly aesthetic roots had become swamped by the sophistication of the social analogue, with literature as satisfaction and status rather than as symbolic exploration. Here there is an essential contrast between her principle of poetry or muse, Zamorna, and Emily Brontë's 'sterner power', 'My slave, my comrade and my King', who trained Emily in a more strenuous, struggling mentality than Zamorna did Charlotte. [54] Emily's internal god concentrated on principles of intensification of vision, rather than on the distribution of prizes. For Charlotte, the source for this intensification, or increase in dimensionality, was (unlike Emily) observation and relationships in the outside world. She wrote to Ellen Nussey in August 1841 of her 'urgent thirst to see — to know to learn — something internal seemed to expand boldly for a minute — I was tantalized with the consciousness of faculties unexercised'. [55] She was not, as is usually interpreted, suffering from an excess of phantasy life but from an impoverishment of the imagination, Zamorna's tyrannical repression of 'something internal'. During the years 1837–9 she wrote the series of relatively sophisticated 'novelettes', improving her grasp of storytelling and of narrative and psychological focus. But what she really needed, by now, to bring her out of the juvenilia and into creative writing, was not technical progress *per se*, but a new internal system of identifications: a new dynamic aegis under which to approach the whole process of writing. It took Charlotte some years to achieve this. Her 'solemn resolve' of 1838 to 'write no more till I had somewhat to write about',[56] applied to her internal world as much as to external subjects. In *Caroline Vernon* (1839), her last romance, she is still engaged in the fruitless occupation of bolstering the Zamorna image. Here she tries to inject some life into the image by slightly satirising herself through the young Caroline's naive notion of a hero: 'something there was of a Hero — yet a nameless, a formless, a mystic being — a dread shadow'.[57] But this streak of satire is presented only to be undermined and replaced by Zamorna's dominance, through a 'thrill of nameless dread': 'all at once she knew him — Her Guardian was gone — Something terrible sat in his place'. After this for several years, Charlotte wrote nothing which seemed to have any meaning for her. She needed the external world to enrich the dynamism of her phantasy life, where movement and aesthetic contrast were stultified. Her 'Farewell to Angria' (after *Caroline Vernon*) heralded 'a cooler region where the dawn breaks grey and sober', to expand the single-toned 'burning clime' of the juvenilia.[58] Brussels in 1842 made the grey dawn of *The Professor* possible, which in turn made her return to Angria from a new perspective in *Jane Eyre*, a creative and transforming move.

In terms of imaginative functioning, *Caroline Vernon* and the first two novels belong to different worlds. In *The Professor*, despite or perhaps by means of the uneven texture and episodes which are tonally unassimilated to the overall structure, Charlotte emerges from her chrysalis and explores new vertices for observation and juxtaposition. Although it is not always successful, there is a new and interesting self-consciousness about the novel form and about modes of observation, including the 'surveillante' aspect of the observer-observed: an experimentation that in its freshness has more in common with the early juvenilia (such as 'Strange Events') than with later repetitions of the pattern. But in *Jane Eyre*, these modes are newly integrated within the double 'autobiography' of child and adult developing simultaneously, with interplay between the 'master' and the 'fairy' vertices on literature. Jane is the juvenilia's peeping-Tom style narrator become protagonist and heroine: one who, though frequently in the position of an out-cast, is in fact a prime mover of events — which in this novel, are primarily mental events. Between 1842 and 1845, therefore, the years of Charlotte's time in Brussels as pupil and teacher and of her dismal 'slavery' to sorrow which followed, a change took place in her total attitude to the process of writing, and in her implicit idea of its function in her life. Its claustrophobic perspectives opened out. It would seem that this change was effected, in some mysterious way, through her relationship with M. Heger, who could be said to have replaced Branwell in Charlotte's mind as an internal partner in the aim of achieving a 'stake in life' through literature. As with Branwell, Heger's significance derives more from his function as an agent in a personal myth of Charlotte's than from his actual advice, which was always strictly proper and cautious. Thus she gave him a selection of her juvenile writings, but he — like her other paternal advisers — told her to consider the career of letters closed, just as in one of his last communications to her he forbade her to speak of her feelings and state of mind.

The relationship with Heger fell into two distinct parts: the actual relationship in Brussels (a period of mutual 'teaching' followed by the withdrawal of 'the light of his countenance'), and the one-sided relationship of the correspondence from Haworth, which was in a sense fictional, and in which she defied his instructions. Charlotte utilised both aspects of the relationship in her adult writing: the first for newly-inspired character observation in *The Professor* and *Villette*. These novels employ, with variations, the type of mental stance expressed through Charlotte's penetrating cartoonist's vignette of Heger: a 'man of power as to mind', though 'sometimes he borrows the lineaments of an insane tom-cat, sometimes those of a delirious hyena'.[59] This mental stance pervades the texture of the novels, not just its representative portraiture. Secondly, Charlotte employed the absent Heger as an internal blank page, through whom to reform the master or god of her imagination. As late as May 1843, towards the end of her stay in Brussels, she wrote to Branwell that in her isolation she reverted 'as fanatically as ever to the old ideas, the old faces, and the old scenes in the world below'.[60] Yet in the same month she noted down a 'Scheme for a May Tale' full of good technical sense. Technically she was ready, but imaginatively she was not, although her recent experiences had brought her to a point at which some kind of internal revolution seemed imminent. This imminence is suggested perhaps, by such 'freaks' as her visit to the confessional, when she felt 'as when alone on the Thames at midnight' — that is, on the point of a new imaginative departure.[61]

Emily complained that Charlotte was 'vegetating' in Brussels.[62] In a sense she was; both then and during the further painful period at home when her inability to write was protracted and intensified, and associated with 'blindness'. It was a period of hibernation or dormancy, away from the 'light' of Heger's active direction. It is as if the old book magic and everything connected with the process of writing in the old way, had to be silenced before new work could begin: including Zamorna himself as literature master and 'mental king'. Through her relationship with Heger, 'a man of power as to mind', Charlotte worked through and in a sense exorcised the unproductive aspects of her attitude to Zamorna. Her letters to him were not only unanswered but unanswerable, as they needed to be in order for him to fulfil a function as the new Zamorna or literature master. In July 1844 she wrote:

> I should not know this lethargy if I could write . . . Were I to write much I should become blind. This weakness of sight is a terrible hindrance to me. Otherwise do you know what I should do, Monsieur? — I should write a book, and I should dedicate it to my literature-master — to the only master I ever had — to you, Monsieur.[63]

Heger himself was alarmed by language which he could only interpret as romantic infatuation indulged to dangerous excess. For Mina Laury, Zamorna 'superseded all things . . . Unconnected with him my mind would be a blank'.[64] Now, freed by distance, and perhaps also by language restraints (writing in French), Charlotte projects this aspect of Zamorna which had kept her a 'slave', onto Heger:

> That, indeed, is humiliating — to be unable to control one's own thoughts, to be the slave of a regret, of a memory, the slave of a fixed and dominant idea which lords it over the mind.[65]

By the end of her correspondence (this was November 1845),

Charlotte had silenced the tyranny of Zamorna through the un-answerability of her language to Heger.

Charlotte seems to have unconsciously created a situation of self-imprisonment, surrounded by silence and — she felt — blindness; she persistently identified with her father's failing sight at this time, which she used as her reason for remaining at home, refusing at least one well-paid teaching post. Ultimately, as is well known, she began *Jane Eyre* on the morning of her father's eye operation. Meanwhile it was important for her to remain in the place where she used to daydream effortlessly, and to feel the silence reflecting from this unproductive imaginative situation. In January 1845 she wrote:

> For me the universe is dumb,
> Stone-deaf, and blank, and wholly blind;
> Life I must bound, existence sum
> In the strait limits of one mind;
>
> That mind my own. Oh! narrow cell:
> Dark — imageless — a living tomb!⁶⁶

Her mind had to become 'imageless' before she could exorcise her slavery to a 'fixed and dominant idea' with its hallucinatory images. Despite its overt pessimism and misery, this poem suggests Charlotte sensing the limits and structure of her mind and identity, 'that mind my own'. As in Milton's *Samson* which these lines seem to echo (and which enters explicitly the end of *Jane Eyre*), imprisonment brings the potential for a new self-knowledge and use of the imagination; Charlotte was living out one of the great literary metaphors, of blindness before insight. The final stage towards this was initiated by Emily, who during these years was keenly aware of the reasons for Charlotte's depression, and who offered a new 'stake in life' when she allowed Charlotte to discover the manuscript of her poems (despite the cost to her own peace of mind). These, Charlotte wrote later, 'stirred my heart like the sound of a trumpet'.⁶⁷ Charlotte read Emily's poems in October 1845, and wrote her last letter to Heger, whose role was now obsolete, in November. In this way she used her apparent dependence on 'a man of power', to come to terms with her own mind and become independent. Out of the vegetative nullity of those chrysalid years of hibernation and ghostliness, Charlotte metamorphosed with enriched vision and a proliferation of new perspectives. From this point, the book magic was internalised; she became her own literature master.

The four Brontë children all grew out of their childhood writing in different ways, fulfilling — or not — their idea of the internal heritage of the 'geography book'. It was Emily who made the greatest change in orientation, a 'final bound' from the world whose escapist and childish qualities she had resolutely maintained as inextricable from her poetic powers. Despite fending it off until the last minute, the imaginative leap which she made with the aid of her 'sterner power' was both uncompromising and irrevocable. Branwell never made the break at all: persisting in living out a role as 'one of the FALLEN',[68] an outcast and martyred genius, which he had written and Charlotte had satirised many times through various characters; as Alexander Percy, for example, who 'first launched from Eternity' while

> Expectation's eager gale
> Swelled and sounded in my sail;
> Ambition's ever-rousing power
> Urged me on in morning's hour;

and awoke to find the 'dream gone': 'Life alone with its midnight sea/Howled on me in stern reality.[69] As if all part of a family myth, these lines are echoed in Emily's poem of 1844:

> O, fairly spread thy early sail,
> And fresh, and pure, and free,
> Was the first impulse of the gale
> Which urged life's wave for thee! (H.171)

Branwell, who had excellent imitative abilities but never developed any internal strength, was left to fulfil the role of the empty poetaster. Anne, in contrast, never pursued that sort of involvement in literature; from the beginning there is a clear distinction between her Gondal and personal poems, unlike Emily's; Gondal was always a game, under Emily's impetus, and she kept her soul or religion separate — its struggles recorded in verse, but not actively worked out through poetry. Her determination to make literature encompass the details of everyday actuality, had its effect on the substantiality of her sisters' work; she was writing 'Passages in the Life of an Individual' (later *Agnes Grey*), while they were still fully absorbed in Angria and Gondal. She was essentially a moralist and teacher, and her notion of 'truth' as something which 'conveys its own moral to those who are able to receive it' [70] underlies the surface objectivity of the 'facts' which she portrays; the narrative of her works carries a moral which is worked out separately, even if in parallel, rather than evolved through an organic unity. For Anne, literature was the didactic expression of internal arguments, rather than self-exploration. *The Tenant of Wildfell Hall* echoes *Wuthering Heights* in many details of theme, motif and narrative form, but only in a superficial way, and such as makes it appear to be her correction of the immorality and romantic illusions of Emily's book. Indeed the writing of the novels of 1845 and after, emphasized a distinction and distance between the Brontës in their attitude to the book as an expression of identity, and therefore to life. As Anne wrote on 'Monday Night May 11 1846', when *Agnes Grey*, *The Professor* and *Wuthering Heights* were finished and ready to be sent off, 'something from our hearts is gone':

Each feels the bliss of all destroyed
And mourns the change — but each apart. [71]

The notion of a childhood Edenic unity, when speech did not have to struggle to communicate, and 'Peace . . . flowed from heart to heart . . . And gave us language to impart/The blissful thoughts itself had given', and writing was 'a web of sunny air', itself took its place in a realm of myth.

\*　　\*　　\*　　\*　　\*

*Jane Eyre* was Charlotte's answer to the autobiographical *Agnes Grey* with governess as heroine, and to the symbolic drama of *Wuthering Heights*. The young Brontës inherited the Romantic Agony context of a search for self-realisation culminating in an image of love and death fused together, and transformed it in different ways. Like Heathcliff's 'strange way of killing', the story of *Jane Eyre* may be seen in terms of a search for an image of creation within Jane's search for self-fulfilment and a home for her identity, a 'marriage'. Charlotte's and Emily's use of

165

Romantic content is similar, although at a deeper level their methods of portraying emotional states, and their ultimate conceptions of creativity, are as distinct as are the styles of their novels. Charlotte was disturbed and mystified by *Wuthering Heights*, as her comments about Emily as a 'theorist' who would not be 'seen in [her] full strength till [she] is seen as an essayist',[72] show; at the same time she found it an inspiring example. Emily achieves her negative-capability stance, fundamental to the novel's structure, by approaching her Romantic material through — initially — an alien and outcast viewpoint; Lockwood is not an outcast in the familiar Byronic sense but, more difficult for her to empathise with, a stumbling, innocent, worldly mind whose real passions are latent but unwoken and unrealised. Charlotte in *Jane Eyre* has an opposite but related way of disentangling herself from Angria and revising its familiar theme of the young girl confronting Zamorna and coming to know herself; she converts her peeping-Tom style narrator of the juvenilia, into the protagonist and heroine: one who, though frequently in the position of watching from an outcast, secluded position, is in fact a prime mover of events. In this way Charlotte takes responsibility for her visions through Jane; all the characters in an allegorical sense exist within Jane, embody aspects of her worldview and have some function in her progress towards independence and mastery. She begins the process in *The Professor* with Crimsworth having to 'work his way through life'; but the strength of that novel lies in its shrewd realistic character observation, whereas the moments which approach symbolism appear offkey and like undiluted Angria. Crimsworth has a tendency to monitor his progress in the terms of a novel ('Hunsden, you've only seen the title page of my happiness'); but his stilted self-consciousness is very different from Jane Eyre's structural function as narrator of her own 'autobiography'.

The fusion of the point of view of Jane as a child and Jane as narrator in the Gateshead section of *Jane Eyre*, marks a new way of writing in Charlotte. The older Jane watches her younger self watching; sees her in tableau-like pictures (as, framed within the window-seat), whilst she seeks, through books and pictures or through the outside world framed by the window, for means to express her inner state. The child Jane in her environment is suspect because she 'always looked as if she were watching somebody', 'sullen and sneaking', a 'precocious actress'; later Mrs Reed on her deathbed recollects 'her continual, unnatural watchings of one's movements', a sinister passivity from which she broke out in her true colours 'like something mad, or a fiend'. Charlotte's dual perspective dramatises the experiment she made very early on in 'Strange Events', when Charles Wellesley finds himself of miniature dimensions in the hands of his creator and doubts his own reality, on the lines of *Gulliver's Travels* (one of the child Jane's favourite books). Jane maps out her mind with the aid of Bewick's arctic 'death-white realms', Bessie's fairy tales and Gothic superstitions; becomes herself 'a picture of passion'; and then a type of ghost in the mirror of the Red Room, embodying aspects of all these as she watches herself:

> All looked colder and darker in that visionary hollow than in reality: and the strange little figure there gazing at me, with a white face and arms specking the gloom, and glittering eyes of fear moving where all else was still, had the effect of a real spirit: I thought it like one of the tiny phantoms, half fairy, half imp, Bessie's evening stories represented as coming out of lone, ferny dells in moors, and appearing before the eyes of belated travellers. (Ch.2)

It follows naturally, as an extension of this picture of her mind, that the next light flickering before her in the gloom should appear to bring her uncle's ghost, a 'herald of some coming vision from another world'. The vividness with which Jane imagines and watches not just others but herself, makes her appear 'unnatural', 'fiendish', artificial ('I abhor artifice' says Mrs Reed). In her nightmare of the Red Room are prefigured aspects of her future story — Bertha's visitation (her red visage and white veil), Jane a 'stranger' to herself in her wedding clothes in the mirror, herself as 'fairy' to Rochester, her sojourn in 'lone, ferny dells in moors' as a child of 'Nature'. She awakes from her species of death in this prophetic 'visionary hollow', in a kind of hellfire: 'a terrible red glare, crossed by thick black bars'. Then she has her outburst as 'something mad, or a fiend', after which the mature Jane as narrator explains to the reader: 'A ridge of lighted heath . . . would have been a meet emblem of

my mind when I accused and menaced Mrs Reed'; the older
Jane reinforces the emblematic quality of the young Jane's
visions. Her later adventures, unlikely by the standards of
actuality, are made aesthetically appropriate in the sense of
fulfilling her own picture of herself.

At Lowood, Jane learns self-containment in the context of
grotesque distorted pageantry and hypocrisy, introduced
through the figure of Mr Brocklehurst, a 'black pillar' with a
'carved mask' on top. The red curls of 'nature' are cut off and
the girls are literally labelled with placards of 'Slattern' etc.,
like figures in a primitive morality play. Even the 'good'
characters have some of this mask-like character — Miss
Temple (the house of true religion), Helen Burns whose image
is replaced fifteen years later by the gravestone pointing up-
wards with the imprint 'Resurgam', as if her stamp on Jane
had overcome Miss Scatcherd's. Jane, after initially standing
out by being placed on a stool and branded 'liar', learns that
this in itself is simply part of a show, irrelevant to her inner self,
for which the potential audience is 'hundreds of millions' of
people in the world, and beyond that 'Eternity'. She becomes
aware of the 'stores of knowledge' and 'secrets of nature'
wielded by Miss Temple and Helen Burns, and becomes
equipped with skills such as drawing which enable her to
express herself through mastering external figures — an instrument of power to fight the world. Apart from these external
skills and the art of self-concealment, the real Jane does not
appear but lies quiescent at Lowood, and she immediately
becomes restless when her temporary haven, Miss Temple,
departs to get married. She has become a lady in all external
respects; Bessie's farewell visit emphasizes Jane's credentials.
The Jane who identifies with Bessie's 'fairy tales' (herself living
a 'fairy tale' as she says ironically later), returns, when her
imagination strays out from Thornfield's upper window (the
station from whence the mysterious 'thrilling laugh' is heard at
intervals), dwelling upon 'bright visions', 'my heart heaved by
the exultant movement', opening 'my inward ear to a tale that
was never ended — a tale my imagination created'. Jane moves
out from Thornfield towards Hay Hill:

My ear too felt the flow of currents; in what dales and depths

168

I could not tell: but there were many hills beyond Hay, and doubtless many becks threading their passes. (Ch.12).

The 'heaving' heart mingles with the 'currents' felt in the air, to invite a 'tale of incident, fire and feeling' which accordingly materialises, as if in response to the intensity of Jane's wish, through the sound of Mr Rochester's horse approaching:

> A rude noise broke on these fine ripplings and whisperings, at once so far away and so clear: a positive tramp, tramp; a metallic clatter, which effaced the soft wave-wanderings; as, in a picture, the solid mass of a crag, or the rough boles of a great oak, drawn in dark and strong on the foreground, efface the aerial distance of azure hill, sunny horizon, and blended clouds, where tint melts into tint.

Jane enjoys the picture of her first impression of Mr Rochester and works to complete it via the emblem of the landscape; as with the vision in the Red Room (echoing Lockwood's dream and Catherine's delirium), this echoes the approach of Heathcliff's horse to the second Cathy, and the way in which the presence of Wuthering Heights is sometimes sensed from the open window of the Grange; but through a more image-conscious, picturesque, stagey technique. Jane's wishful 'wanderings' (the tints of 'aerial distance', a pun on her name) take a new definite imprint — dark and rough Rochester with his horse and dog; the 'oak' prefiguring the 'chestnut tree' later associated with him. Jane deliberately fixes the moment 'as, in a picture'; just as shortly, Rochester's face becomes 'a new picture introduced to the gallery of memory'. Meanwhile the horse and dog approaching are referred to repeatedly as the 'Gytrash' of Bessie's nursery stories, and retain their supernatural or fairy significance simultaneously with their everyday one:

> It was exactly one mask of Bessie's Gytrash, — a lion-like creature with long hair and a huge head: it passed me, however, quietly enough; not staying to look up, with strange pretercanine eyes, in my face, as I half expected it would.

The negative in 'not staying' does not deny the emotional intensity evoked by the supernatural, and is typical of

169

Charlotte's method throughout *Jane Eyre* — described by R. Heilman as 'new Gothic'.[59] (Emily's use of Gothic and anti-Gothic, romance and anti-romance is less easily definable, without the delight in stylistic artifice). As in *Wuthering Heights*, the dog is the first sealer of relationship; Jane returns to Thornfield after her expanded visions (like the moon 'aspiring to the zenith, midnight dark in its fathomless depth and measureless distance'), 'recalled to earth' as she thinks, only to encounter instead of Mrs Fairfax, the dog sitting on the rug, and instinctively to pronounce its name, thereby cementing her unconscious recognition of Rochester.

From this point the Thornfield section of the book is taken up with Jane and Rochester's interaction, in terms of reading, representing, picturing each other, always with the 'mystery' of the ghost-that-is-not-a-ghost intensifying in the background, symbolic of an emotional blockade between them. Initially Jane and Rochester carry on the 'fairy tale' type of private language in front of Mrs Fairfax, who — as they carry on about the 'men in green' and Jane 'bewitching his horse' — 'seemed wondering what kind of talk this was'. Mr Rochester dramatises his 'destiny' as an 'old hag' writing 'lurid hieroglyphics all along the house-front' (Ch.15), prefiguring Bertha and the hieroglyphics of the fire; and enacts it by means of the house-party charade with Miss Ingram and the gipsy 'masquerade', all designed to test and read Jane through the presentation of 'hags' or false women. In the context of 'goblin-laughter' and 'demoniac laughs' from the attack, Jane herself is a 'witch', 'sorceress' and 'fairy', and later a 'provoking puppet', whose mission is to redeem him and 'do him good'. Jane's lurid hieroglyphics are displayed in her gruesome paintings, evidence of — Rochester suspects — 'a kind of artist's dreamland' (Jane, in unconscious vanity, confides: 'While he is so occupied I will tell you, reader, ... that they are nothing wonderful' [Ch.13].) Jane sees Rochester as a picture, with 'excellent materials in him', albeit 'spoiled and tangled', and regards him as her artifact. She sketches her own 'real' and Blanche's (imaginary) face to hold before her as examples; as later, back at Gateshead Hall, she sketches Rochester's to have a 'friend' for company, with a strange confidence in art as direct representation. (Anne and Charlotte both regard pictures as explanations; Emily in

*Wuthering Heights* distrusts portraits as representations; Heathcliff's seizure of the portrait and locket of Catherine does not provide him with the key to her nature, nor does it deprive her daughter of that key.) Rochester, in testing Jane through the flamboyant hieroglyphics of charade, gipsy-impersonation, fire and blood, during which she is apparently a passive observer and helper, falls into her moulding hands: 'lean on me, sir'. She is his 'prop and guide' at the end, as at the end of the gipsy sequence after the 'blow' of Mason, and as she was initially when she 'felled his horse'. As Jane says of the portrait of him which she conjures up at Gateshead,

> Good! But not quite the thing . . . There! I had a friend's face under my gaze, and what did it signify that those young ladies turned their backs on me? (Ch.21).

The image of Rochester is in effect always 'under her gaze'; in a sense the houseparty charade is as much her invention as his; its unreality (reading like pure Angria) is part of its dramatic effect — the dowagers 'like a pair of magnified puppets', the crowd 'shapes in a magic lantern . . . mere shadows of human forms and not the actual substance'. Through it Charlotte places and exorcises her Roe Head hallucinations. Blanche Ingram serves to magnify and make artificial Jane's own attitude to Rochester as Byronic hero with his 'Corsair'-like attractions: 'a man is nothing without a spice of the devil in him'; she admires him 'wild, fierce, a bandit hero'. Jane confesses to Rochester (as gipsy) that they 'seem telling a tale' — the usual tale of courtship which 'promises to end in the same catastrophe — marriage'. The houseparty version of the courtship-marriage theme serves both as grotesque unreal parody of the Jane-Rochester romance taking place under the shelter of its disguise; and also as a flamboyant, artificial portrayal of that romance, much as the Gothic and anti-Gothic elements support one another. Jane's 'artist's daydream' is extended to the gipsy pageant: the 'strange talk . . . wrapped me in a kind of dream':

> I got involved in a web of mystification; and wondered what unseen spirit had been sitting for weeks by my heart watching its workings and taking record of every pulse. (Ch.19).

Jane describes the 'unseen spirit' Rochester in the same terms as

later the mad Bertha, who has always been close to her (symbolically, her room is above Jane's, and Jane has always been
the nearest to her 'laugh'), and who is also an unseen spirit
observing her progress towards marriage. Through the web of
mystification spun around themselves they are, as Rochester
says, 'coming to reality'.

The 'mystery' of Thornfield — its Gothic pageantry, its lurid
hieroglyphics — is thus worked in as an inseparable aspect of
Jane's and Rochester's relationship; she confesses she thought
the gipsy was Grace Poole, 'that living enigma, that mystery of
mysteries', the key to Mr Rochester's secret:

> What crime was this, that lived incarnate in this sequestered
> mansion, and could neither be expelled nor subdued by the
> owner? What mystery, that broke out, now in fire and now in
> blood, at the deadest hours of night? What creature was it,
> that, masked in an ordinary woman's face and shape, uttered
> the voice, now of a mocking demon, and anon of a carrion-
> seeking bird of prey? (Ch.20)

All forms part of the wider picture of Mr Rochester which Jane
has under her gaze, whilst she is simultaneously watching and
being watched: her fate, like Bertha's, being carried between
Heathcliff-like Rochester and Edgar Linton-like Mr Mason
('the contrast ... between a sleek gander and a fierce falcon'),
whose influence in a worldly marriage requires recognition. At
this point Jane finally disposes of her Gateshead past, and turns
her back on the young ladies who had turned their backs on her,
as both constituting false approaches to art or life. Georgiana's
chatter makes up 'a volume of a novel of fashionable life'; Eliza
caricatures an 'independent being', being a 'rigid formalist'
aiming at 'a system which will make [one] independent of all
efforts, and all wills, but [one's] own' (Ch.21). Jane is satisfied
that her own method of portraiture is more realistic. At the same
time the Ingrams disappear from her life like false decoys, and
she concentrates on the 'mystery' of Rochester when she returns
to renew her relationship with him; he is sitting on a stile
awaiting her in a reversal of their original positions of meeting
— 'Well, he is not a ghost'. The 'ring of golden peace', the
'splendid midsummer' which initially enshrines the reunited
Thornfield family (Adèle has her stepmother, Mrs Fairfax her

stepdaughter), is broken once their marriage is decided upon and they face each other 'as if both had passed through the grave — equal — at God's feet':

> But what had befallen the night? The moon was not yet set, and we were all in shadow: I could scarcely see my master's face, near as I was. And what ailed the chestnut tree? It writhed and groaned; while wind roared in the laurel walk, and came sweeping over us. (Ch.23)

The weather and pageant of nature take over from the guests' dressing-up games as objective correlatives for Jane's state of mind, with deliberate and explicit artifice: the famous lightning-struck chestnut tree literally standing for the lovers, and then for the divided and struck-down Rochester. The eclipse in nature occurs as ominous warning that Rochester 'stood as an eclipse' between Jane and God, whom she could not longer see after making an 'idol' of his 'creature'. Rochester's Angrian declamations ('It will atone — it will atone') contrast strongly with Heathcliff's evolution of a symbolic poetic language of self-analysis at points of crisis. Charlotte, unlike Emily, uses nature as a stage-set, itself a kind of dressing-up, a melodramatic declamation, inseparable from the charades and later from the surreal dreams which appear to Jane. Suspense is created during the build-up to the false marriage by these tokens, which as it were declare the existence of Bertha Mason as more than an external impediment (it is not just the 'law' which keeps them apart, as George Eliot complained). [74] Jane's dream of carrying the phantom child up to the battlements and falling off (prefiguring Bertha's leap) is corroborated by the tangible evidence of the ripped veil; her vision of Bertha wearing the veil is another expression of feeling herself a 'stranger' in the mirror when wearing the veil herself; Adele is the 'emblem of my past life' like the child with whom she tumbles from the roof; the Red Room imagery, with sexual connotations is explicitly recalled during Bertha's visitation and Jane's vision of a moon-mother who parts the clouds as Bertha split the veil:

> The light that long ago had struck me into syncope, recalled in this vision, seemed glidingly to mount the wall, and tremblingly to pause in the centre of the obscured ceiling . . .

the gleam was such as the moon imparts to vapours she is about to sever. I watched her come — watched with the strangest anticipation; as though some word of doom were to be written on her disk. She broke forth as never moon yet burst from cloud; a hand first penetrated the sable folds and waved them away . . . (Ch.27)

Jane has other aspects of her orphan fairy-tale existence to live through before union with, or possession of, Rochester; her 'mother' bids her to flee. She needs a new picture of herself, drawn from sources other than the lurid hieroglyphics of Thornfield, which has already become a mélange of fire, blood, charred beams and eyebrows, tumbled battlements. She goes 'upon the moors where the grey rocks are piled', following Bessie's nursery song about the orphan child: becoming a child of the 'universal mother', 'Mother Nature', and then following the guiding light (which proves not to be an 'ignis fatuus') to Marsh End. Parting the foliage and looking through the window, Jane sees clearly the kind of relatives she wants, the kind of picture she wishes to become a part of:

I could see all within. I could see clearly a room with a sanded floor, clean scoured . . . This scene was as silent as if all the figures had been shadows, and the fire-lit apartment a picture: (Ch.28)

The window is Jane's new mirror, the apartment herself clean scoured; she insists to her new friends that she was 'free from culpability . . . no blame attached to me' (and hers is the only reference-point in the novel, endorsed by Charlotte; no-one is in a position to disagree). Her 'broken idol and lost elysium' are stored away in memory, as it were in her portfolio, becoming the sort of picture on which she is not at present engaged. The attitudes in *Jane Eyre* do not so much develop as oscillate, until a complete picture has been formed of all the chambers in Jane's mind. The idealised vision of the three sisters (or two sisters and cousin) is as much a romance as that with Rochester: 'Thought fitted thought, opinion met opinion; we coincided, in short, perfectly' (words echoed in Anne's poem of May 11 1846). Rosamund Oliver finds her a 'lusus naturae' as a village schoolmistress; 'She was sure my previous history, if known, would make a delightful romance'. In her 'breezy mountain nook in the healthy heart of England', Jane revises the place of her 'delightful romance' in her history. The aspect of herself with whom she meets and clashes is St John (who, as Eyre Rivers, calls himself her namesake). Now it is she, not Rochester, who appears mysterious: in St John's eyes, hiding a guilty secret liable to lead her to hell. (The nature of mystery, of the unknown, is very different in *Jane Eyre* and *Wuthering Heights*; Charlotte's is based on the Gothic and requires eventual revealing; whereas no suspense is drawn from Heathcliff's time in the world or other unknown factors, because his mystery cannot be explained by any hidden secret).

Jane uses St John to sharpen her sense of blamelessness, and to strengthen her sense of religious mission with regard to Rochester, by contrasting it explicitly with St John's mission and his desire to make her part of *his* picture of a romantic life, converting the heathen in India. Although she clashes with St John, she draws more upon the similarity in their natures, despite calling his 'antagonistic to my own'. St John's discovery of her name is symbolic; he tears it from the dogeared sheet of paper she was using to protect her drawing of Rosamund Oliver. Jane had felt a 'thrill of artist-delight at copying from so perfect and so radiant a model' (another of her romances); but she is thwarted in her attempts to thereby defuse St John and the harm he might do to herself; he refuses both a copy of the picture and her advice 'take to yourself the original at once'. The battle between Jane and St John has begun: she is 'beset' by him, she says, as intensely as by Rochester; she 'stamps' and 'burns' words on his 'tenacious surface'. She is on the point of losing (which constitutes a type of death, prefiguring an actual death from the Indian climate), until by 'an inspiration' she recognises how she can convert his example to another usage. Her offering of Rosamund's picture fails to appease him; so does her 'emblem' about her fire dissolving his ice; she has become subject to him ever since the acknowledgement of their blood-relationship. (Jane is by nature, as well as fortune, an orphan; all kinship other than that of 'perfect concord' poses a threat such that she must either conquer or be conquered.) The saintly St John threatens to kill her as did the boorish John Reed. He leads her to the head of Moor Glen for the final fight — where

175

'wild' becomes 'savage' and 'fresh' becomes 'frowning'; where the hills enclose the human figures menacingly and claustrophobically:

> ... we reached the first stragglers of a battalion of rocks, guarding a sort of pass, beyond which the beck rushed down a waterfall, and where still, a little further, the mountain shook off turf and flower, had only heath for a raiment, and crag for gem — where it exaggerated the wild to the savage, and exchanged the fresh for the frowning — where it guarded the forlorn hope of solitude, and a last refuge for silence. (Ch.34)

The landscape, with its 'last refuge' and 'battalion of rocks', figures their fight to the death; Jane is tempted to follow the path of the waterfall and 'rush down the torrent of his will into the gulf of his existence, and there lose my own'; whilst his displeasure is couched in terms of an avalanche beginning to crash down on her head ('The avalanche had shaken ... but did not yet crash down'): 'You will kill me ... you are killing me now'. The vision of their marriage is a kind of death, an apocalypse. St John 'seemed in communion with the genius of the haunt ... with his eye he bade farewell to something'; the landscape prefigures for him the time 'when another slumber overcomes me — on the shore of a darker stream'. Jane is on the point of succumbing to his exaggerated, melodramatic, apocalyptic imagery when (as if vibrating in resonance with the heightened Thornfield imagery), she hears her inspired voice:

> I stood motionless under my hierophant's touch ... All was changing utterly, with a sudden sweep. Religion called — Angels beckoned — God commanded — life rolled together like a scroll — death's gates opening, showing eternity beyond ... (Ch.35)

Jane, 'more excited' than ever before, demands of Heaven to 'show me the path'; as always, the melodramatic build-up is not negated or discarded but simply changes course; the impression created is that Heaven calls 'Jane! Jane! Jane!' in 'the voice of a human being — that of Edward Fairfax Rochester'. Jane in a sense accepts St John's vision of creativity but transfers its object, becoming sure that her mission is to rescue Rochester, that she can 'accomplish the will of Heaven, when once that will is distinctly known to me'. She finds a way of using St John's imagery but with herself as mistress of the field: 'It was *my* time to assume ascendancy. My powers were in play, and in force . . . I seemed to penetrate very near a Mighty Spirit':

> The wondrous shock of feeling had come like the earthquake which shook the foundations of Paul and Silas's prison; it had opened the doors of the soul's cell, and loosed its bands — it had wakened it out of its sleep, whence it sprang trembling, listening, aghast; then vibrated thrice a cry on my startled ear . . .

Jane's moment of recognition — of her mission, her identity, her new kind of union with Rochester — foreshadows the description of the purgatorial conflagration of Thornfield which she is soon to hear: the cell whence Bertha and Rochester spring, the earthquake which leaves Rochester mutilated like the chestnut tree, whilst recognising 'the hand of God in my doom'. Rochester's final home, and the home of the revised Jane-Rochester union, is a cross between a leafy church and a classic temple; she walks toward Ferndean down its 'forest aisle' (a revision of the abortive Thornfield church marriage), and he emerges to her view in the midst of an 'amphitheatre of trees' (Ch.37). She undertakes to 'rehumanise' him with his 'shaggy black mane' and 'eagle's features': an undertaking supported by terms echoing the annunciation and coming of Christ ('I kept these things then, and pondered them in my heart'), and not so different from the language describing the fulfilment of St John's mission ('My Master has forewarned me . . . Surely I come quickly!') which provides the novel's closing paragraph. Jane Eyre succeeds in effect in bringing both her lovers within the circumference of the completed picture of herself; as with Diana and Mary, the ultimate picture is of 'perfect concord': 'We talk, I believe, all day long'; the orphan has created her own relatives, offshoots of herself, with no jarring elements, tempering romance with reality. The master-servant tension inherent in all Charlotte's descriptions of creativity is not resolved, but reversed; Jane becomes the master of her world after testing her powers in a succession of fights or temptations; just as through her heroine, Charlotte in a series of vivid

177

tableaux demarcates the reaches of her art, and demonstrates the tempering marriage of Angrian romance with Christian morality which in her juvenilia had always required separate opposing voices. Rochester is the Byronic hero 'redeemed', not pursuing Heathcliff's 'arrow-straight course to perdition' which so horrified Charlotte.

Charlotte's ultimate image of creation, involving the mutilation of Rochester, is essentially different though superficially similar to Heathcliff's 'strange way of killing'. Her narrative method is one in which she keeps hold of the reins by virtue of circumscribing her subject's universe: the elder mature Jane as narrator, keeps a watchful eye on the evolution of her younger self. Her honesty is of the 'surveillante' type which she portrayed so acutely in Mlle. Reuter and Mme. Beck: no hidden corners of herself can escape uncorrected and unartificed; all aspects are justly placed, rewarded or punished, within the bounds of an individual consciousness — the artist as God. The tensions involved in her self-analysis are simple; she is victorious in her struggle against her own innate tendency to 'sink into a bathos of sentiment' (in Jane's words) at the expense of art. Charlotte's relation to her reader is a parallel one, slightly teasing and manipulative; through her use of Gothic and anti-Gothic she plays with the reader like Jane with Rochester in terms of the creation of suspense, what she does and does not let him know about the 'mystery' of Thornfield; her revelations are given in the context of a master and servant relationship. Her apostrophes to the reader are not excisable or incidental; they are part of her total aesthetic approach, in which she organises his viewpoint, settles or unsettles him, prepares him for the picture to follow (as, most strikingly, in the re-approach to Thornfield as a ruin). In *Jane Eyre*, as opposed to *Wuthering Heights*, the reader is left satisfied rather than troubled; because the supervising Charlotte (not the uncomfortable Lockwood) becomes his 'prop and guide' as Jane does Rochester's. The harmonious, in the sense of conflict-free, ending is very different from Emily's more musical harmony, which reverberates onwards with a sense of life continuing to develop on many levels; her ghosts live, whereas Bertha Mason is stone dead. Charlotte and Emily have different implicit ideas of aesthetics, as they have different notions of morality or the evocation of the inner life; in both, aesthetics and spirituality are inextricable. Thus Charlotte's method of presenting objective correlatives through a magnificent stream of display, contrasts with Emily's less static evocation of emotion, which finds its very existence outside and all around the characters (Forster's 'thunder clouds'), not merely a comparison or mirror for the thing itself. Charlotte like her characters believes in art as representation, from which follows the primitive idea that once you've got someone's image ('under her gaze' like Jane with Rochester), they are in your power. Emily sets up a network of tensions as opposed to a successive series of tableaux, thereby relaxing her previous omnipotent control over her imaginary world; fixed images are, for her, the suspect beguiling of the 'spectre of a hope'. She never commits herself to a preconceived form or moral judgement. She transcends the idea of images having a fixed significance, a growth-stopping power. Her entire landscape is a mental space, not a pageant of objective correlatives, traversing the 'gulph' between mortality and eternity which is the constant theme of her poetry; metaphor rather than a series of similes. There is no drama between the two Janes of *Jane Eyre* — the actor-protagonist, and the artist-narrator who has reached a smooth plateau in her existence, and is now shaping her childhood and adolescence in retrospect; whereas the first and second Catherines are in continuous unconscious communication over two levels of existence, with themselves and with Heathcliff, in the process of writing another story altogether which is 'above and beyond' the life-picture of either of them separately. Charlotte conforms essentially to the revenge-tragedy pattern, though she makes it a revenge comedy; Emily reverses it altogether through a different artistic method, which allows for the evolution of a dynamic, two-generation image of creativity, complex rather than simple.

# IV
# EMILY BRONTË AND THE ROMANTIC SPIRIT OF CREATION

# Introduction

The following sketches of Emily Brontë's relation to four of the great Romantic poets — Wordsworth, Shelley, Byron and Coleridge — are not studies of influence in the usual straightforward sense. They are not part of an investigation into the 'sources' of *Wuthering Heights*. They are, however, concerned with deep affinities (and divisions) in the creative spirit. Emily Brontë was in many ways a child of the Romantic movement. *Wuthering Heights* is as much a Romantic poem as an early Victorian novel; it could be said to represent the Romantic version of the Shakespearian drama which all the Romantic poets wanted to convert into a genre of their age. Apart from Shakespeare, whose influence is so fundamental that it is always acknowledged rather than analysed, sources for *Wuthering Heights* are generally sought in Romantic and Gothic prose fiction ('read Scott alone', recommended Charlotte to Ellen Nussey, in relation to novels.)[1] Parallels with Scott and Hoffmann, however, tend inevitably to be of a superficial and literal-minded nature, and do not illumine, except negatively by contrast, the quality of Emily Brontë's poetic creative spirit. It is very difficult to determine precisely what Emily Brontë had read. Certainly internal evidence indicates that she was influenced by all these four poets, in differing ways. Byron, for example, was the Brontës' idol from childhood, so his influence appears at different levels of complexity. The influence of Coleridge is more elusive and less evident on the surface, but the deep metaphysical parallels are stronger. This might apply also to Blake, though he is not discussed here. In comparing Emily Brontë's Romantic spirit to that of some of her great predecessors, I am not searching for an ultimate unifying generalisation, although the Romantic-agony association of creation with 'a strange way of killing' is obvious, as an organising metaphor current in the age. Rather, I have emphasised primarily the parallel concern of Emily Brontë and each individual poet, with the developing idea or spirit of creation which is manifest in the structure of their work.

# 1    Emily Brontë and Wordsworth

Wordsworth was by Emily Brontë's time the grand old man of the Romantic movement; Branwell wrote to him as such for advice (though he did not receive any); and versions of the *Lyrical Ballads* were lisped in nurseries and drawing-rooms. The influence of the early Wordsworth permeates Emily's work, sometimes — despite their total difference in character and principles — on the lines of Heathcliff and Catherine, 'more myself than I am'. Wordsworth's character led him always towards enshrining the vision or the poetic principle in a search for permanence, making poetry (though in fact a present experience) into a past experience, thereby ultimately losing it; Emily's whole cast of mind and inner struggles led her into the principle of change and the vision of futurity. But before these differences of character take over, during the moments of poetic reverie or 'mysticism' or reception of vision through a certain use of nature, the poetic process in both has an essential similarity. Their identification with nature as an initial stage in poetry, is equivalent; Wordsworth's Vale, Emily's Moor is the landscape of their being, with no sense of a gap for simile or symbol or the pathetic fallacy. As Charlotte said of Emily, her native hills were not a 'spectacle', but 'what she lived in, and by';[2] and as Wordsworth of Michael, 'these hills/ Which were his living Being, even more/ Than his own blood'.

Michael is Wordsworth's image of the essential poet, who — once his younger self (his son) has left and been corrupted by city values — remains a part-ruined but permanent aspect of nature like his unfinished sheepfold, the pile of rocks by Greenhead Ghyll, a record for future poets 'who among these hills/ Will be my second self when I am gone', as Wordsworth describes his own tale. Despite the difference in development between this tale, for example, and *Wuthering Heights* with its final picture of rocky tombs sinking into the landscape, the initial setting for a poetic experience has a similarity. Wordsworth leads the reader (the apprentice poet?) out of the 'public way' to a hidden valley with its monument to passion:

The mountains have all open'd out themselves,
And made a hidden valley of their own.
No habitation there is seen; but such
As journey thither find themselves alone
With a few sheep, with rocks and stones, and kites
That overhead are sailing in the sky,
It is in truth an utter solitude.[3]

Lockwood, removing himself from the stir of society to the moorland valley detached from Gimmerton, is as much a follower of Wordsworth as of Byron or the romantic novelists, in his quest for the reality and poetry beyond fiction. Emily Brontë, like Wordsworth, has this quality of making the landscape (and the houses and rustic objects grown into it) significant or real in an emotional sense, pregnant with possibility, whilst apparently simply transferring naked objects to paper (and so arousing confusion with being everyday or common perception; a confusion aggravated by Wordsworth's own theoretical principles). In both poets, Nature *is* The Dream; with human beings, animals, inanimate aspects all existing on interchangeable levels and emanating the 'spirit' that 'rolls through all things'. Wordsworth's Leech-Gatherer (in 'Resolution and Independence') emerges out of a barren moor 'unawares', when the poet is ready to receive his image and significance, like a 'huge Stone' lying on an 'eminence':

So that it seems a thing endued with sense:
Like a Sea-beast crawled forth, which on a shelf
Of rock or sand reposeth, there to sun itself.

He is 'not all alive nor dead,/ Nor all asleep'; the sense of man as landscape, both familiar and alien, emerging from it and fading back into it, is also in *Wuthering Heights*: as when Heathcliff appears with inevitability from the 'frowning Nab', in response to a spiritual arrangement.

The figure of the Child, like the Old Man (in Emily Brontë it is only the Child), is associated with an intensifying of identity through nature, a point of interchangeability with nature which is in a sense a kind of death, but is also part of an image of creation. In the 'Lucy' ballads Lucy, a 'solitary Child' dwelling 'on a wide Moor', is really part of the moor: 'A violet by a mossy

stone/ Half-hidden from the Eye', a 'Thing' growing 'Beside a
human door' rather than within humanity. 'She seemed a thing
that could not feel / The touch of earthly years'; she becomes
party to Nature's secrets and is formed by them: 'hers the silence
and the calm/ Of mute insensate things'. Lucy's 'death' is an
inevitable part of her whole history from the beginning, not just
an accidental termination, but an aspect of her significance for
the poet's poetry; it is coincidental with the 'sealing' of his spirit
in a poetic dream, when he as well as she loses motion and force:

> No motion has she now, no force;
>   She neither hears nor sees,
> Roll'd round in earth's diurnal course
>   With rocks and stones and trees!

As in 'Tintern Abbey', nature's 'forms of beauty . . . felt in the
blood, and felt along the heart' as the landscape is impressed
upon him, undergo a transformation once they are internalised:

> And even the motion of our human blood
> Almost suspended, we are laid asleep
> In body, and become a living soul . . .

The awakened blood is 'suspended' in a kind of death in order
to 'see into the life of things'. Emily's 'little and a lone green
lane' of home, opens out to

> A distant, dreamy, dim blue chain
> Of mountains circling every side;
>
> A heaven so clear, an earth so calm,
> So sweet, so soft, so hushed an air
> And, deepening still the dream-like charm,
> Wild moor-sheep feeding everywhere — (H.92)

The state of dreamlike trance, absorption into nature, forms the
basis later for the visionary leap in 'He comes with western
winds', which begins with 'a hush of peace . . . unuttered
harmony/ That I could never dream till earth was lost to me'. In
both poets the intensification of 'earth' leads to a loss or death of
earth simultaneously, imaging a new reality; although it is only
the calm reverie which Emily Brontë shares with Wordsworth,
not her desire to 'burst the fetters and break the bars', to

participate in the Tempest and leap outwards or forwards into infinity and eternity.

*The Prelude* as a whole, was not published during Emily Brontë's lifetime, although certain key, representative passages were:[4] enough to indicate the nature of the heart of Wordsworth's creative experience (and interweaving with the *Lyrical Ballads* and the *Poems* of 1807). It does not describe the growth of an individual mind so much as present a stream of consciousness with moments of revelation pressed out of it ('spots of time'), in which the Boy or youth's unthinking immersion in action is suddenly suspended and the energy instantaneously converted into contemplation, based on the sensuous power of the preceding passage. As in the sonnet 'On Westminster Bridge', a type of death takes place in which mind and nature are fused. Thus, the boy birdnesting finds himself 'suspended by the blast'

> When on the perilous ridge I hung alone
> With what strange utterance did the loud dry wind
> Blow through my ears! The sky seemed not sky
> Of earth, and with what motion mov'd the clouds! (Bk.1)

The 'perilous ridge' represents a mental balancing-point, a turning of experience from without to within, similar to the way nature becomes super-nature in Emily Brontë, and the earth 'instinct with spirit' speaks with its 'myriad voices'. During the boat-stealing, the Cliff

> Rose up between me and the stars, and still
> With measured motion, like a living thing
> Strode after me. (Bk.1)

— as do aspects of nature form into godlike spirits in Emily Brontë's poetry ('forerunners of a sterner power ... Heralds of me'), or pillars and rocks become apparitions in *Wuthering Heights*. During the skating episode, the vivid and semi-earthly sounds (the pack 'bellowing', the precipices ringing aloud, the crag tinkling like iron, the hills sending 'an alien sound of melancholy'), together with the shadowy gradations of the light, are suddenly negated: or rather their essence is channelled into a reversed perspective, as the earth wheels and rolls round him, leaving him 'tranquil as a dreamless sleep'; the sudden reversal

187

of perspective between the boy and the earth again results in the paradoxical sense of perceiving a deeper motion through becoming motionless. Again, after shouting and making 'all the mountains ring',

> the calm
> And dead still water lay upon my mind
> Even with a weight of pleasure, and the sky
> Never before so beautiful, sank down
> Into my heart, and held me like a dream. (Bk.2)

This literal identity of the mind and nature, dispensing with all rhetorical figures and symbols, is the essence of Wordsworth's poetic originality; the sky enters his heart, without any hint of personification; his mind is impressed and given shape ('held') by the weight of the 'dead still water' which is a 'dream'. His mind is shaped to the precise limits of the visionary experience, becoming the earth beneath the lake and then the lake beneath the sky. Emily Brontë has something of this quality in *Wuthering Heights*; though less in her poetry. Her version is Heathcliff 'sleeping the last sleep by that sleeper, my heart stopped and my cheek frozen against hers': a frozen movement which pairs with a ghostly walking, paradoxically dead and alive. The spirit rolling through all things and felt along the blood, is only captured and known through a state of suspension, a stillness founded on a heart-beat. This central image of receptive reverie is expanded in the Winander Boy passage, being a miniature allegory of poetic process: beginning with 'mimic hootings' in imitation of the owls, nature's musicians, and building up to a cacophany of 'long halloos and screams and echoes loud'. Suddenly this imitation poetry is stopped dead and the boy is 'mock'd' by the ensuing deep silence:

> Then sometimes, in that silence, while he hung
> Listening, a gentle shock of mild surprise
> Has carried far into his heart the voice
> Of mountain torrents; or the visible scene
> Would enter unawares into his mind
> With all its solemn imagery, its rocks,
> Its woods, and that uncertain Heaven, receiv'd
> Into the bosom of the steady Lake. (Bk.5)

The characteristic sense of depth is expanded by the sense of distance as the 'voice' of flowing water is carried 'far into his heart' (not the voice coming from far: the internal distance expands to meet the external distance); again in contrast to deliberate intent, the boy's 'mind' is occupied 'unawares' by a different kind of poetry — the solemn imagery, the restless 'uncertain' clouds, gathered deep into the all-containing all-reflecting 'steady Lake'. Despite all differences in the foregoing dramas, there is a similar quality of a peace deeper than any disturbance or tempest, which holds Lockwood like a dream, in the last paragraph of *Wuthering Heights* 'under that benign sky', with the vibrating moths and harebells (the 'imagery' of a past 'concourse wild'), governed by the concept of a 'sleep' below the earth like the deep bosom of the Lake.

Wordsworth characteristically uses the term 'haunted' to describe nature's effect upon him. In 'Tintern Abbey' the 'sounding cataract/ Haunted me like a passion'; in *The Prelude*, nature's 'presences' 'haunt' his boyish sports; these presences or spirits impose themselves 'as with slacken'd step we breath'd/ Along the sides of the steep hills', as if nature's body as well as mind (in the terms of his myth) were an extension of his own. Nature in Wordsworth, as in Emily Brontë, has an integral element of the supernatural or spiritual, so instinctively at home that it needs no apology or explanation. He does not offer nature objectively, any more than his language is really that of everyday rural parlance, or than his 'childhood' is an actual condition, but rather as an image of a poetic state.

> I would stand,
> Beneath some rock, listening to sounds that are
> The ghostly language of the ancient earth
> Or make their abode in distant winds.
> Thence did I drink the visionary power. (Bk. 2)

The moment this 'nature' enters within the confines of his mind-body, or that mind-body changes shape in order to accommodate nature in the shape of a dream, it becomes 'spirit' or 'infinitude', 'the types and symbols of Eternity':

> in such visitings
> Of awful promise, when the light of sense
> Goes out in flashes that have shewn to us
> The invisible world . . . (Bk. 6)

The invisible word is the 'harbour' of man's spirit, the steady Lake of his mind: 'our home/ Is with infinitude, and only there'. This recognition, however, immediately interposes a gap between man and nature, separating the adhesive relationship of instinctive mystical oneness. In Emily Brontë the theme of the spirit's affinity yet distance from the Heavenly Earth has long been introduced, though she does not dramatise it until *Wuthering Heights*: Wordsworth, towards the end of *The Prelude*, writes: 'I seemed about this period to have a sight/ Of a new world', and he writes the Immortality Ode in response (in Emily Brontë's time, his most controversial poem); where the 'new world' appears in his own version of the ancient myth of the soul's pre-existence.

Unlike a later ode ('Composed upon an Evening of Extra-ordinary Splendour and Beauty'), which refers back to the 'light/ Full early lost, and fruitlessly deplored', the 'Intimations of Immortality from Recollections of Early Childhood' expresses a present experience, in the sense of a sudden new understanding of his poetic path so far; it enshrines a creative principle whilst leaving the nature of future poetry ambiguous; like the boy in *The Prelude*, he hangs on a 'perilous ridge'. Like Emily Brontë's 'No coward soul', it is a statement of faith in poetry, immortality, reality; and the myth of different existences within one soul adds a new potentially dramatic dimension to his poetry (albeit a drama which Wordsworth never took up). The poet begins with a sense of separation from nature — not the 'ghostly language of the ancient earth' type of nature, but the innocent, unthinking relationship in which 'May' means 'joy', every Beast keeps holiday and all creatures apart from himself appear 'blessed' and unified in spirit: 'To me alone there came a thought of grief'. He 'wrongs' 'the season'; but his repeated sense of the loss of 'glory' begins to suggest that the kind of glory he means is not present in the season wherever he looks: 'The things which I have seen I now can see no more'; 'there hath pass'd away a glory from the earth';

Whither is fled the visionary gleam?
Where is it now, the glory and the dream?

Our birth is but a sleep and a forgetting;
The Soul that rises with us, our life's Star,
    Hath had elsewhere its setting,
      And cometh from afar;

The essential glory of the soul belongs to another realm of existence, nothing to do with birds singing and lambs bounding; it is the soul trailing clouds of glory which apparels the earth in celestial light. Indeed Nature, 'the homely Nurse', like everything else earthly, conspires to make her 'Foster-child, her inmate Man/ Forget the glories he hath known' and accustom himself to poor substitutes for creativity without even realising that he is entombed within a 'prison house'. The Child as 'little actor' cons his part to fit in with what is expected of him 'As if his whole vocation/ Were endless imitation' — where imitation contrasts with original or real creative response. Yet the Child itself (symbolising the growing Poet) is deceptive in appearance, having a foot in both worlds, its 'exterior semblance' belying its 'Soul's immensity': in terms of insight, it is 'best Philosopher' and 'Eye among the blind',

> That, deaf and silent, read'st the eternal deep,
> Haunted for ever by the eternal mind,
> . . .
> Thou, over whom thy Immortality
> Broods like the Day, a Master o'er a Slave,
> A Presence which is not to be put by . . .

The two aspects of the Child are for the first time separated by Wordsworth, like two potential paths for the poet: the weight of worldliness, imitation, acting, and custom is heavy — 'Heavy as frost, and deep almost as life!' (like Emily's 'Cold in the earth, and the deep snow piled above thee!'): a kind of depth which reminds but contrasts with his characteristic images of visionary experience. But the power of the 'Eye among the blind' as a living function, reading the eternal deep and haunted by brooding presences, is greater; the lines are echoed by Emily Brontë in

> So surely anchored on
> The steadfast rock of Immortality
> . . .
> Thy spirit animates eternal years
> Pervades and broods above
> . . .
> Every existence would exist in thee

— she who describes her God of Visions as 'My slave, my

comrade, and my King'. Wordsworth then differentiates more specifically the 'simple creed of childhood' from the visionary gleam which has now become more complex: 'shadowy recollections' still 'a master light of all our seeing'. He acknowledges a sense of disorientation, the 'Blank misgivings of a Creature/ Moving about in worlds not realiz'd', which is different from his characteristic moods of 'despondency' and flatness (as in 'Resolution and Independence'), because it gives a sense of worlds yet to become 'realised', a new dimension to poetry. The Child is the poetic principle within mankind, bearing 'something that doth live', the potential poetic link with 'that immortal sea/ Which brought us hither':

>            Uphold us, cherish us, and make
> Our noisy years seem moments in the being
> Of the eternal Silence . . .
>
>            Though inland far we be,
> Our Souls have sight of that immortal sea . . .

The imagery is of *The Prelude*, where presences of nature make the 'surface of the universal earth' 'Work like a sea', alive with passion; yet, as in all the moments of vision, the animation is stilled and in one sense negated when another reality, the 'eternal Silence', is perceived. The passage which can be made 'in a moment' back to the sea of eternity however far inland, however heavy the weight of custom, is equivalent to the breach in the mist which Wordsworth described in the last book of *The Prelude* as bearing the 'Soul':

>                    but in that breach
> Through which the homeless voice of waters rose,
> That dark deep thoroughfare had Nature lodg'd
> The Soul, the Imagination of the whole. (Bk.13, version of
> 1805 – 6).

The power is lodged in the word 'homeless' which (as well as helping convey the sound of moving waters) indicates an alien element, a passage to a world not realised in ordinary forms, a breach in the ordinary texture of vision, a reading of the eternal deep. Although Wordsworth ends the Ode with platitudinous consolations (the intrusive 'philosophy' from which his poetry is

ROMANTIC SPIRIT OF CREATION

rarely free), he has during its progress encountered a new note of genuine yearning and clarified his concept of the nature of poetry and the imagination, intimating Immortality albeit in a past existence; focussing on the poetic principle itself; celebrating as well as bidding farewell to the child within the man, the eye among the blind.

Emily Brontë was clearly impressed by the Immortality Ode in particular; she echoes it persistently, as in (for example) 'Tell me, tell me, smiling child . . . What is the future? — 'A mighty, glorious, dazzling sea,/ Stretching into infinity' (H.3); in 'In the same place, when Nature wore/ The same celestial glow' (H.153); in the theme of visionary childhood becoming over-shadowed; and in the breach between man and nature, when the dreamer has intimations of infinitude:

Shall Earth no more inspire thee,
Thou lonely dreamer now?

— though 'none would ask a Heaven/ More like this Earth than thine' (H.147). Unlike Wordsworth however, she early on indicates awareness of an innocence beyond experience, of an inevitable period of storm and battle and darkness. She partly regrets the passing of the adhesive state of 'forming my mood to nature's mood' (H.154) but is prepared to dramatise the mind's battle thereafter which, like Keats, she regards in the light of soul-making or achieving Identity:[5]

Is it not that the sunshine and the wind
Lure from its self the mourner's woe-worn mind,
And all the joyous music breathing by,
And all the splendour of that cloudless sky,
Re-give him shadowy gleams of infancy,
And draw his tired gaze from futurity? (H.114)

Unlike Wordsworth, she has a concept of sin and redemption, of internal darkness: her 'iron man' was once an 'ardent boy' who has lost 'Remembrance of his early home —/ So lost that not a gleam may come' (H.99); he may remain 'chained to sin', or alternatively may come a different kind of revelation:

Perhaps this is the destined hour
When hell shall lose its fatal power

And heaven itself shall bend above
To hail the soul redeemed by love.

Although in expression her poetry only occasionally equals
Wordsworth's, yet her mentality is more complex and consequently her poetic capacity more resilient; she works towards
an earned as opposed to an instinctive 'love'; not content to
yearn for a return to 'shadowy gleams of infancy' she sets her
sights on 'futurity'. Wordsworth's preparation for 'the faith that
looks through death', the 'years that bring the philosophic
mind', does not have the energy nor the capacity to endure pain
manifest in Emily Brontë's 'final bound', when 'the soul feels
the flesh and the flesh feels the chain', or in her equivalent statement of the immortality principle:

There is not room for Death
Nor atom that his might could render void
Since thou art Being and Breath
And what thou art may never be destroyed.

# 2    Emily Brontë and Shelley

It seems likely that Emily Brontë had read Shelley's *Complete Works* which came out in 1839, and she probably first came in contact with him earlier. Both poets, in evolving their image of creativity, focus upon the boundary or tension (the 'veil') between sense and spirit, and the quest for a 'real' communication between poet and Spirit, or lost Beloved, or dead Poet (as in *Adonais*), the simultaneous gain and loss of identity through union with Eternity: 'could we lift the veil . . . Thou would'st rejoice for those that live,/ Because they live to die' (H.170). They have a similar contempt for worldly creeds, mass religion, the world's 'withered weeds'; a similar rage against worldly injustice, though Shelley's led him in restless wandering and Emily's kept her moorlocked: hence dispersal of his words amongst mankind is characteristic of Shelley's image, while absorption of the self away from mankind is Emily's. Despite this difference, both have a similar underlying view of evil as ultimately unreal, with love being the only active force in the universe, and fear being the state of mind least conducive to a sense of 'reality' (in the Platonic sense).

The 'Ode to the West Wind' serves as a point of departure for both Shelley and Emily Brontë (who frequently echoes it), in terms of considering how inspiration relates to eternity. In the Ode, the poet — like Prometheus — is chained, by a 'heavy weight of hours'; awaiting inspiration by the creating and destroying Spirit, through recognition of a correspondence ('one too like thee, tameless and swift and proud'). The affinities present in boyhood, 'when, to outstrip thy skiey speed/ Scarce seemed a vision', are like those of the *Wuthering Heights* childhood ('half savage and hardy and free'), which also requires recalling yet modifying as the creative process proceeds. The problem in both poets concerns how to expand, divide and multiply, the original primitive adhesive visionary state:

> Be though, Spirit fierce,
> My spirit! Be thou me, impetuous one!

Drive my dead thoughts over the universe
Like withered leaves to quicken a new birth!
And, by the incantation of this verse,

Scatter, as from an unextinguished hearth
Ashes and sparks, my words among mankind![6]

Emily Brontë's 'Aye, there it is! It wakes to-night' (H.148),
describing the wind which becomes 'spirit', 'a principle of life',
'The essence of the Tempest's roaring/ And of the Tempest's fall'
(like Shelley's 'sails to the tempest given' in *Adonais*), ends with
a conventional formulation dividing sense from spirit:

Thy prisoned soul shall rise,
The dungeon mingle with the mould —
The captive with the skies.

This is not the 'final bound' of the later image heralding *Wuthering Heights*, when 'My outward sense is gone, my inward essence feels'. Shelley, however, in the 'West Wind', develops the idea of the quickening spirit further, through the dimensions of 'this verse' and the soil of 'mankind' receiving the spirit (not losing it to the skies). The image of the 'Pestilence-stricken multitudes', 'Yellow, and black, and pale, and hectic red', gives way to the leaves-as-embers carrying sparks of life rather than symptoms of disease, but still retained in earth's mould like the corpse-like seeds. The poet's 'unextinguished hearth', through an implicit cremation or crossing of the boundary of death, leads to a type of oneness of spirit more ambiguous, but also with more potential fulfilment, than does the simple escape from sense to either Emily Brontë's 'skies' or to the 'white radiance of Eternity' which concludes *Adonais*. Both Emily Brontë and Shelley in different poems work on this boundary or point of tension, to evolve a 'strange killing' image of creation; and their poems are fullest and most intense when the boundary is crossed and re-crossed to create a wider penumbra of meaning — given not by the visionary image alone, but by its context, when the soul feels the flesh and the flesh feels the chain. In reaction against this struggle, Emily Brontë at times seeks the dreamless sleep 'without identity', formulating what she calls the 'coward cry/ To cease to think and cease to be' (H.181), because she — as the 'Philosopher' — cannot find the Spirit that unifies 'divided sources' into white eternity.

196

The climax of *Wuthering Heights* focusses on Heathcliff's struggle with the reality of 'spirit' through its earthly manifestations: the distinction between a genuine poetic image and an assortment of dead elements, a 'collection of memoranda'. In *Adonais*, Shelley evolved a premature end to this story, curtailing the ambiguity of the West Wind. Whilst following the classical pattern of lament for a dead brother-poet (Keats), Shelley concentrates on evoking the image of a kind of death more real than life:

> he is not dead, he doth not sleep —
> He hath awakened from the dream of life —
> 'Tis we, who lost in stormy visions, keep
> With phantoms an unprofitable strife,
> And in mad trance, strike, with our spirit's knife
> Invulnerable nothings. — *We* decay
> Like corpses in a charnel; fear and grief
> Convulse us and consume us day by day,
> And cold hopes swarm like worms within our living clay.

The violence of the 'spirit's knife' striking 'nothings' (echoing *The Tempest*'s 'with bemock'd at stabs . . . Wound the loud winds'), represents a state of illusion equivalent to Heathcliff's when he is tormented by 'the spectre of a hope' and has his life in the grave — in the destructive not the ghostly transcendental sense. The cause of death in *Adonais* is the 'nameless worm', the reviewer who (in Shelley's myth) killed Keats; the satanic serpent within mankind who substitutes false action, 'mad trance', the 'eclipsing curse of birth' for the love, fire, power which sustains the universe. The tomb of Adonais is Rome, ancient civilisation grown back into nature; the command 'Go thou to Rome' initiates investigation of a different kind of charnel house, where 'flowering weeds, and fragrant copses dress/ The bones of Desolation's nakedness'. The outsider, like Lockwood, is led to a revised image of a corpse in a grave, decorated not with worm-like hopes but with bones and flowering weeds and other 'fragments' belonging to Life's 'dome of many-coloured glass':

> the spirit of the spot shall lead
> Thy footsteps to a slope of green access

> Where, like an infant's smile, over the dead
> A light of laughing flowers along the grass is spread.

Yet the picturesque evidence of the 'stain' on the 'white radiance of Eternity' is still, like 'words' themselves, not gathered into a fitting dynamic relationship:

> Flowers, ruins, statues, music, words, are weak
> The glory they transfuse with fitting power to speak.

And the solution offered by *Adonais* is a seductive, sinister invitation to 'burn through the inmost veil of Heaven', to an image of creative union with Adonais' inspiring spirit, 'far from the trembling throng', which is an assertion of willpower rather than a dramatic manifestation as in *Wuthering Heights*:

> The breath whose might I have invoked in song
> Descends on me . . .
> I am borne darkly, fearfully, afar . . .

This difference is not due to genre, but rather to Shelley's insistence on forcing a conclusion, on finishing the story of his invocation to the West Wind and fixing the destination of the tempest-driven spirit in 'the abode where the Eternal are'. Even in Emily Brontë's lyric 'No coward soul', the conviction of 'As I Undying Life, have power in Thee' is quite different in quality from *Adonais*, in terms of the imaginative leap from worldly 'froth' or 'throngs' into essence.

*Prometheus Unbound* (from which Charlotte quotes in 1839), being a full-scale tragedy, might be thought to bear a similar relation to Shelley's lyric poetry as does *Wuthering Heights* to Emily's poetry: a three-dimensional dramatisation of familiar tensions, again centring on the problem of how the imprisoned poet-within-mankind can express himself. However if anything, the opposite is the case; the *Prometheus* has the texture of an argument clothed in poetry. *Wuthering Heights* invites interpretation perversely, owing to its mysterious quality; the Prometheus invites allegorisation from within: transferring the Promethean mind from 'crag-like agony' to 'Love' with its 'awful throne of patient power'. It is an allegory of creativity as well as of social reformation, with Prometheus and Asia (as Forethought and Imagination) mobilising the volcanic powers of Demogorgon into a triumphant exchange of power. Jupiter is excised from the final configuration in Shelley's version, resulting in a loss of poetic power, due also to the fact that Prometheus has no 'satanic' qualities; he is, as Shelley says in his preface, a version of Satan as hero without his badness. This is a different, even antithetical, technique from the permutations of oppressor and oppressed in *Wuthering Heights*, which progress with balance and incvitability over two generations, without loss of the original elements. The resulting image of creativity and poetic reformation through love, in the *Prometheus*, is consequently an idealised and nostalgic one, rather than an essentially new one growing organically out of conflicts in the poem. The 'mind' of 'human kind' becomes 'an ocean/ Of clear emotion'; the elements of nature take their plan 'from the new world of man/ And our work shall be called the Promethean'. This is based on an idealised relation between man and words, as 'veil by veil, evil and error fall'; thus Prometheus to Asia:

> we will sit and talk of time and change,
> As the world ebbs and flows, ourselves unchanged . . .
> . . . and make
> Strange combinations out of common things,
> Like human babes in their brief innocence.

The vision of a new poetic world of man is not emotionally earned by the poem. Lifting the veil, letting the 'loathsome masks' fall away, making strange combinations out of common things, is based on a goal of security rather than exploration. The ultimate nature of poetic expression is idealised rather than ideal; by Act IV

> Language is a perpetual Orphic song,
> Which rules with Daedal harmony a throng
> Of thoughts and forms, which else senseless and shapeless
> were.

All this contrasts with the new world achieved at the end of *Wuthering Heights*, and its version of absorbing the life-death boundary and the uncouth, uncivilised shapelessness of language (Hareton's lack of letters), into a new type of conversation touched by an inspired softly-breathing wind. Despite

199

similar attitudes and rhetorical figures, there is no similarity of emotional effect; consequently the ultimate image of creativity growing from the total texture of each drama, is different.

Behind the whole impetus of the *Prometheus* lies the sense of love as power, and the poet as omnipotent, in effect exchanging Jupiter's tyranny for his own. Early on we know Prometheus is possessed of a 'secret' which could 'transfer the sceptre of wide Heaven' (fear of which 'perplexes the Supreme'), should he just 'clothe it in words'; and in effect, by more roundabout means, this describes what happens in the poem. Through Prometheus controlling the 'Spirit of the Hour' and understanding the 'mysteries of the universe', the poet organises a transfer of power in order to make room for his presentation of a reformed world. Shelley does not achieve negative capability in the *Prometheus* (or even attempt to); and it is this, rather than any superficial catalogue of the poetic new world's characteristics, which differentiates its image of creation from that of *Wuthering Heights*. The relinquishment of power is precisely what enables Heathcliff to perceive and help evoke a poetic image from a suffocating 'throng' of meaningless forms.

In this last poem, *The Triumph of Life*, Shelley begins to allow poetry to work on him to evolve a more complex image of creation. As in the 'West Wind', though antithetical in feeling, he writes as a poet rather than as a reformer; and he uses the same stanza form (Dante's *terza rima*) with its relentless onward movement. Here he finally confronts the ambivalence and ominous warning ignored but implicit in the last stages of *Adonais*, of the veil by veil approach to the core of reality. The form is dream within dream, like Keats's *Fall of Hyperion*, to which it bears an uncanny resemblance (Shelley had not read *The Fall*, but was reading Keats's earlier poems at the time). It proceeds by a step by step anti-revelation; and in its concern with the destructiveness of unreality and with anti-knowledge, it comes closer to Heathcliff's struggles and to the feeling of Emily Brontë's last poem (H.192) than does Shelley's idealist philosophy. Shelley in a sense painfully negates every move towards a superinduced resolution by the propagandist in himself (Emily Brontë's 'Enthusiast'). First the 'mask' of everyday reality is penetrated, and the dreamer enters an ambiguous visionary state, part obscuring and part revealing:

his 'strange trance' grows a 'shade' which is yet 'transparent', like a 'veil of light'; 'And then a vision on my brain was rolled'. This vision is a strange reversal of the 'Ode to the West Wind', whose leaf-elements are here resolved back into 'a great stream/ Of people', compared to 'dust' and 'gnats', whirling along mindlessly in a crowd like 'the million leaves of summer's bier', 'Mixed in one mighty torrent'. Shelley refocusses on the colours of the world's stain on white etermity. None of the 'multitude' is real or engaged in real, purposive movement; their 'fear' is not only baseless but based on their own unreality, fleeing from their 'own shadow' or pursuing or shunning 'the shadows the clouds threw':

> Some flying from the thing they feared, and some
> Seeking the object of another's fear.

They form part of a false tempest animated not by the wind but by 'a chariot on the silent storm/ Of its own rushing splendour': the anti-revelatory chariot of Life, which is occupied by an entombed and deformed 'Shape'.

Within this vision is given the inner history of the dreamer's 'guide', Rousseau, a man even more lost than himself, and who enters the poem through a gradual image suggesting a grim process of resurrection. Caricaturing Adonais' swift flight to eternity, Rousseau appears to come alive, fossil-like, from a death-like posture as 'an old root which grew/ To strange distortion out of the hill side'; his eyes as it were materialise from the holes between the roots. But he is reanimated only to testify to his living death as one of the 'deluded crew' in life's meaningless progress (which in Shelley's image, is not even a race), whose failure is due to inadequate self-knowledge. Not only the political Napoleons but also the lords of philosophy, with their 'signs of thought's empire over thought', have been 'taught not . . . to know themselves',

> And for the morn of truth they feigned, deep night
> Caught them ere evening.

This is the plight not only of those who were 'given power only to destroy', but more significantly, of those erstwhile heroes represented by Rousseau, who 'have created' in their time and who 'partly seem to know' who they are. Insufficient internal substance shrouds them in unreality. The narrative moves back to Rousseau's 'morn of life', to the simple single vision befor ehe became his own ghost, to investigate the failure in development. At this point the emotional link between guide and dreamer is reinforced, as it is at key points in its model the *Divine Comedy*, and likewise in *Wuthering Heights*. The passive dreamer is told he must pay for his secondary knowledge by a commitment to life himself,

> and from spectator turn
> Actor or victim in this wretchedness,

> And what thou wouldst be taught I then may learn
> From thee.

This symbiotic relationship of mutual need is echoed in the Lockwood-Heathcliff path towards knowledge through reviewing and re-experiencing the past.

At the centre of the narrative layers is Rousseau's dream: 'In the April prime . . . I was laid asleep'. It describes an awakening from the innocence or naivety of the Promethean new world, through his relationship with a 'Shape all light . . . as if she were the dawn'; in appearance antithetical to the 'Shape' in the chariot, yet related through the noncommittal name. His awakening is effected by the steady sinister movements of her feet, gliding first over the idealised landscape and then over his mind:

> 'And her feet, ever to the ceaseless song

> 'Of leaves, and winds, and waves, and birds, and bees,
> And falling drops, moved in a measure new
> Yet sweet . . .

> 'And still her feet, no less than the sweet tune
> To which they moved, seemed as they moved to blot
> The thoughts of him who gazed on them; and soon

> 'All that was, seemed as if it has been not;
> And all the gazer's mind was strewn beneath
> Her feet like embers; and she, thought by thought,

> 'Trampled its sparks into the dust of death;

The progression through 'feet' 'blot' 'not' 'thought', eradicates previous vision, in a movement the reverse of the West Wind's blowing an 'unextinguished hearth' into live embers. This is Shelley's version of a 'strange killing' 'inch by inch', a paradoxical step towards reality from the midst of a plethora of unreal phantoms: 'like day she came,/ Making the night a dream', to show 'Whence I came, and where I am, and why'; although the means she gives toward self-knowledge involve further erasure: 'And suddenly my brain became as sand', in preparation for a new vision 'bursting' like a wave.

The new vision is a gradual return to the chariot of Life — which rather appears to return to him, its noise crossing the forest, 'as if from some dread war/ Triumphantly returning'. This overlapping of experience, visions, boundaries, ways of seeing, involves the greatest strain. The mind-stamping muse (her prints compared implicitly to both deer and wolf), remains for a while 'beside my path, as silent as a ghost', in 'obscure tenour', waning yet still present like the moon:

'And the fair shape waned in the coming light,
As veil by veil the silent splendour drops
From Lucifer, . . .

Even in the new light's 'severe excess', he is still aware of the Shape's presence: the moon in daylight being a characteristic image for a source of poetry, as in 'The Skylark': 'Until we hardly see — we feel that it is there'. The two kinds of light are felt together, like the sun and stars in Emily Brontë's 'Stars', or Lockwood on his return to the Heights after another sojourn in the world; ghosts hover in the background, guiding and tormenting the dreamers. The next stage in the visionary's progress involves a more testing plunge into unreality, 'dense with shadows . . . grey with phantoms . . . dim forms . . . flock of vampire bats . . . Phantoms diffused around . . . shadows of shadows . . . lost in the white day'; 'others like elves/ Danced in a thousand unimagined shapes'. The plague of shadows, making up the contagion of the world's slow stain, appears to emanate from the human beings as much as attacking them, and expresses their mental atmosphere: like 'gnats and flies, as thick as mist . . . discoloured flakes of snow' forming a veil 'like tears', 'obscure clouds'. This incessant cloud of shadows, 'numerous as

the dead leaves blown' (as in the 'West Wind'), a matrix of
tearful and meaningful emotionality, is shaped by the 'car's
creative ray . . . As the sun shapes the clouds'; while

> Mask after mask fell from the countenance
> And form of all;

Shelley's parody of his usual description of the stripping of the
veils which obscure reality or eternity, in fact has the effect of
coming closer to the truth, as 'the sleepers in the oblivious
valley' awake to join the hideous pageant of Life.

The last line of the unfinished poem — " ' Then, what is life?' '
I cried' — expresses a triumphant nadir which nevertheless
suggests a new kind of involvement with poetry, different from
the *Prometheus'* pre-ordained conclusion with its 'swift shapes
and sounds' growing 'More fair and soft, as man grows wise and
kind', and different from Adonais' reformation of the ruins of
classical antiquity. It is a new kind of surrender to the whirling
leaves of the West Wind, no longer riding on the blast as in
carefree boyhood, but within the centre of the storm. The poet's
re-encounter with Life's chariot is intensified through the
guidance and identification with Rousseau, who himself invokes
the example of Dante, 'him who from the lowest depths of hell
. . . Love led serene, and who returned to tell/ The words of hate
and awe'. This suggests that Shelley is hoping for a 'return'
from the depths whilst bearing 'the words of hate' within him
(rather than excising them as in the *Prometheus*), yet by
surrendering himself to the poem rather than controlling it, and
using the different narrative layers of dream with dream, poet
within poet, as stabilising factors in the midst of the maëlström
of experience. In this strenuous mentality, *The Triumph of Life* is
concerned with a creative spirit and vision of creativity more
akin to *Wuthering Heights* than the *Prometheus*, which is
superficially more similar in theme; and, like Emily Brontë's
novel, it dramatises images of creation which had appeared in
simpler lyric poetry.

# 3    Emily Brontë and Byron

Patrick Brontë possessed the complete works of Byron, and the children read the extensive *Life, Letters and Journals* by Thomas Moore, in early adolescence. From the moment they came in contact with this 'great man' (as Charlotte called him)[7] they became obsessed with a fever of Byronism. Charlotte concentrated on the myth of sexual seduction through Zamorna; Branwell on the 'gloomy egoism' of an idealised and self-doomed hero both flattered and outcast by the world. Emily found a resonance in Byron, a poetic legitimacy, for the violence of her passions, as well as adopting his persona to some extent in her diary notes whose style (as Winifred Gérin has noted) was modelled partly on his.[8] Heathcliff is often regarded as an archetypal 'Byronic' hero, with his mysterious origins, lawlessness, fatal love, and self-induced death. Yet most readers of *Wuthering Heights* would accept that ultimately Heathcliff is a Byronic hero who outgrows and undermines his genre, being in fact part of a wider dialetic of romance and anti-romance. But Byron also subsumed this dialectic within himself; and asserted that though the common identification of himself with his own romantic heroes might be 'near the truth', yet 'I doubt the equivocation of the fiend that lies like truth'.[9] The image of the society hero was a kind of lie about himself as a poet. Both Emily Brontë and Byron therefore have a more complex vision of the hero than that encompassed by the 'Byronic hero' *per se*; and it is on this deeper level of affinity that the most interesting correspondences between them are to be found. Emily Brontë's assimilation of Byron did not (as is usually assumed) end with the lyrics, the romances and *Manfred*; it also included the 'other side' of Byron expressed in *Don Juan* and in his prose. Although she began with the romantic hero, the 'wandering outlaw of his own dark mind', as she matured she became more interested in the metaphysics of the restless search for Poetry which, through paradox and ambivalence, Byron exemplified through the total struggle of his mind: as he defined it, 'the feeling of a Former world and a Future'.[10]

A swift survey of lines in Emily Brontë's earlier poems

indicates the reflection of Byron's lyrics and romances in sentiment, phraseology and cadence, on the most straightforward
level of influence. The lines 'Sometime the loved and the loving/
Shall meet on the mountains again', 'Twice twelve short years,
and all is over', 'Let us part, the time is over', 'And never more to
be a rover', echo — without any of its power or beauty — the
famous lyric 'So we'll go on more a-roving'. *The Giaour*'s 'But
Heaven itself descends in love . . . A Glory circling round the
soul' is seen in 'Heaven itself shall bend above/ To hail the soul
redeemed by love'; Byron's poem 'Remember thee, remember
thee' lies behind Heathcliff's 'May she wake in torment!' spoken
to Nelly Dean after Catherine's death. Byron, in his 'Epistle to
Augusta', has 'The Passions which have torn me would have
slept/ *I* had not suffered, and *thou* hadst not wept.' Emily, in
different poems, has '*He* rests, and *I* endure the woe' (H.134);
'May I . . . turn away from passion's call' (H.10); and 'Old feel-
ings gather fast upon me/ Like vultures round their prey'
(H.120) (the image of the vulture tearing the heart, from the
Prometheus myth, also being used by Byron). Byron, to his sister
Augusta, complains 'With false Ambition what had I to do?/
Little with Love, and least of all with Fame'; and in *Don Juan*,
'Ambition was my idol, which was broken/ Before the shrines of
Sorrow, and of Pleasure' (1.ccxvii) — a theme taken up by Emily
frequently, as in H.146: 'And lust of Fame was but a dream/
That vanished with the morn', or the long-superseded false
'shrine' she had once erected to Wealth, Power, Glory and
Pleasure, who 'once indeed seemed Beings divine' (H.176). Her
Byronic heroine, also named Augusta, confesses on her deathbed
to being 'shut from Heaven', a 'spirit lost in crime', a 'wanderer,
all my life', and 'self-destroyed at last':

> The baited tiger could not be
> So much athirst for gore:
> For men and laws have tortured me . . . (H.143).

Contemptible law and lawyers, like Mr Green of *Wuthering
Heights*, are taken as the antithesis to the tigerish poetic spirit, as
in Byron's 'I am like the tyger (in poesy) — if I miss the first
Spring — I go growling back to my Jungle'. [11] The following lines
from 'I would I were a careless child', find variations again and
again in the Gondal poetry:

Few are my years, and yet I feel
The world was ne'er designed for me,
Ah! why do darkening shades conceal
The hour when man must cease to be?

— compare Emily Brontë's 'coward cry/ To cease to think, and
cease to be', and the whole myth of a darkened childhood, when
the 'freeborn soul/ Which loves the mountains wild' (Byron) or
'walk [s] by the hill-river's side' (Brontë) becomes imprisoned
by its dark inheritance. Thus *The Prisoner of Chillon* provides
material for all the Gondal situations of solitary imprisonment
or living death, along with their allegorical connotations of a
death-like state intensifying self-knowledge and creativity: 'So
much a long communion tends/ To make us what we are'.

This is the world of the Byronic hero proper — the themes, the
imagery and expression, the values. Its ethos predominates in
Gondal; though even there, its main attraction for Emily Brontë
seems to have been the hero's mixture of light and shade,
indicating the possibility of dramatic evolution in his story —
whether backwards or forwards in time. The 'mingled tone/ Of
seraph's song and demon's moan' (H.168) echoes the Giaour
whose mind is 'not all degraded' even by his crimes, showing
'brighter traits with evil mixed . . . hues not always faded' (all
tracing back to Milton's 'archangel ruin'd', where 'care/ Sat on
his faded cheek'). Likewise the Corsair's 'murkiness of mind'
covers his 'feelings fearful, yet undefined' and the mysterious
warping of his nature in early years, for he was 'not by Nature
sent/ To lead the guilty'. However, any comparison with
*Wuthering Heights* indicates how far Emily Brontë has gone
beyond the world of the Byronic hero (and of Gondal) in terms
of the dramatic interplay of values, by contrast with the Byron
of the romances and even the 'metaphysical' dramas. Thus
Byron's mysteries always have a teasing, directed-at-the-public
quality, on the lines of his own semi-ironic comment in a diary:
'passion is a whirlpool . . . I must not go on with these reflections
— or I shall be letting out some secret or other — to paralyze
posterity'. [12] Whereas Nelly Dean's question about Heathcliff,
'Where did he come from, the little dark thing?', placed only at
the end of the book, has a deeper metaphorical significance, and
serves to stress that the heart of the book is a mystery, not a

secret. Heathcliff's unaccountability is very different from the Corsair's or from the role-playing with which Byron teased the public. Likewise, though Nelly or Isabella watching Heathcliff or Catherine's paroxysms of passion have some resemblance to the fisherman watching the Giaour or the chamois hunter watching Manfred from the standpoint of everyday life, yet Emily Brontë's narrators have a more complex, integral function in the total emotional constellation. Byron's romantic narratives are basically simple structures of passive spectators and flamboyant protagonists living in the public eye. Emily Brontë also makes more of the hero's dissociation from ordinary values (as symbolised by leaving 'no recording stone', like the Corsair or Lara), when she uses the Corsair's lily and rock as materials for the complex of images around Heathcliff's grave-stone. Struck by thunder, the lily withers,

> And of its cold protector, blacken round
> But shiver'd fragments on the barren ground.

These provide some of the elements for Brontë's final landscape of assimilation and disintegration — mould overgrowing solid rock, slates falling off the church roof, the flowers and 'benign sky' yet hinting at coming 'autumn storms'. But the intensity and emotional vibrancy in which every element reaches back into the total structure of the book, becoming loaded with meaning, is absent in Byron.

In her investigation of the further implications of the Byronic hero, Emily Brontë makes use of the relation between the two brothers in *Cain*, which has aspects of that between Heathcliff and his rival 'brother' Hindley on the one hand, and his rival in love Edgar, on the other. Abel, in his sheeplike masochism, refusing to understand Cain's feelings of rejection by God, is instrumental in bringing 'death and all our woe' into the world for the second time. It is *Manfred*, however, which Emily Brontë cannibalised (in a sense) and revolutionises more systematically and thoroughly. *Manfred* has been called 'the only work which bears a sustained likeness to *Wuthering Heights* in English literature'. [13] (Charlotte Brontë calls one of her early characters Manfred, indicating the strong appeal of the play from the beginning, for the Brontës). Byron explains in his preface that he takes for his hero 'a magician, who is tormented by a species of remorse, the cause of which is left half unexplained'; the drama is of a 'very wild, metaphysical, and inexplicable kind', peopled mainly by spirits — like *The Tempest* or *Faust*, its models for allegorising the perils of creative power. Manfred, in order to catharsize his torments, goes to 'the very abode of the Evil Principle, in propria persona, to evocate a ghost': the ghost of Astarte for whose death he is somehow responsible. Like Satan, 'on his brow/ The thunder-scars are graven'. Like Heathcliff, by the end of his machinations toward revenge, he is in a position of apparent total power with everything at the command of his will. He calls up spirits 'By the strong curse which is upon my Soul . . . I do compel ye to my will!' But the one position he desires is death (as Heathcliff has 'not a presentiment, nor a fear, not a hope of death'): not the death attainable by jumping off a cliff, but the 'self-oblivion' of peace within himself, which is obscurely and inevitably related to contact with the lost Astarte, as Heathcliff's mental torture is related to his tantalising contact, or loss of contact, with the dead Catherine. To this, 'Philosophy and science, and the springs/ Of wonder, and the wisdom of the world . . . avail not'; his knowledge is useless, his poetic power false, lacking communion with its governing spirit. A female spirit tantalises him as if she were Astarte; he feels that if he could 'clasp' her he 'yet might be most happy', like Heathcliff trying to grasp Catherine's spirit by unearthing her corpse. His delusions, likewise, condemn him to be his 'proper Hell':

My solitude is solitude no more,
But peopled with the Furies; I have gnashed
My teeth in darkness . . . (II.ii)

(like Heathcliff 'grinding his teeth' after Catherine's death, in preparation for a 'moral teething'). He reviews his history: as a 'stranger' among men who, after his élite and etherial wanderings, made him feel 'degraded' back to 'clay'; Astarte, as the female counterpart of himself, being the only exception to this, a companion in 'The quest of hidden knowledge', with 'the same lone thoughts and wanderings'; just as Heathcliff feels degraded and deprived of knowledge when kept apart from Catherine. Again, theirs was a forbidden love, 'the deadliest sin', though bound 'by blood' (Byron's incest theme): she the

'sole/ Companion of his wanderings/ And watchings'. Like
Heathcliff's 'Haunt me then', Manfred asks a Witch to 'wake
the dead, or lay me low with them . . . in any shape . . . With any
torture', since 'I loved her, and destroyed her!'; his 'heart . . .
broke her heart' ('You and Edgar have broken my heart', says
Catherine). Astarte rises from her grave, life-like (like Catherine
whose 'features are hers yet'): 'Can this be death? there's bloom
upon her cheek'. They 'torture' one another again, in almost
the same words as those of Heathcliff to Catherine's ghost, as
overheard by Lockwood:

> I cannot rest . . .
> Speak to me! though it be in wrath; — but say —
> I reck not what — but let me hear thee once —
> This once — once more! (II.iv)

The action ends in a secret recess within a tower in Manfred's
castle, the scene of 'mysteries', equivalent to the inner closet-
chamber which had been Heathcliff's and Catherine's, and
where — according to the servants — Manfred has been con-
ducting his nightly vigils 'without a witness', in this 'chamber
where none may enter', yet where Astarte watched with him in
the past. Manfred ultimately goes to the interior of the tower to
meet his death, of which Astarte's ghost had finally given him
the reassurance. His departure to unknown regions is observed
with awe by the Abbot who, like Nelly, had tried at the last
minute to draw him back into the fold: 'He's gone — . . .
Whither? I dread to think'. Nevertheless, despite these echoes of
phraseology, and the resemblances of plot on the metaphysical
level, even to the chamber of knowledge-through-dreams, the
affinity between *Manfred* and *Wuthering Heights* is not deep. The
narrative texture, not just the genre, is quite different: to the
extent that different means result in essentially different ends.
Brontë's is a dramatic poem of mental development: Byron's of
self-dramatisation. It is written on the lines of 'All convulsions
end with me in Rhyme': an attempt to evacuate the 'volcanic
lava' within him before he became crushed by the weight of
'imagination and reality'. [14] Byron himself felt that he was being
'a devil of a mannerist' in producing it. The metaphysical
Byronic hero could not contain the total mental and emotional
activity of Byron himself any more than could the romantic

Byronic hero. Written after crossing the Alps, *Manfred* could not enable him — any more than could glaciers, forests, clouds, mountains or avalanches — to 'lose my own wretched identity in the majesty, and the power, and the Glory, around, above, and beneath me'.[15] The play did not really encompass his identity or encourage him to explore his predicament. To Emily Brontë, it gave materials and preoccupations, but not the transforming spirit which could make its world a container for aspects of identity and emotional reality

Byron had an antagonistic, self-destroying, love-hate relationship with poetry, of which Brontë was clearly aware at a deep level of influence, and fascinated by its implications. He could never commit hiimself to poetry in the sense of directional self-development; from early days, frequently, he pronounces himself 'cured' of 'scribbling'. Closeness to poetry gave him the sense of his mind exploding, 'dying at top', in a sense different from the heroic departure of Manfred at the top of his tower, yet more real, and expressed only in his letters (and in ironic vein in *Don Juan*):

> I feel a something, which makes me think that, if I ever reach near to old age, like Swift, 'I shall die at top' first. Only I do not dread idiotism or madness so much as he did. On the contrary, I think some quieter stages of both must be preferable to much of what men think the possession of their senses.[16]

The Byron who could experience mind's existence as 'a sad jar of atoms',[17] is much closer to Heathcliff in the shattered, disjointed state when Catherine is a 'collection of memoranda', than to any of his own heroes; in Heathcliff's words to Nelly, 'The most ordinary faces of men, and women — my own features mock me with a resemblance. The entire world is a dreadful collection of memoranda that she did exist, and that I have lost her!' Byron *as hero*, as distinct from the Byronic hero, is in evidence when Byron comes closest to being himself through words: namely in *Don Juan* and in his letters and journals; and Emily Brontë was influenced by his style, his mixture of the colloquial and pontifical, his sense of the potential derived from juxtaposing the sublime and the ridiculous, his metaphysical preoccupations, and his image of the forces which

211

made and unmade him as a poet — including the pull between
Words and Action. This side of Byron, demonstrating his mind
in the process of working, had in some ways a deeper if less easily
traceable effect on *Wuthering Heights* than the romantic Byronic
hero, since it presents imagination in the context of the over-
riding pressures of necessity: the imagination as real and a part
of life, however ill-assorted the juxtapositions. There is, for
example, Byron's entry in his 1813 journal, describing his
awakening from a dream from a 'Lockwood' point of view:

> I awoke from a dream! — well! and have not others dreamed?
> — Such a dream! — but she did not overtake me. I wish the
> dead would rest, however. Ugh! how my blood chilled, — and
> I could not wake — and — and — heigho! . . . And am I to be
> shaken by shadows? . . . Since I rose, I've been in con-
> siderable bodily pain also . . . [18]

Grammatically the dream itself is 'she', as well as perhaps its
subject (recalling Lockwood's dream of Catherine followed by
his bodily collapse): giving another dimension to Byron's
constant reiteration that he has been the 'martyr' of women,
victimised and 'ravaged'; [19] the form of Woman is an apparent
manifestation of the spirit of Poetry or Beauty, but always in a
sense unattainable though burning up the poet in its pursuit.

Byron's letters to Lady Melbourne show his partial desire for
a containing, motherly figure to contain and assuage his restless
sense of persecution better than he does himself: 'Am I sure of
myself . . . No — but *you* are'. [20] His ill-fated marriage with his
'Princess of Parallelograms' Anabella Milbanke, could in a
sense be seen as another false attempt to circumscribe the
explosive effect of poetry and dreams. And in his letters and
journals Byron pursues more concretely the myth of his early
rejected love for 'Mary' and the picture of his childhood's
passionate nature scorned and thwarted, in a way which clearly
interested Emily Brontë. Biographers have often noted the
influence on the plot of *Wuthering Heights* of the famous episode
(recounted in Moore's *Life*) in which the adolescent Byron
overhears his neighbour, Mary Chaworth, say to her maid 'Do
you think I could ever care for that lame boy?', and runs away
from the house, like Heathcliff. Byron said this rejection by
Mary Chaworth 'threw me out again "alone on a wide — wide

sea" ';[21] and his picture of the effects of this particular fall from
innocence is confirmed and pressed by Moore, who writes that
to this 'ill-fated attachment . . . he himself attributed the
desolating change then wrought in his disposition'. In *Don Juan*
(5.iv) he explains 'I have a passion for the name of "Mary" . . .
Where I beheld what never was to be'. There were in fact three
Marys (like the Catherines' triple surname), though for the
purpose of Byron's myth they may as well be one — including
Mary Duff aged eight, 'my first of flames',[22] as well as Mary
Gray the governess who 'played tricks with his person'. Byron
felt that 'one of the deadliest and heaviest feelings of my life was
to feel that I was no longer a boy' (like Catherine in her delirium
at Thrushcross Grange); that his early passions recoiled on him,
'my heart thrown back upon itself';[23] that in those days 'I could
have left or lost the world with or for that which I loved' (like
Emily's 'For truth, for right, for liberty,/ I would have gladly,
freely died': H.119). The explosive uncontainability of
emotion, as in 'I abhor cruelty . . . except on an impulse, and
then I am savage — but not deliberately so',[24] is transposed into
the 'half savage' Catherine's cry, 'I did nothing deliberately!',
after striking Edgar. In later years Byron never wanted to meet
Mary Chaworth but preferred to preserve the myth associated
with an idyllic period of intense, adhesive union. As he describes
it in 'The Dream' (paralleled by Catherine's 'I *am* Heathcliff'):

> He had no breath, no being, but in hers;
> She was his voice; he did not speak to her,
> But trembled on her words; she was his sight . . .
>                    . . . he had ceased
> To live within himself; she was his life,
> The ocean to the river of his thoughts,
> Which terminated all.

And 'yet', he reflects in the journal, '*We* are *not* united' (despite
her unhappy marriage); although 'our Union would have
healed feuds in which blood had been shed by our fathers'.[25]
The whole picture of an early adhesive passion in which identity
is contained to the point of being swallowed up, and its failure
to progress into a worldly union of houses (the Linton-Earnshaw
relationship), indeed the impossibility of a worldly union on
those terms, is dramatised by Emily Brontë in *Wuthering Heights*:

213

not simply as a plot, but as Byron himself saw it, in terms of a poetic principle struggling to find expression, through words or action, or words *as* action.

Emily Brontë saw that Byron's restlessness in relation to women and to poetry was part of a single phenomenon, a species of haunting, driven by the search for (and ambivalent escape from) a self-containing form; and she drew on this concept of Byron's mind in her presentation of the tormented Heathcliff. Heathcliff's 'monomania' for Catherine, has more in common with Juan's wandering, than with the romantic pilgrimage of a figure such as Childe Harold (whom Byron called a 'repulsive personage', whilst always being affectionate about Juan). The central preoccupation of the anti-epic is how to portray live knowledge or thought in the making, without being circumscribed by preconceived limits of philosophy or of genre — to write, as Byron put it, a 'human' rather than a 'divine' poem. 'One system eats another up', and his poem is allowed to progress through a process of continuous devouring, even though 'there's no such thing as certainty', and forever 'the spouseless virgin Knowledge flies'. At least it is not knowledge curtailed by a Princess of Parallelograms. Juan flees his conventional education under the Annabella-like Donna Inez (studying 'The languages, especially the dead' and avoiding anything 'that hints continuation of the species'); just as his narrator defies the example of those 'Aeneids, Iliads or Odysseys' whilst in fact drawing on them in the effort to produce a new type of live epic that actually 'continues the species', not merely homage to a dead monument. Attempts at permanent union or containment are satirised, along with other Romantic postures, through such things as the story of King Cheops's pyramid — which, far from keeping 'his memory whole, and mummy hid', was burglariously rifled:

> Let not a monument give you or me hopes,
> Since not a pinch of dust remains of Cheops. (1.ccxix)

The underlying allegorical preoccupations with how an 'idea' can remain alive, within a culture or a personality, are the same as those of Emily Bronte when she shows the futility of Heathcliff's grave-rifling or the fate of the different houses and cultural monuments and their dependence for reality upon the

214

spirit of the living. Heathcliff has to subsume false attempts at union with Catherine (who is his 'idea' or goal) until, finally in sight of it, he becomes 'swallowed up' by the 'anticipation' of his idea's fulfilment — in the same metaphor of 'devouring' which Byron also uses for the poem's progression. Both Heathcliff and Juan are searching for the kind of formal existence (in *Don Juan*, it is the form of the poem itself) which can perpetuate an idea live, not entombed:

> But it was all a mystery: Here we are,
>    And there we go: — but *where*? ...
>          ... we dead?
> *We*, whose minds comprehend all things? No more;
> But let us to the story as before. (5.xxxix)

He takes up the favourite Romantic posture via Hamlet (the 'solitary hobgoblin' who pervades his letters), then — as realist — catches himself in his tracks before proceeding in a manner that first devalues, then revalues the famous question:

> 'To be, or not to be?' — ere I decide,
>    I should be glad to know that which *is being* ...
> For me, I sometimes think that Life is Death ... (9.xvi)

Juan's wandering leads him circuitously, again and again, not only into the arms of different women, but to what Woman or Poetry in a sense symbolises — an ultimate goal, an existence which is not illusory but real. When Heathcliff finally attains his 'goal', his 'harbour' or 'heaven' (distinguishing it from unreal heavens), his idea of Catherine-beyond-death is very different from that which prompted his grave desecration twenty years earlier. The first union in death represented a state of illusion, the second a state of reality, of 'being' itself. In a similar way, Byron distinguishes between the unreal transactions made through words in non-poetic activity, and the reality of a union or goal which is only defined in *Don Juan* by negative means, yet is nonetheless more real than any of the deliberate pilgrimages made by his purely romantic heroes. The form of the poem allows him to 'hit on' truth by means of unexpected juxtapositions evolved to cope with imperious 'Rhyme', at the expense of limited 'Reason' ('Reason ne'er was hand-in-glove with rhyme'):

> I cannot stop to alter words once written,
> And the *two* [i.e. Love and Lust] are so mixed with human dust,
> That he who *names one*, both perchance may hit on. (9.lxxvii)

In Juan's anti-pilgrimage, the arch-enemy — for his narrator — is represented by the 'intellectual eunuch Castlereagh', 'that monstrous hieroglyphic' who can only command

> . . . strange displays
> Of that odd string of words, all in a row,
> Which none divine, and every one obeys. (9.xlix)

The anti-poet commands not thought, but obedience, and gains his power through wielding a 'queer *no* meaning'. He has an unreal use of words. Like Heathcliff's 'lost' meaningless corpse of Catherine, the 'collection of memoranda' without the spirit, there is a superficial relationship through contiguity ('all in a row'), but without any essential meaning or 'being'. In the last cantos of the unfinished *Don Juan*, Byron introduces the figure Aurora, who appears to be intended to represent a new dawn of woman as poetic spirit, being 'more Shakespearian' and having more 'depth of feeling':

> The worlds beyond this World's perplexing waste
>   Had more of her existence, for in her
> There was a depth of feeling to embrace
> Thoughts, boundless, deep, but silent too as Space. (16.xlviii)

She contrasts with the other English ladies: Adeline with her intellectual affectation (Juan wondered 'how much of Adeline was *real*'), and Fitz-Fulke who, dressed as the monkish ghost, has another sort of unreality but one which is contrasted with immateriality. 'Immaterialism's a serious matter' but, far from being a wandering spirit, she is of the 'substantial company engrossed/ By matter', who make one wonder how 'bodies could have souls, or souls such bodies!' It is as if Byron were fed up with the incessant sideways movement of his interminable poem, and wished to bring in a more distinct symbolic goal through Aurora. The preoccupations of this sector of the poem are similar to those of Heathcliff at the end of *Wuthering Heights*.

216

As his 'strange change' approaches, Hareton and Cathy are 'the only objects which retain a distinct material appearance'; yet their materiality is dependent upon 'the thousand forms of past associations, and ideas he awakens, or embodies'. The sense of reality in existence is being transferred onto a new level of abstraction.

Yet *Don Juan*, unlike *Wuthering Heights* does not and could not lead to a vision of a new world. Revising the archetypal burnt-out Byronic hero, Emily Brontë and Byron found different solutions to the old world which (in Emily's words) 'goes rolling on'. At this stage in his life, Byron was fascinated by the idea of the world's being destroyed and recreated many times, with Man as 'the relic of some higher material being, wrecked in a former world — and degenerated in the hardships and struggles through Chaos into Conformity';[26] as if this somehow formulated his conception of the working of a poetic spirit in the world, and the type of 'future' possible for his mind. Yet like Byron himself, *Don Juan* is an eternally restless poem, never fulfilling his own criterion of poetry as 'the feeling of a Former world and a Future'; although its disillusion is worth more, and was more to Emily Brontë, than any lesser Romantic's illusion. For Byron even in *Don Juan* is essentially an omnipotent writer, rather than one of exploratory negative capability; satirising his own method of self-criticism through the 'poetical commandments' which he has made for himself in lieu of Aristotle's, for his new epic form:

> Thou shalt not write, in short, but what I choose;
> This is true criticism, and you may kiss —
> Exactly as you please, or not, — the rod;
> But if you don't, I'll lay it on, by God! (1.ccvi)

In his 1813 journal he had noted: 'My restlessness tells me I have something "within which passeth show"';[27] yet his omnipotent mode and his insistence upon action, in a sense prevented him from allowing what was within to come out and take its own form: 'To withdraw myself from myself . . . has ever been my sole, my entire, my sincere motive in scribbling at all'. Writing ('scribbling', as the Brontë children also called it, after him) is for Byron a form of action, in self-defence against the forces hunting him down — the pursuing devil of Woman or Poetry.

217

'No one should be a rhymer who could be anything better', he wrote; and increasingly adjured himself, '*onward*! — It is now the time to act, and what signifies *self*, if a single spark . . . the *spirit* of liberty must be spread.'[28]

All his life Byron was obsessed with achieving effectiveness in a field other than literature; though literature, also, he regarded as a kind of fight against external forces — the world, the public, his publishers — who tried to typecast him. 'If I took you all in hand — it would not be difficult to cut you up like gourds . . . making all your ribs — Gridirons for your hearts', he wrote Heathcliff-style to Murray;[29] continuing to explain that, in order to let his 'genius take it's natural direction', he makes sure his 'feelings are like the dead — who know nothing and feel nothing'. At the same time as the external fight, and almost in antithesis, Byron has the idea of a philosophical action which is genuinely independent — the 'action of Mind', with which his 1821 journal 'Detached Thoughts' is much concerned:

> Attend for the moment to the action of Mind. It is in perpetual activity . . . independent of body: in dreams for instance incoherently and madly, I grant you; but it still is *Mind*, and much more Mind than when we are awake.[30]

The 'mainspring of Mind' has an 'innate tendency to Good', but is 'at present a sad jar of atoms' — again, lacking a poetic principle, something to connect the 'former world' with the 'future'. Ultimately, as if unable to realise the former and future world in poetry, he chose 'a soldier's grave', something which seemed to straddle the dilemma — 'the very *poetry* of politics.'[31] Instead of 'dying at top', he chose the battlefield of Greece which, for him, symbolised the 'former world' of poetry itself: 'Hers the loveliness in death', where 'all the Muse's tales seem truly told' (as he described Greece in *The Giaour* and *Childe Harold*).

> 'Tis time this heart should be unmoved,
>     Since others it hath ceased to move,

are the lines beginning his last poem, 'On This Day I Complete my Thirty-sixth Year'. They suggest a deliberate relinquishment of the restless relation with Beauty, which still moves him, although

> unto thee
> Indifferent should the smile or frown
>   Of Beauty be.

But they are without the self-blinding mania of his previous invocations to the alternative goddess Liberty. Byron was unable to resolve the metaphysical questions which obsessed him about 'the action of Mind' and the nature of its existence 'independent of body'. So, echoing *Hamlet* for the last time, he gracefully resigned himself to chance at Missolonghi:

> Seek out — less often sought than found —
>   A soldier's grave, for thee the best;
> Then look around, and choose thy ground,
>   And take thy Rest.

Emily Brontë echoes this poem in 'I am the only being whose doom' (H.11). But more importantly, she in a sense re-wrote his internal history, when she took up the conflicts of the post-Byronic hero at the point where Byron himself had reached deadlock, and gave him through Heathcliff, a different kind of 'soldier's grave'.

Coleridge's spirit of creation spans the Romantic period and also survives a change in medium from poetry to philosophy. Apart from an occasional, almost incidental parallel between *Wuthering Heights* and *The Ancient Mariner*, the relation between Emily Brontë and Coleridge has not been investigated by Brontë scholars. This is probably owing to the elusive nature of any 'facts' about her private reading, in addition to conclusions which might be drawn from her own statement that she was temperamentally lazy in pursuing systematic courses of studies. [32] Her poems, indeed, are full of echoes of the *Mariner*; but apart from this, there is also a sympathetic resonance between some of their central ideas, implicit and explicit, which suggests that she had read enough of his prose work to gather an essential idea of the working of his mind. She may, for example, have read the *Biographia Literaria*; perhaps *The Statesman's Manual* or *On the Constitution of the Church and State*, which was written in connection with the issues of the Reform Bill of 1832 — a subject of great excitement amongst the young Brontës and their father. Emily Brontë's explicit philosophy is most openly and simply expressed in her poetry. But the deeper metaphysical parallels which I wish to draw out here, require comparison with *Wuthering Heights*, where she comes to grips with the issues of mental growth which Coleridge formulated in a particularly profound and poetic way. As always, when comparing poetic principles, the degree of direct 'influence' must remain conjectural. My aim here, is to describe how Emily Brontë's evolving pattern of a hero has essential links with Coleridge's conception of a man of genius — which itself has its roots in the vibrant emotionality of *The Ancient Mariner*.

The central principles in Coleridge's poetic philosophy, which are relevant to Emily Brontë, are: the foundation of all true thought in feeling, and the distinction between the 'man of genius' who is able to think symbolically (using the 'shaping spirit of Imagination'), and the man of power whose thought-processes are essentially dead and mechanical because they are divorced from their dynamic roots in feeling and the 'One Life'.

The poetic-philosophic quest of the mature Coleridge has the sense of always bearing some necessary relation to the colours of pure feeling portrayed in his most 'poetic' poem, *The Ancient Mariner*; while Emily Brontë's poetic novel, *Wuthering Heights*, contains within it a philosophic quest parallel to Coleridge's, internally evolving rather than super-imposed, so corresponding to his own characteristic principle about 'form as proceeding' rather than 'superinduced'. Exposure to feeling is the first stage in the evolution of thought. Thus the poet Bowles, whom Coleridge once idolised, he came to consider had sensibility but 'no native Passion, because he is not a Thinker'. [33] Noted in Coleridge's *Table Talk* is the advice:

> The best way to bring a clever young man, who has become sceptical and unsettled, to reason, is to make him *feel* something in any way. Love . . . will . . . bring him to a sense and assurance of something real and actual; and that sense alone will make him think to a sound purpose, instead of dreaming that he is thinking. [34]

Any philosophy not proved upon the pulses is an illusion, a dream of thinking, a substitute, Platonic shadow-thought. Catherine in *Wuthering Heights* needed to express 'a feeling of how I feel' as a basis for realising the very nature of her existence, and how her identity with Heathcliff gives reality to the entire 'universe':

> 'I cannot express it; but surely you and every body have a notion that there is, or should be, an existence of yours beyond you . . . If all else perished, and *he* remained, I should still continue to be; and, if all else remained, and he were annihilated, the Universe would turn to a mighty stranger.'

As Catherine feels for 'an existence beyond' herself despite Nelly's revulsion, so Coleridge suddenly addresses the reader in *The Friend*: 'Hast thou ever raised thy mind to the consideration of EXISTENCE . . . the mere act of existing?' — which had aroused in the greatest early philosophers 'a sort of sacred horror' at the notion of 'something ineffably greater than their own individual nature'. [35] And in Book X of the *Biographia* he writes: 'what proof had I of the outward *existence* of anything? . . . as a thing in itself, separate from the phenomenon or image

221

in my perception'.[36] For Coleridge the investigation of 'existence' is inseparable from the investigation of perception, which is itself a function of feeling — in so far as this is 'real and actual'; and this becomes precisely Emily Brontë's preoccupation towards the end of *Wuthering Heights*, imaged through Heathcliff's relation to Catherine's ghost.

In *The Ancient Mariner*, Coleridge depicts unaccommodated man nakedly exposed to violent and incomprehensible feeling; the passive victim of relentless forces which alternately attack and soothe him, whilst moving from one state of primitive exposure to another. This is done with the same sense of compulsion and inevitability as in *Wuthering Heights*. The significance of the poem is to be found in its intense, dreamlike evocativeness, rather than in its moral or its allegorical interpretability — which, as Coleridge himself said, makes it 'incomprehensible,/ And without head or tail'.[37] The poem is a foundation for thought rather than its finalisation. It could be said to represent Coleridge's central recurring dream; and as he wrote in a letter, 'Dreams with me are no Shadows, but the very Substances and foot-thick Calamities of my Life'.[38] As with Catherine, certain dreams have gone 'through and through me, like wine through water, and altered the colour of my mind'. The reality of their feeling makes them substantial life events. The prerequisite for the tale is the inexplicable link between the Mariner and the Wedding Guest, whose function resembles Lockwood's. It is a compulsive irrational pairing equivalent to those which maintain the 'story' of *Wuthering Heights*, with a sense of one person or aspect thereof, possessed and taken over by another: held by his 'glittering eye', 'The Mariner hath his will'. The Mariner instinctively recognises 'the man that must hear me', and in a sense it is the listener's subconscious experience which he verbalises, 'wrenched/ With woful agony', himself driven to storytelling by forces outside his will.

The organising principle of a marriage, or different kinds of marriage, true and false, lies behind *The Ancient Mariner* and *Wuthering Heights*: really as symbolic of the juxtaposition of different emotional states, and the trauma resulting from their approach to one another. The outer story of the marriage feast is both backdrop and springboard for the inner sea-story with its successive states of consciousness:

The bride hath paced into the hall
Red as a rose is she;
Nodding their heads before her goes
The merry minstrelsy. [39]

The red bride, in her stilted pageantry, both contrasts with and prefigures the nightmare 'red' sections at the centre of the poem, with the sun 'Nor dim nor red like God's own head' in its sinister punitive dawn, or the Nightmare Life-in-Death who is suddenly recognised against the sun's backdrop when it becomes 'flecked with bars': 'Her lips were red, her looks were free . . . Her skin was white as leprosy'. Only one stanza separates the figure of the bride pacing, from that of the personified Storm-Blast, who 'Struck with his o'ertaking wings' and likewise drives all before him:

With sloping masts and dipping prow,
As who pursued with yell and blow
Still treads the shadow of his foe,
And forwards bends his head,
The ship drove fast . . .

In this way, the Bride is related to the violent pursuing forces; to the spirit of the spectre-ship with its veering, darting movement before the moment of visual attack; to the avenging Polar Spirit who moves the ship along from the keel then suddenly sinks it; to the Mariner's sense of being pursued by supernatural or spiritual forces, 'Because he knows, a frightful fiend/ Doth close behind him tread', and his consequent association with the dark side of the sun as he passes 'like night from land to land'. Throughout, the ship seems an extension of the Mariner's body. His introductory words are 'There was a ship'; and there is a clear sense of its existing on three levels — its mast in the upper air, its deck at water level, its keel beneath: all zones with their own territorial powers, almost on the lines of Coleridge's rule:

In every living form, the conditions of its *existence* are to be sought for in that which is *below* it; the grounds of its *intelligibility* in that which is *above* it. [40]

There is a similar sense of exploration-lines drawn across a mental landscape in *Wuthering Heights*, with a similar jolt whenever invisible boundaries are crossed: 'We were the first that ever burst/ Into that silent sea'. Every change of state brings disorientation, like Lockwood finding his known landmarks obliterated after a dream and a snowfall; and a recognition of different animating spirits at work.

After a gruesome species of marriage with the spectre-ship ('The naked hulk alongside came'), the Mariner takes on some of that ship's identity. His effort to pray, which ends in 'a wicked whisper' that 'made my heart as dry as dust', echoes the spectre's sudden bound away towards the horizon:

> The Sun's rim dips; the stars rush out;
> At one stride comes the dark;
> With far-heard whisper, o'er the sea,
> Off shot the spectre-bark.

Later the ship 'bounds' like a pawing horse: 'It flung the blood into my head/ And I fell down in a swound', and at the end of the story his own ship is taken for a death-ship by the Hermit and Pilot. When, at that point, his ship sinks 'like lead' (following the path of the Albatross), carrying with it the curse embodied by the dead men's accusing eyes, the Mariner undergoes a transformation rather than a release: a type of death in which the sense of curse within him, is simply transferred into another medium — a 'strange power of speech':

> Stunned by that loud and dreadful sound
> Which sky and ocean smote,
> Like one that hath been seven days drowned
> My body lay afloat.

The energy of that subaqueous 'stunning' sound then serves to stun the Wedding Guest: 'He went like one that hath been stunned,/ And is of sense forlorn'. Like Lockwood at the end of *Wuthering Heights*, who feels 'irresistibly impelled' to escape the moonlit vision of Cathy and Hareton on the 'doorstones', he 'turns from the bridegroom's door'.

In a poem of 1844 Emily Brontë echoes *The Ancient Mariner* in a ballad-style reverie:

> On a sunny brae alone I lay
> One summer afternoon;

It was the marriage-time of May
With her young lover, June. (H.170)

The dreamer, alone 'of all the wedding guests', is 'sullen', until
he hears the 'strange minstrelsy' of 'A thousand thousand
glancing fires . . . kindling in the air', while 'The little glittering
spirits sang,/ Or seemed to sing, to me'; like the spirit-sounds
from the dead men's mouths in the *Mariner*: 'Around, around,
flew each sweet sound';

Sometimes a-dropping from the sky
I heard the sky-lark sing
Sometimes all little birds that are,
How they seemed to fill the sea and air . . .

One type of wedding is negated and an alternative vision is
received. At the centre of *The Ancient Mariner*, after the union
with Life-in-Death which begins his own nightmare 'Alone on a
wide wide sea', the Mariner perceives the union between sun-
and moon-light which awakens in him a new sense of beauty,
despite the horror and grossness of his subject and situation:

Beyond the shadow of the ship
I watched the water-snakes:
They moved in tracks of shining white,
And when they reared, the elfish light
Fell off in hoary flakes.

'Within the shadow of the ship' the colours are bright and flash
with 'golden fire'; the snakes, which seem an embodiment of the
curse in the numerous eyes of the dead men, become beautiful
in the light of the sun and moon which have both been persecu-
tory and ominous; a perception resulting in the 'spring of love'
gushing 'unaware' from his heart. This central section is echoed
in Emily Brontë's 'Stars', which contrasts the 'fierce beams' of
the sun ('Blood-red he rose, and arrow-straight') with the 'cool
radiance' of the stars (H.184).

These sudden changes in the state of feeling, with marriages
of opposing 'lights', all apparently irrational yet responding to
a deeper inevitability, constitute the basic substance of
Coleridge's poem and of *Wutherinig Heights*. They image what
Coleridge would call a new perception of the 'relations of

225

things', leading towards a 'higher reality'.[41] Thus the gush of love resulting in a heaven-sent sleep which 'slid into my soul', seems to be echoed in Heathcliff's account of his grave-desecration, when he becomes aware of Catherine's spirit not in the grave but above the ground: 'A sudden sense of relief flowed, from my heart, through every limb — I relinquished my labour of agony, and turned consoled . . . Her presence was with me . . . it led me home'. At the same time, as the opposite pole of a dialectical process, Catherine is also for Heathcliff a Nightmare Life-in-Death condemning him to 'intolerable torture'; destroying his sleep like the Mariner's, and ultimately leading him through a slow path towards death, a 'strange way of killing' in which his eyes like the Mariner's are bound up with the eyes of the dead: 'his eyes pursued' the unearthly vision of Catherine 'with unwearied vigilance', and 'were never weaned away'. Heathcliff's body and mind, as the possibility of death approaches, are described in terms like those of the Mariner's ship-body straining towards the 'harbour': 'you might as well bid a man struggling in the water, rest within arm's length of the shore!' With 'glittering, restless eyes' like the Mariner's 'glittering eye', his 'frame shivering . . . as a tight-stretched cord vibrates', he echoes the ship's rocking back and forth 'with a short uneasy motion' before it takes its final bound like a 'pawing horse'. Heathcliff describes himself as 'in the shadow' of an approaching change; like the shadow of the Mariner's ship at the point where the lights mingle and 'love' gushes ('Nelly, there is a strange change approaching — I'm in its shadow at present'); and finally, like the ship before it sinks into the bay, struck by the Polar Spirit even within the bounds of the harbour, he is 'swallowed up' by 'one universal idea . . . it has devoured my existence — I am swallowed in the anticipation of its fulfilment'.

Thus the bright, primitive colours of feeling acting in *The Ancient Mariner* find a deep affinity with *Wuthering Heights*, both in their expression and in their modes of interaction and rhythmic inevitability, with alternating qualities of nightmare and blissful reverie. It is hard to avoid noting, in passing, how in this both works show a vivid realisation of sexuality and the feelings behind 'marriage' which is ahead of their time, and deeper than Charlotte's more overt concern; though Coleridge's exploration

226

is bounded and inhibited by the overlying framework of Christian guilt and retribution superimposed by the poem's 'moral'. Comparison heightens one's recognition of Emily's achievement in pushing through to a genuine ethical solution through her two-generation story; embodying a mental development, not simply a voyage and return with endless, repetitive telling of the tale 'from land to land'. The overall structure of *Wuthering Heights*, indeed, is much more complex than the *Mariner*, and carries within it ideas and a dialectic which bear a closer relation to Coleridge's poetically expressed prose work. The feeling of existence, the 'sacred horror' of the 'mere act of existing', is the first step towards creative thought in both Emily Brontë and Coleridge. Beyond this, the investigation of further problems of perception is focussed in *Wuthering Heights* on Heathcliff's final struggle, and in Coleridge, on his admiring but ambivalent attitude towards Wordsworth.

For many years (during the period between the *Lyrical Ballads* and the *Biographia*) Coleridge seems to have held a dual view of Wordsworth. On the one hand he wanted him to become the First Philosopher-poet and present to the world an authoritative and redemptive model; on the other hand he recognised that this would constitute a form of 'superinduced' shaping, of smooth and ready-made solutions, in fact contradicting true poetic genius and the 'shaping spirit of Imagination' which Coleridge felt (after his relationship with Wordsworth) had become lost or suspended within himself. In 'Frost at Midnight' he envisaged his baby Hartley as a sort of Wordsworthian baby-poet who would find fulfilment in a way that his father had not:

> But thou, my babe! shalt wander like a breeze . . .
>
> so shalt thou see and hear
> The lovely shapes and sounds intelligible
> Of that eternal language . . .

In his *Table Talk* he describes a failed 'plan' for Wordsworth's *Prelude*, in which Wordsworth was supposed to 'assume the station of a man in mental repose, one whose principles were made up, and so prepared to deliver upon authority a system of philosophy'. This system would 'reconcile all the anomalies' and promise 'future glory and restoration'; it would constitute, in effect, 'a redemptive process in operation' and substantiate in

227

a neat and authoritative way 'what I have been all my life doing in my system of philosophy.'[42] And indeed his desire for an ultimate philosophic 'authority' expressed through poetry, seems to be associated with his own projected yet impossible Opus Maximum, and with the wish of one part of himself to rest in peace and harmony with a 'cultivated surface' of poetry, 'instead of delving in the unwholesome quicksilver mines of metaphysic depths'.[43] The dialectic within Coleridge is not so much one of poetry versus philosophy (as creative media), as of a smooth, super-induced idea versus a mysterious, troubling, evolutionary idea. The true 'man of genius' (he said in a lecture of 1819) has the 'power of existing universally'; he 'finds a reflex to himself, were it only in the mystery of being'.[44] And in chapter II of the *Biographia*, he distinguishes 'absolute genius' from 'commanding genius': the former being creative and poetic, living 'in an intermundium of which their own living spirit supplies the *substance*, and their imagination the ever-varying *form*'; while the latter 'must impress their preconceptions on the world without, in order to present them back to their own view with the satisfying degree of clearness'.[45] This type of mental activity (which corresponds in effect to his desire to make Wordsworth an 'authority'), is in fact a danger to creative thought, resulting in omnipotently organised works of art. In 'tranquil times' it makes 'a perfect poem in palace, or temple, or landscape-garden'; but in 'times of tumult' it cannot stand the test, and such men 'come forth as the shaping spirit of Ruin'.

This distinction between antithetical types of genius is intimately related to all Coleridge's thought-organising contrasts: the mechanical versus the organic; Fancy versus Imagination; and the idea which carries a commandment or expresses an authority, versus 'idea' in 'the highest sense of the word': and 'An IDEA, in the *highest* sense of that word, cannot be conveyed but by a *symbol*'.[46] Coleridge distinguished, therefore, between sign-systems and symbolic systems. Likewise the Fancy simply rearranges its mechanical 'counters', 'fixities and definites', linked only by 'the law of association'; but the Primary Imagination is the living Power and prime Agent of all human Perception, and ... a repetition in the finite mind of the eternal act of creation in the infinite I AM.[47]

And the secondary Imagination echoes this activity: 'It dissolves, diffuses, dissipates, in order to recreate ... It is essentially *vital*, even as all objects (as objects) are essentially fixed and dead.' This is the distinction which informs the dynamic dialectic of Heathcliff's struggle in *Wuthering Heights*. At the end, he suddenly switches his mode of mental operation, from that of a 'commanding genius' obsessed by mechanical links of association, to that of 'absolute genius'. He becomes a man of Imagination rather than Fancy; and foregoes his position as the 'shaping spirit of Ruin' when he discovers his internal shaping spirit of Imagination. When Heathcliff tells Nelly that 'there is a strange change approaching' which he cannot define but only describe his feelings, he is referring to this switch in mentality. He is aware that it is 'the precise time to revenge myself' and his power over the two houses is complete, yet he has 'lost the will' to do so, owing to his dawning insight that this mental attitude is what makes Catherine (whom he calls his 'life', his 'soul') appear dead to him:

> 'I cannot look down to this floor, but her features are shaped on the flags! ... I am surrounded with her image! ... my own features mock me with a resemblance. The entire world is a dreadful collection of memoranda that she did exist, and that I have lost her!'

The image of Catherine, the soul of his whole world-view, is made up of mechanical components linked purely by memory and association, but lacking the spirit which dissolves in order to recreate. Heathcliff is tormented by the dawning realisation that, despite his commanding genius, he is separated from his soul, his imagination, the governing dynamic principle of his existence. He has lost the 'living Power and prime Agent' of his perception, the power which is 'essentially vital' by contrast with objects, memoranda, which 'are essentially fixed and dead'.

In Coleridge's thought, ideas are the poetry of the mind, just as imagination is its soul. He distinguishes ideas from 'conceptions', which are abstractable from their context and so enter the field of mechanical existence; and he distinguishes poetry or the poetic spirit from the rhetorical construct which is a poem, and which may or may not contain poetry. Poetry is the highest form of philosophy in man, just as imagination is his highest faculty. In Book IX of the *Biographia*, Coleridge describes the 'Mystics' who 'helped to prevent my mind from being imprisoned within the outlines of any dogmatic system':

> They contributed to keep alive the *heart* in the *head*; gave me an indistinct, yet stirring and working presentiment, that all the products of the mere reflective faculty partook of *death*, and were as the rattling twigs and sprays in winter, into which a sap was yet to be propelled from some root to which I had not penetrated, if they were to afford my soul either food or shelter. [48]

Coleridge's rhetoric of natural growth and death is consonant with the first Catherine's description of her need for Edgar and Heathcliff, foliage and rocks, the latter being 'a source of little visible delight, but necessary'. Emily Brontë makes use of what Coleridge calls the 'delving' mind in action in the 'metaphysic depths', unearthing graves, ghosts and the rocks beneath, to create the dynamic linkages of a 'redemptive process in operation', rather than a superinduced philosophy 'partaking of death'. The crisis for her hero occurs when he comes tantalisingly close to the governing dynamic principle of his mental existence, while still being as distant as death from life, hell from heaven. The tormenting 'signs' of Catherine need to be converted into a symbolic language, to become the kind of idea which 'cannot be conveyed but by a symbol'; which embodies 'the God-like within us', and

> flies homeward to its Parent Mind enriched with a thousand forms, itself above all form and still remaining in its own simplicity and identity. [49]

Ultimately, the metamorphosis of Heathcliff, Catherine's 'strange way of killing' him, embodies this very process of symbol-formation. It begins with the congregation of a 'thousand forms' intensely charged with personal associations, and beginning a sort of 'homeward' journey backwards in time:

'If I try to describe the thousand forms of past associations and ideas he [Hareton] awakens and embodies . . . Five minutes ago, Hareton seemed a personification of my youth, not a human being — I felt to him in such a variety of ways . . .'

Heathcliff's journey to Catherine begins with his adopted son, the child within himself. For Heathcliff, Hareton is becoming a 'symbol' in the Coleridgean sense, entering another world of reality. His image both belongs to the world of noumena — so linking his existence with the ghostly unattainable Catherine — whilst finding an existence in the phenomenal world; so showing 'the translucence of the Eternal through and in the Temporal', and partaking of 'the Reality which it renders intelligible'. [50] When Heathcliff feels the need to 'turn out' his mind to Nelly (as she puts it), he is not merely employing a rhetorical device, but prefiguring the internal transformation which is soon to be imaged in his bodily metamorphosis, as he becomes subject to the shaping power of Imagination. The key point in Heathcliff's change of perception occurs when he sees the eyes of Hareton and the second Catherine confronting him in unison, and recognises — not a similarity which he has known for a long time — but an identity; that they 'are those of Catherine Earnshaw'. This change in mentality is presented through the entire symbolic system of the final part of the book. Imagination, in Coleridge's terms, 'gives birth to a system of symbols, harmonious in themselves, and consubstantial with the truths, of which they are the conductors'. [51] The eyes both 'conduct' the truth and partake of its substantiality. Through them, Heathcliff receives a sort of electric charge of reality, a new relation between noumenon and phenomenon, a system of symbols which then flowers on all levels of the book's story, as in Lockwood's final painful 'dream' of a marriage beyond romance.

Thus the dialectic between opposing modes of feeling which has characterised the struggle throughout *Wuthering Heights* is finally resolved, not on a winning or losing basis (revenge and inheritance), but through dissolving in order to recreate (metamorphosis). The metamorphosis of Heathcliff completes the evolution from an original intense adhesive passion, through 'delving in the unwholesome metaphysic depths' and an illusory

231

union in the graveyard (indicating false thought), to a true symbolic system which realises 'an idea in the highest sense of the word'. Emily Brontë fulfils in artistic form, the central principles of Coleridge's thought. The second generation lovers inhabit the earth's surface; the first generation the soil and air; only together do they constitute a total symbolic system. The 'heaven' Heathcliff finds is not an escape into death, from phenomenon to noumenon direct; rather, it superimposes layers of existence or consciousness in a poetic, aesthetic manner, 'enriched with a thousand forms'. This is the wailing spirit of Catherine 'come home' to its 'Parent Mind'. The resulting mental landscape is one which — like Coleridge's man of genius — can weather 'times of tumult': not just the coming 'autumn storms' of nature but, as Lockwood ruefully observes, 'Satan and all his legions'. The ambiguous and disruptive demonic power which had threatened to put a curse on both the houses of Linton and Earnshaw, instead participates in 'a repetition in the finite mind of the eternal act of creation in the infinite I AM'.

# NOTES

## ABBREVIATIONS

CB    Charlotte Brontë
EB    Emily Brontë
*MUW*  *The Miscellaneous and Unpublished Writings of Charlotte and Patrick Branwell Brontë* (The Shakespeare Head Bronte), ed. T. J. Wise and J. A. Symington, 2 vols., 1936 and 1938
*SHL*   *The Brontës: Their Lives, Friendships and Correspondence* (The Shakespeare Head Bronte), ed. T. J. Wise and J. A. Symington, 4 vols., 1932

## NOTES TO INTRODUCTION (pages ix – xiii)

1. E.M. Forster, *Aspects of the Novel* (1927), p.187.
2. See A. MacLeish, *Poetry and Experience* (1960), p.7.
3. CB, letter to W.S. Williams, *SHL*, II.245.
4. From the *Britannia*, 15 January 1848, and the *Spectator*, 18 December 1847. For these and the following review extracts see *The Brontes: The Critical Heritage*, ed. M. Allott, 1974; also *Wuthering Heights: A Casebook*, ed. M. Allott, 1970.
5. *Examiner*, 8 January 1848.
6. *Douglas Jerrold's Weekly*, 15 January 1848.
7. *Tait's Edinburgh Magazine*, February 1848.
8. *Leader*, 28 December 1850.
9. *Atlas*, 22 January 1848.
10. *Palladium*, September 1850.
11. *Britannia*, 15 January 1848.

## NOTES TO PART II: *WUTHERING HEIGHTS* AND CATASTROPHIC CHANGE (pages 119 – 129)

1. Milton, *An Apology for Smectymnuus.*
2. On the psychoanalytic concept of 'catastophic change', see W.R. Bion, *A Memoir of the Future* (3 vols., 1975 – 79); W.R. Bion, *Brazilian Lectures* (1973 – 74); *Bion in New York and Sao Paulo* (Lectures, 1980); W.R. Bion, *Attention and Interpretation* (1970); D. Meltzer, *The Kleinian Development*, vol. III (1978).
3. Susanne Langer, *Philosophy in a New Key* (1947), p.41.
4. Milton, *Of Education.*
5. I.A. Richards, *Practical Criticism* (1929), p.314.
6. CB's Preface is reprinted in most modern editions of *Wuthering Heights.*
7. Shelley, *Defence of Poetry.*
8. Yeats, 'An Acre of Grass'.

NOTES TO PART III: EVOLUTION OF THE POETIC SPIRIT
(pages 133 – 179)

1. Elizabeth Gaskell, *Life of Charlotte Bronte* (1857; Everyman edition, 1971), p.151.
2. Numbers refer to those in C.W. Hatfield's edition of EB's *Complete Poems* (1941).
3. Cited by W. Gérin in *Emily Bronte* (1971; Oxford paperback, 1978), p.67, from C.K. Shorter, *Complete Poems of Emily Bronte* (1910).
4. *SHL*, II.273, I.113.
5. *SHL*, II.51
6. CB wrote to EB from Brussels in 1841: 'Regards to the fighting gentry' (*SHL*, I.300).
7. *SHL*, II.49.
8. CB, 'Biographical Notice of Ellis and Acton Bell', 1850; reprinted with her Preface, in most modern editions of *Wuthering Heights*.
9. W. Gérin, *Emily Bronte*, p.181.
10. *SHL*, I.262.
11. According to CB in her Preface to *Wuthering Heights*.
12. See Gérin, *Emily Bronte*, p.110.
13. Letter to W.S. Williams; *SHL*, II.165.
14. 'Biographical Notice of Ellis and Acton Bell'.
15. *MUW*, I.1.
16. Gaskell, *Life of Charlotte Bronte*, p.124.
17. See Gérin, *Emily Bronte*, p.18.
18. An account is given in C. Alexander, *The Early Writings of Charlotte Bronte* (1983), p.11.
19. CB to Henry Nussey, *SHL*, I.232.
20. CB to Hartley Coleridge in December 1840; see *Times Literary Supplement*, 14 May 1970, p.544.
21. CB, *Poems*, ed. T. Winnifrith (1984), p.184: 'We wove a web in childhood,/ A web of sunny air'.
22. 'Tales of the Islanders', quoted by W. Gérin, *Charlotte Bronte* (1967), p.16.
23. *SHL*, I.97.
24. *SHL*, I.91.
25. As Ellen Nussey saw them: *SHL*, I.112.
26. 'Ode on the African Games', *MUW*, I.168. The 'Chief Genii' Brannii, Tallii, Emii and Anii were Branwell, Charlotte, Emily and Anne respectively.
27. 'The Country of the Genii', *MUW*, I.3 – 4.
28. Gérin, *Charlotte Bronte*, p.26.
29. Gaskell, *Life of Charlotte Bronte*, p.57.
30. CB, 'The trumpet hath sounded', *Poems*, pp.133 – 35.
31. 'Albion and Marina', *MUW*, I.28 – 29.
32. *MUW*, I.19 – 20.
33. 'The Duke of Zamorna', *MUW*, II.350.
34. 'The Bridal', *MUW*, I.205.
35. Melodie Monahan, 'Charlotte Brontë's *The Poetaster*: Text and Notes', *Studies in Romanticism*, 20 (1981), p.480.

36. See 'Ellen Nussey's Narrative', *SHL*, I.96.
37. The 'Roe Head Journal', cited by Gérin, *Charlotte Bronte*, p.103.
38. *SHL*, I.243.
39. 'The Poetaster', p.493.
40. *MUW*, I.364.
41. *MUW*, II.12.
42. *MUW*, II.9.
43. *Poems*, p.294.
44. *MUW*, I.304.
45. *SHL*, I.155.
46. See for example 'Tales of the Islanders', in Alexander, *Early Writings*, p.51.
47. *MUW*, I.205.
48. Winnifrith (*Poems*, p.293) has 'mortal king', but Alexander (*Early Writings*, p.142), also quoting from the MS, has 'mental king', which makes more sense.
49. *SHL*, II.3.
50. *SHL*, I.143.
51. The 'Roe Head Journal', cited by Gérin, *Charlotte Brontë*, p.106; also the following quotations.
52. *SHL*, II.117.
53. *Poems*, p.205.
54. EB, *Poems*, nos. 37, 76.
55. *SHL*, I.240.
56. Foreword to 'Caroline Vernon', in Charlotte Brontë, *Five Novelettes*, ed. W. Gérin (The Folio Press, 1971), p.277.
57. *Five Novelettes*, p.312.
58. *MUW*, II.404.
59. *SHL*, I.260.
60. *SHL*, I.297.
61. *SHL*, I.304.
62. *SHL*, I.298.
63. *SHL*, II.13.
64. 'Mina Laury', *Five Novelettes*, p.147.
65. *SHL*, II.70.
66. CB, *Poems*, p.24.
67. *SHL*, II.256.
68. *SHL*, II.114.
69. 'An Hour's Musings' by Branwell in 1934; *MUW*, II.60.
70. Preface to the second edition of *The Tenant of Wildfell Hall*.
71. *The Poems of Anne Brontë*, ed. E. Chitham (1979), pp.128–29.
72. Letter to W.S. Williams, *SHL*, II.189.
73. R. Heilman, 'Charlotte Brontë's "New" Gothic', in *From Jane Austen to Joseph Conrad*, ed. R. Rathburn and M. Steinmann, Jr. (1958).
74. George Eliot, letter to Charles Bray, 11 June 1848 (in *Jane Eyre and Villette: A Casebook*, ed. M. Allott, 1973; p.61).

NOTES TO PART IV: EMILY BRONTË AND THE ROMANTIC
SPIRIT OF CREATION (pages 183 – 232)

1. For CB's list of recommended reading to Ellen Nussey in 1834, see *SHL*,
   I.122.
2. CB's Preface to *Wuthering Heights*.
3. *Michael* and other poems of Wordsworth are quoted from *Wordsworth:
   Poetry and Prose*, ed. W. M. Merchant (1955).
4. The skating passage 'From an Unpublished Poem' was printed in *The
   Friend* (December 28 1809), beginning 'Wisdom and Spirit of the
   Universe!' and ending 'tranquil as a summer sea'; the Winander Boy
   ('There was a Boy') in 1800; the Simplon Pass ('Brook and road/ Were
   fellow-travellers') in 1845.
5. See Keats's journal-letter of February-May 1819; Keats regarded
   Wordsworth as 'a great Poet if not a Philosopher' (21 February 1818).
6. *Adonais* and other poems of Shelley are quoted from *Selected Poems*, ed. E.
   Blunden (1954).
7. CB to Ellen Nussey in 1834 (*SHL*, I.122).
8. Gérin, *Emily Brontë*, p.38.
9. Journal, 10 March 1814; *Letters and Journals of Lord Byron*, ed. L.
   Marchand, 12 vols (1974 – 80), III.250. This and most of the following
   references to Byron's letters and journals may be found in Thomas
   Moore's *Life of Byron*, 1833; see I.362.
10. Ravenna journal, 28 January 1821; Marchand, VIII.37; Moore, II.244.
11. Letter of 18 November 1820 to John Murray; Marchand, VII.299; Moore
    (dating 9bre 18), II.219.
12. The 1821 journal called 'Detached Thoughts', no.76; Marchand, IX.38
    (not in Moore, who does not give this journal as a whole, but quotes
    extracts here and there, whilst using it indirectly as a basis for insight into
    Byron's character).
13. Margiad Evans, 'Byron and Emily Brontë, *Life and Letters Today*, LVII
    (1948), pp.216, 214.
14. Letters of 30 November 1813 to Moore (Marchand, III.184; Moore,
    I.313), and 29 November to Annabella Milbanke (Marchand, III.179).
15. Alpine journal, 29 September 1816; Marchand, V.105; Moore, I.492.
16. Ravenna journal, 6 January 1821; Marchand, VIII.16; Moore, II.232.
17. 'Detached Thoughts' no.96; Marchand, IX.46; Moore, II.515.
18. Journal, 23 November 1813; Marchand, III.216; Moore, I.323.
19. As, for example: 'I have been more ravished myself than anybody since
    the Trojan war' (letter of 29 October 1819 to R.B. Hoppner: Marchand,
    VI.237).
20. 18 September 1812; Marchand, III.199.
21. 'Detached Thoughts' no. 34; Marchand, IX.24; Moore, I.137. Moore
    describes Byron's 'disposition to form strong attachments', in relation to
    Mary Chaworth; and how he was 'thrown back, isolated, on his own
    restless desires' (Moore, I.136 – 38).
22. Journal, 17 November 1813; Marchand, III.210; Moore, I.319.
23. 'Detached Thoughts', no.72; Marchand, IX.37.

24. Ravenna journal, 12 January 1821; Marchand, VIII.26; Moore, II.237.
25. 'Detached Thoughts' no.65; Marchand, IX.34.
26. 'Detached Thoughts' no.101; Marchand, IX.467; Moore, II.516. See also *Don Juan* 9.xxxvii.
27. 27 November 1813; Marchand, III.225; Moore, I.328.
28. Journal, 24 November 1813; Marchand, III.217; Moore, I.323; and the Ravenna journal of 9 January 1821 (Marchand, VIII.20; Moore, II.234).
29. 24 September 1821; Marchand, VIII.220; Moore, I.362.
30. See 'Detached Thoughts' no. 96; Marchand, IX.45; Moore, II.515.
31. Ravenna journal, 18 February 1821; Marchand, VIII.47; Moore, II.251.
32. See EB's diary note of July 1841; *SHL*, I.238.
33. As for example in Coleridge's lecture 'On Poesy or Art', reprinted in *Biographia Literaria*, ed. J. Shawcross, 2 vols (1907), II.262; or *Biographia Literaria*, chapter XIV.
34. *Table Talk*, 17 May 1830; Oxford edition (1917), p.96.
35. Essay XI, *The Friend*, 3 vols (1837), III.203.
36. *Biographia Literaria*, ed. Shawcross, chapter X; I.133.
37. See Coleridge's 'anonymous' epigram, subsequently printed as a note to *Biographia Literaria* at the end of chapter I.
38. Letter to T. Wedgwood, 16 September 1803; *Letters*, II.991.
39. *The Rime of the Ancient Mariner* and other poems of Coleridge are quoted from *Poetical Works*, ed. E.H. Coleridge (1980).
40. Appendix to *On the Constitution of the Church and State*, ed. J. Colmer (1976), p.183.
41. Ibid., p.183.
42. *Table Talk*, 21 July 1832, p.188.
43. *Biographia Literaria*, chapter I, I.10.
44. Lecture of 18 January 1819, in *Coleridge's Philosophical Lectures*, ed. K. Coburn (1949), p.179.
45. *Biographia Literaria*, chapter II, I.20-21.
46. *Biographia Literaria*, chapter IX, I.100.
47. *Biographia Literaria*, chapter XIII, I.202.
48. *Biographia Literaria*, chapter IX, I.98.
49. *The Statesman's Manual*, in *Lay Sermons*, ed. R. J. White (1972), p.50.
50. Ibid., p.30.
51. Ibid., p.29.

# BIBLIOGRAPHY

Recent editions of THE TEXT OF WUTHERING HEIGHTS are based on the first edition of 1847. As that was inaccurately printed and presented, and EB's own corrected copy is lost, some emendations are made (including reference to CB's over-corrected edition of 1850). EB's original paragraphing is usually retained, and on the whole variations are minor matters of personal taste in punctuation and spelling. Some easily available editions are: the Penguin English Library, ed. D. Daiches (1965); the Norton Critical Edition, ed. W.M. Sale, Jr. (1963, 1972), which has a short list of textual variants, extracts from some contemporary reviews, and a selection of modern critical essays; the Everyman, introd. by M. Drabble, 1978 (CB's paragraphing: no glossary), which includes a substantial selection from EB's poems ed. P. Henderson; the World's Classics, ed. I. Jack (1981), which has explanatory notes, and chapters numbered as in the original two-volume edition (I:1 – 14, II:1 – 20); this text is that of the Clarendon edition, ed. I. Jack and H. Marsden (1976), which has textual variants and a series of appendices by different scholars intended to provide authoritative statements on EB's use of dialect, the legal background, the book's publishing history, the importance of EB's juvenilia. All these editions reprint CB's 'Biographical Notice of Ellis and Acton Bell' and her Preface to the 1850 edition of *Wuthering Heights*. The present study quotes from the Penguin edition.

An excellent CRITICAL INTRODUCTION to the whole novel is F. Goodridge's *Emily Brontë: Wuthering Heights* (1964) — on theme, narrative and metaphoric structure; D. Daiches' shorter introduction to the Penguin edition evokes well its disturbing qualities. Modern criticism could be said to begin with D. Cecil's classic 'storm versus calm' interpretation (*Early Victorian Novelists*, 1934) which, together with the different lawyer's analysis by C.P. Sanger ('The Structure of *Wuthering Heights*', 1926), both often reprinted, initiated serious study of the novel's intellectual qualities — in Cecil's terms 'logical as a fugue'. G. D. Klingopoulos ('The Novel as Dramatic Poem: *Wuthering Heights*', *Scrutiny* XIV, 1946 – 7), compared the novel's elemental strength to Greek tragedy in literal Wordsworthian terms, as 'found amongst genuine peasants' in 'places which yield only the permanent essentials of experience'. A. Kettle's humanist-Marxist interpretation 'rescuing *Wuthering Heights* from the transcendentalists' saw Heathcliff as partly a moral force, in the sense of inverting the standards of bourgeois morality (*An Introduction to the English Novel*, 1951). A different sort of rescue was effected by D. Van Ghent (*The English Novel, Form and Function*, 1953; often reprinted), focussing more sharply on the organic form of the novel in her description of how barriers such as the 'window image' suggest an interaction between different kinds of reality; also by M. Schorer ('Fiction and the Matrix of Analogy', *Kenyon Review* XI, 1949) who described the wild imagery of animals and elements running throughout and how this related to the human forces and passions. Also on its poetic qualities, I. Nixon ('A Note on the Pattern of *Wuthering*

239

*Heights'*, *English Studies* XLV, 1964) describes how action, past and future, is grouped around key lyrical and dramatic passages. E. Shannon (*Nineteenth Century Fiction* XIV, 1959) discussed 'unforgivable sin' in 'Lockwood's Dreams and the Exegesis of *Wuthering Heights*': 'Instead of prescriptive morality, [EB] offers a transcendent ethic.' W.A. Madden ('*Wuthering Heights*: The Binding of Passion', *Nineteenth Century Fiction* XXVII, 1972) describes the binding force of Joseph through his negative qualities.

A seminal essay was written by R. Chase ('The Brontës, or Myth Domesticated', *Kenyon Review* IX, 1947; often reprinted), describing the Brontë novels as portraying the domestication of a mythic or romantic element, with Heathcliff as 'sheer dazzling sexual and intellectual force'. Its influence appears in most subsequent interpretations: thus D. Donoghue ('Emily Brontë: On the Latitude of Interpretation', *Havard English Studies* I, ed. M.W. Bloomfield, 1970) sees the 'declaration of Romantic rights' in the first part leading to 'a long process of accommodation'; K. Sagar ('The Originality of *Wuthering Heights*', in *The Art of Emily Brontë* ed. A. Smith, 1976) sees a demolition of conventional morality followed by a 'reconstruction which is also a repudiation of romanticism'. T. Moser ('What is the matter with Emily Jane? Conflicting Impulses in *Wuthering Heights*', *Nineteenth Century Fiction* XVII, 1962) gives a Freudian interpretation with Heathcliff as 'the id, the source of psychic energy', and the novel's last paragraph 'profoundly ironic' as the second-generation lovers are 'oblivious to the primitive forces that underlie life'. Other views of Heathcliff as a semi-allegorical figure include V. Buckley ('Passion and Control in *Wuthering Heights*', *Southern Review* I, 1964) and an interesting analysis by W.A. Craik (*The Brontë Novels*, 1968): 'if Catherine is the impetus of the story, Heathcliff is its structure', a focus of 'figurative language'. T. Eagleton, in an ideological-Marxist formulation which allows little of the novel's flesh to shine through (*Myths of Power*, 1975) reinterprets Chase in terms of a clash between an old-world 'civilised delicacy' and industrial 'stoicism and energy and brashness' which EB unlike CB maintains to the end unresolved — the novel's 'inner ideological structure' being imposed by 'the real history of the West Riding'. M. Allott ('The Rejection of Heathcliff?', *Essays in Criticism* VIII, 1958), which is illuminating on patterns of imagery associated with Heathcliff, prefigures I. – S. Ewbank (*Their Proper Sphere*: A Study of the Brontë Sisters as Early-Victorian Female Novelists, 1966) in an overall viewpoint of a split between 'head and heart' in which Heathcliff as an exaggeratedly Byronic hero is 'placed morally' and EB ultimately affirms the 'healthful' 'domesticated virtues' despite her 'powerful vision of the other life as well'. Q.D. Leavis ('A Fresh Approach to *Wuthering Heights*', *Lectures in America* by F.R. and Q.D. Leavis, 1969), in a controversial essay, offers a commonsensical moral view in amateur-psychological terms of EB's artistic confusion — being the result of her psychological confusion when trying to disentangle herself from a Romantic incest theme, to a 'more mature intention'.

A more telling examination of the novel's pulsing dialectic is made by T. Vogler ('Story and History in *Wuthering Heights*'), in *Twentieth Century Interpretations of Wutheriong Heights*, ed. same author, 1968), describing 'images of change' which suggest a larger process of change but ultimately no 'resolution' of contraries. In *The Disappearance of God* (1963), J. Hillis Miller gives a stimulating if abstract metaphysical reading of figures embodying 'elemental energies' with some necessary connection between first and second generations: 'The destructive love of Heathcliff and Catherine is the necessary ground of the benign love of Hareton and the second Cathy'. In general however, recent criticism of *Wuthering Heights* would appear to have reached a kind of impasse, although the same debates are perpetuated in varying clothing — by contrast with CB who, with her well documented literary career, has been a fruitful object of academic study. In a useful book J. Hewish (*Emily Brontë: A Critical and Biographical Study*, 1969), aimed to decrease EB's 'inaccessibility' through a general survey of all the relevant extraneous materials including literary 'models' for *Wuthering Heights*. J. F. Goodridge ('A New Heaven and a New Earth', in *The Art of Emily Brontë*, ed. A. Smith, 1976) gives a more subtle analysis of the nature of EB's use of Scott's fiction and of ballads as 'sources' for her narrative. T. Winnifrith (*The Brontës and Their Background*, 1973) also surveys the literary and social background, from which EB appears the most socially conscious of the sisters, though her 'enigmatic' novel receives only a 'partial and perverted' recognition from social or other interpretations; he concludes therefore that 'any attempt to give a total picture of *Wuthering Heights* is bound to be incoherent, because in the last resort *Wutheriing Heights* is incoherent'. F. Kermode (*The Classic*, 1975) from a similar standpoint, takes *Wuthering Heights* as an example of a classic enigma open to infinite interpretation without ever becoming 'closed'; the text's 'openness' is taken as synonymous with 'indeterminacies of meaning' requiring completion by the reader each time it is read. *Wuthering Heights*' refusal to respond to academic ideological (as opposed to descriptive) approaches, has been recognised by its more perceptive critics but at the expense of arousing a lot of unconscious hostility, directed back against the book whose creative spirit cannot be reductively manipulated.

*     *     *     *     *

The standard edition of EB's COMPLETE POEMS, used in this study, is that of C.W. Hatfield (1941). There are many selections, such as that of P. Henderson (1947) with a good introduction (see also the Everyman edition of *Wuthering Heights*), and that in S. Davies, *The Brontë Sisters: Selected Poems* (1976), and by D. Thompson (1972). Interesting studies of EB's poems include: M. Visick, *The Genesis of Wuthering Heights* (1958, often reprinted), a classic though literal-minded relation of the content of Gondal to that of the novel; I.H. Buchen, 'Emily Brontë and the Metaphysics of Childhood and Love' (*Nineteenth Century Fiction* XXI, 1967); R. Miles, 'A Baby God: The Creative Dynamism of Emily Brontë's Poetry' (in *The Art of Emily Brontë*, ed. A. Smith, 1976) on the nature of EB's mysticism; B. Hardy ('The Lyricism of Emily Brontë', also in *The Art of Emily Brontë*); D. Donoghue, 'The Other Emily' (in *Twentieth Century Views*, ed. I. Gregor, 1970), on the relation of EB's 'subjective religion' to the working of metapor in her poems, which stand, generically, somewhere in between 'soliloquies' and 'dramatic monologues'. There are several BIOGRAPHICAL STUDIES of EB; some love their

241

author, others hate her. Thus the sympathetic, balanced nature of W. Gérin's biography (*Emily Brontë*, 1971), despite the paucity of primary sources available, may be stressed by comparison with the idiosyncratic and antagonistic view of M. Spark (*Emily Brontë: Her Life and Work* by M. Spark and D. Stanford, 1953), which formulates the myth — still underlying much modern criticism — that EB, 'obsessed by the ideology of her work', 'would have died mentally deranged'. (Gérin also prints EB's French *devoirs* in an appendix.)

The main source for the BRONTË JUVENILIA is still the Shakespeare Head edition ed. T.J. Wise and J.A. Symington: *The Miscellaneous and Unpublished Writings of Charlotte and Patrick Branwell Brontë* (2 vols., 1936 and 1938) (none of Emily's or Anne's prose juvenilia remaining); though this is incomplete and in some respects inaccurate, and often gives illegible facsimiles instead of transcripts. Also invaluble, in the same series, is *The Brontës: Their Lives, Friendships and Correspondence* (4 vols., 1932); this includes Emily's and Anne's diary notes, and the reminiscences of Ellen Nussey and Mary Taylor. A new edition of CB's juvenilia is being prepared by C. Alexander, who has made a systematic survey of *The Early Writings of Charlotte Brontë* (1983). There are recent editions of CB's *Poems* (ed. T. Winnifrith, 1984; unfortunately the poems are not in chronological order), and of Anne's *Poems* (ed. E. Chitham, 1979; with an introduction relevant to Anne's and Emily's experience of the Gondal saga). Elizabeth Gaskell's original *Life of Charlotte Brontë* (1857; Everyman, 1908, 1971) is fascinating and contains apt quotations from the juvenilia. Likewise W. Gerin's biographies of *Charlotte Brontë* (1967) and *Anne Brontë* (1959, 1976). R. Keefe, in *Charlotte Brontë's World of Death* (1979), explores CB's struggle to absorb the impact of the family deaths through symbolic expression. Other recent studies which also pay detailed attention to the juvenilia are: M. Blom, *Charlotte Brontë* (1977); C, Burkhart, *Charlotte Brontë: A Psychosexual Study* (1973); E.A. Knies, *The Art of Charlotte Brontë* (1969); H. Moglen, *Charlotte Brontë: The Self Conceived* (1976). Some critical studies on the nature of CB's imagination in *Jane Eyre* include: D. Lodge, 'Fire and Eyre: Charlotte Brontë's War of Earthly Elements' (*The Language of Fiction*, 1966); R.B. Heilman, 'Charlotte Brontë's "New" Gothic' (*From Jane Austen to Joseph Conrad*, ed. R. Rathburn and M. Steinman,, Jr., 1958; often reprinted) and 'Charlotte Brontë, Reason, and the Moon' (*Nineteenth Century Fiction* XIV, 1960); R.B. Martin, *The Accents of Persuasion* (1966). Also, in relation to *Wuthering Heights*, 'The Place of Love in *Jane Eyre* and *Wuthering Heights*' by M. Kinkead-Weekes (in *Twentieth Century Views* ed. I. Gregor, 1970). An article on 'Charlotte Brontë as a Critic of *Wuthering Heights*' by P. Drew (*Nineteenth Century Fiction* XVIII, 1964) still considers CB's moral condemnation of Heathcliff the correct and 'crucial point in her criticism of the novel'.

\* \* \* \* \*

Some account of the relation of EB to the ROMANTIC POETS is given in the general critical and biographical studies cited above (for example, Gérin, Spark and Stanford, Hewish, Winnifrith), and in essays on her poems. Often the nature of poetic influence is seen in a rather literal-minded way. Articles focussed more specifically on EB and the Romantics include: J. Wordsworth, 'Wordsworth and the Poetry of Emily Brontë' (*Brontë Society Transactions* XVI, 1974); E. Chitham, 'Emily Brontë and Shelley' (*Brontë Society Transactions* XVII, 1978); H. Brown, 'The Influence of Byron on Emily Brontë' (*Modern Language Review* XXXIV, 1939); M. Evans, 'Byron and Emily Brontë' (*Life and Letters Today* LVII, 1948); W. Gérin, 'Byron's Influence on the Brontës' (Royal Society of Literature: *Essays by Divers Hands* XXXVII, 1972); A.R. Brick, '*Wuthering Heights*: Narrators, Audience and Message' (*College English* XXI, 1959), which makes a comparison with *The Ancient Mariner*; while R. Holmes, in his introduction to *Coleridge* as 'Writer, Thinker and Mariner' (1982) elucidates the essentially poetic nature of Coleridge's philosophy.

\*     \*     \*     \*     \*